The Bush-Cheney Administration's Assault on Open Government

The Bush-Cheney Administration's Assault on Open Government

Bruce P. Montgomery

Westport, Connecticut
London

Library of Congress Cataloging-in-Publication Data

Montgomery, Bruce P., 1955–
   The Bush-Cheney administration's assault on open government / Bruce
P. Montgomery.
      p. cm.
   Includes bibliographical references and index.
   ISBN: 978-0-275-99904-9 (alk. paper)
   1. Freedom of information—United States. 2. Government information—
United States. 3. Public records—Law and legislation—United States. 4.
Public records—Access control—United States. 5. Executive advisory
bodies—United States. 6. Intelligence service—Law and legislation—
United States. 7. Presidents—United States. 8. Bush, George W. (George
Walker), 1946–9. Cheney, Richard B. I. Title.
   KF5753.M64 2008
   342.7308′53—dc22   2007043616

British Library Cataloguing in Publication Data is available.

Library of Congress Catalog Card Number: 2007043616
ISBN: 978-0-275-99904-9

First published in 2008

Praeger Publishers, 88 Post Road West, Westport, CT 06881
An imprint of Greenwood Publishing Group, Inc.
www.praeger.com

Printed in the United States of America

The paper used in this book complies with the
Permanent Paper Standard issued by the National
Information Standards Organization (Z39.48–1984).

10 9 8 7 6 5 4 3 2 1

Contents

Introduction

The Bush-Cheney administration has launched the most aggressive campaign in modern times to expand executive authority at the expense of the nation's key open government and accountability laws. Soon after taking office in 2000, administration officials declared their intent to reverse what they viewed as thirty years of legislative encroachment onto the constitutional prerogatives of the presidency. Spearheaded largely by Vice President Dick Cheney, who has repeatedly spoken of the need to restore executive authority, the administration has sought to weaken or nullify the laws passed beginning in the 1960s to establish a more transparent and accountable government. Congress passed or strengthened these laws after the abuses of power surrounding Watergate, the Vietnam War, and the intelligence scandals of the 1970s. Although most Americans saw these dismaying events as well as the Iran–Contra debacle in the 1980s as evidence that the presidency had grown too powerful, secretive, and dismissive, the Bush-Cheney administration has viewed these same events in terms of the executive not being powerful enough and too susceptible to inspection and calls for transparency.

In each case involving the Freedom of Information Act (FOIA), the Presidential Records Act (PRA), the General Accountability Office's (GAO) statutory authority to investigate the White House, the Federal Advisory Committee Act (FACA), and the Federal Intelligence Surveillance Act (FISA), the administration has moved more aggressively that any presidency before it to rollback and invalidate these statutes. Each of these laws involved a historic commitment by Congress to enable the public to view the internal workings of their government or to check unrestrained executive power. And each has come under assault by an administration that has seen these statutes as a violation of the separation of powers and presidential authority. In one sense, the efforts to negate these laws may be seen as an ideological crusade of sorts—one that has been predicated on an ideology of executive supremacy against the constitutional ghosts of past Democratic Congresses, even though these laws were passed largely with bipartisan support. However one may view the administration's efforts to overthrow these statutes, key White House officials—especially the vice president—have expressed a profound belief in their cause to restore executive powers. Indeed, despite the discarding of the War Powers Act, the legislative veto, the independent counsel statute, and other legacies of the 1970s, the vice president and other executive officials have evidently believed that the administration inherited a severely weakened presidency and that the remaining accountability laws inflicted on mostly prior Republican administrations had to be dismantled.

The Bush-Cheney administration has waged its campaign against these landmark statutes in part by appealing to national security in the war on terror. It also has been helped by a feckless Congress whose members have done little to rein in the growth of presidential power during the administration's two terms in office. This abdication of power and oversight has been even more remarkable than the president's claim of greater executive authority. The result has been to greatly weaken the laws that were passed to guarantee an informed citizenry and check America's growing culture of secrecy. It has always been difficult for the government to strike the proper balance between secrecy and openness, especially during times of war when national security concerns are at their highest. But the underpinnings of American democracy depend on an informed citizenry and a people who are kept in the dark by their government can scarcely chart the course of their own country. Or as James Madison warned in 1822, "A Popular Government, without popular information, or the means of acquiring it, is but a Prologue to a Farce or a Tragedy; or, perhaps, both."[1]

Few would disagree that the government must keep certain types of information secret. American laws have long protected information regarding national security, intelligence sources, military plans, or diplomatic negotiations, as well as matters related to personal privacy. Moreover, in this new age of terrorism in which militant groups seek to carry out terrorist outrages in the United States and around the world, the government has prudently limited access to certain kinds of information that was once publicly available regarding vulnerabilities of nuclear power plants, chemical facilities, and other industrial sites and infrastructure that could provide a blueprint for future terrorist assaults. The terrorist attacks of September 11, 2001, impelled a necessary reexamination of U.S. information policy. Federal officials needed to prevent vital information from falling into the wrong hands. But it was perhaps inevitable that the government's political impulse to control information and the administration's declared intent to extend executive authority would foster information restrictions that went far beyond the needs of national security.

Indeed, the administration's twin aims of extending executive powers and winning the war on terror have fueled an especially potent form of secrecy at the considerable expense of the freedom of information law. Even before the events of September 11, 2001, the Justice Department was already drafting a new FOIA policy ordering federal agencies to deny public information whenever possible. In addition to issuing executive orders limiting the Freedom of Information Act and the Presidential Records Act, the administration has increased the power to classify information for national security reasons and created an expansive withholding regime encompassing a broad range of new classes of "sensitive" information beyond public reach.[2] Information also has been secretly reclassified, while thousands of records have been stripped from government websites. The administration, moreover, has fought to withhold information documenting prisoner abuses in the war on terror as well as photographs of the caskets of fallen soldiers. According to critics, the government's limitations on information have been so restrictive as to further threaten public health and safety.

But if the Bush-Cheney administration has tried to shield government from the people, it also has tried to hide history from historians, journalists, and the public. On November 1, 2001, President Bush issued an extraordinary executive order (EO 13233) that erected new barriers to obtaining access to former presidents' White House materials under the 1978 Presidential Records Act (PRA). The effort to rewrite the PRA by executive order began before the September 11 attacks, allowing former presidents and even their heirs to withhold presidential records from the public in seeming perpetuity. The result has been the same—a greater shroud of secrecy over the actions of government, and in this case, over the history of the American government itself. Before passage of that law, presidential records were treated as private property, resulting in significant losses to the historical record. From George Washington to Franklin D. Roosevelt, presidents and their heirs treated their papers as they saw fit, bequeathing, selling, destroying, donating, or depositing them in libraries or historical societies. In 1978, however, a bipartisan Congress passed the PRA as a result of the constitutional struggle over Nixon's tapes and records for the Watergate trials and investigations. Congress passed the act to assure that future presidents could not repeat Nixon's efforts to try to permanently obstruct access to or destroy their White House materials. The law declared that after January 20, 1981, the records of all presidents and vice presidents would be the property of the American people. The Bush administration's assault of the PRA, however, represented its first major policy move to enforce greater secrecy and strengthen executive authority. By inverting the law's presumption of openness, the administration rewrote a congressional statute by executive decree, redefining presidential records as if they were a personal property right and prompting numerous scholars and others to denounce it for "stabbing history in the back."

Even months before President Bush issued his executive order rewriting the Presidential Records Act, the vice president was engaged in constitutional battles with the GAO and liberal and conservative interest groups to keep the proceedings of his national energy task force secret. From February to May 2001, the vice president oversaw an energy task force that solicited input mostly from representatives of the energy industry to devise a new energy plan for the country. The vice president's stealthy deliberations attracted scrutiny from Democratic members of Congress and environmental and consumer groups that claimed they were being shut out of the process and that policy was being hijacked by corporate interests who were big campaign donors to Republican coffers. At the request of ranking House Democrats, the General Accountability Office, the investigative arm of Congress, asked for information concerning whom the task force had met with. The vice president's unyielding refusal to release the information, citing executive confidentiality, ignited an unprecedented and escalating battle of interpretations of the GAO's statutory authority to sue the White House into a constitutional test of the power of the presidency. There seemed little doubt the records would show that the administration had met predominately with energy industry executives who significantly shaped the administration's energy policy. But the records seemed beside the point. The Bush-Cheney administration seized upon the GAO's request, which comported with the agency's numerous past investigations of executive branch activities, for a much larger purpose—to eviscerate the agency's statutory authority to investigate the White House and strengthen executive authority.

At the same time, the administration saw opportunity in welcoming lawsuits filed by the Sierra Club, the liberal environmental group, and Judicial Watch, the conservative government watchdog organization, which were seeking much the same information on the workings of the energy task force. The public interest groups charged that energy representatives and lobbyists who were major donors of the administration constituted de facto members of the task force under the meaning of the Federal Advisory Committee Act, the 1972 open government law that requires that meetings and records of presidential advisory committees be open to the public if they involve participation of nonfederal individuals. Congress passed the law to curb the influence of special interests on major policy decisions stemming from presidential and other federal advisory committees. The vice president claimed, however, that the requests for information on the workings of the energy task force intruded into the heart of executive deliberations and that for the courts to require even preliminary disclosure would violate the constitutional separation of powers between the executive and judicial branches. By staking this claim, the vice president aimed to deal a fatal blow to the open disclosure law covering presidential advisory committees and wrap the White House in a greater blanket of immunity from public and judicial scrutiny into its operations without having to invoke executive privilege.

The administration's attempt to invalidate the 1978 Federal Intelligence Surveillance Act, however, has perhaps represented one of the sharpest expressions yet of its willingness to expand the scope of executive power and secrecy. Although FISA was never meant to promote open government, it was passed to make the executive branch and its security apparatus more accountable. In 1978, after the intelligence-gathering abuses of the Nixon years when the NSA (National Security Agency) and FBI spied on civil rights and anti–Vietnam War activists, Congress passed the surveillance law, requiring the NSA and FBI to obtain a warrant any time it sought to monitor communications inside the country. The new law aimed to check unrestrained executive power by establishing the FISA court, an eleven-member secret panel whose purpose was to hear surveillance requests and issue or deny warrants.

The president's domestic spying program by the NSA was first reported by the *New York Times* on December 16, 2005. The next day, President Bush admitted that secret, domestic wiretapping had been conducted without warrants since late 2001, and that he had issued secret orders in this regard more than thirty times since then. The administration contended that the NSA was looking into only the communications of people with known links to al Qaeda. It further declared that the process of obtaining FISA warrants was too burdensome and outmoded in an era of new technologies that allows the NSA to perform data mining, sifting by computer through billions of phone calls and internet messages for patterns that might indicate terrorist activity.

Nonetheless, rather than seeking to amend the law, the White House bypassed it altogether, claiming that the president had the inherent constitutional authority as commander in chief. The White House further claimed that the president's constitutional powers were supplemented by a congressional resolution that authorized the president to use "all necessary and appropriate force" in the war on terror, even though the administration failed to persuade congressional leaders to include language covering warrantless wiretapping in the resolution. Armed with expansive and questionable theories of presidential power, the White House pushed forward with the unrestrained program, igniting lawsuits and controversy among Democrats, conservative Republicans, and civil liberties advocates that the program constituted an excessive encroachment on Americans' Fourth Amendment rights and gave too much power to the executive branch. As the administration's congressional allies attempted to ratify the warrantless NSA program, a number of conservative Republicans broke ranks in open rebellion. Democratic victories in the congressional elections of November 2006 also compelled the administration to seek legislation to revise the law—something it had refused to do until political and public pressure forced it to seek accommodation.

The administration's sweeping assertions of executive power at the expense of accountability laws have largely come with a compliant Congress that has willingly sacrificed its own constitutional prerogatives. Throughout much of these controversies with the looming concerns of national security, the legislative branch has failed to keep its historic commitments of an open and accountable government to the American people; it has been complicit in creating an expansive secrecy regime that has gone far beyond protecting the nation from external and internal threats to closing down information to which the public has an indisputable right to know. "When governments claim that a broad mandate is essential to protect national security," said the late historian Arthur Schlesinger Jr., "they mostly mean that it is essential to protect the political interests of the administration."[3] Governments have always known that secrecy is a source of power and a means of "covering up the embarrassments, blunders, follies and crimes of the ruling class."[4] But secrecy is also the irrefutable handmaiden of public cynicism and distrust of government. With the exception of sensitive national security and privacy information, Americans have an incontrovertible right to learn what has been done in their name. They also have a fundamental expectation that their civil liberties will be protected under the Constitution. "Liberty," said John Adams, "cannot be preserved without a general knowledge among the people, who have a right, from the frame of their nature, to knowledge ... and a desire to know; but besides this, they have a right, an indisputable, undeniable, indefensible, divine right to that most dreaded and envied kind of knowledge, I mean, of the characters and conduct of their rulers."[5] Further, said Patrick Henry, "The Liberties of a people never were, nor ever will be, secure, when the transactions of their rulers may be concealed from them."[6]

One

The Freedom of Information Act in Retreat

The Freedom of Information Act (FOIA) has suffered the greatest erosion in its history under the presidency of George W. Bush, whose war on terrorism and reassertion of executive power has come at the expense of open government. Bush has said that he believes in open government, but his critics have argued that his administration has gone to extraordinary lengths to control information. The White House has claimed that national security after the 9/11 terrorist attacks has justified limiting disclosure to protect the nation from vulnerability threats. After all, the same data that was available to the public regarding the location and operating status of nuclear power plants, chemical facilities, pipelines, and other vulnerable infrastructure also was available to terrorists. Nevertheless, the administration's secrecy initiatives began well before the bombings with the proclaimed intent of strengthening the presidency after what it perceives as thirty years of legislative encroachment onto its executive prerogatives. From withholding information from Congress, to ordering federal agencies to deny public information requests whenever possible, to spawning new species of secrecy designations for unclassified information, the White House has gone beyond shutting down information for security reasons to often treating it "as the sovereign property not of the people but of the executive branch."[1] Indeed, in the battle of imperatives involving national security and executive prerogatives versus open government, the seminal freedom of information law has been in retreat.

Background

Passed in 1966, the Freedom of Information Act inaugurated the great American experiment in open government. The act was the idea of California

Democratic Congressman John E. Moss, whose zeal for making government information public overcame the opposition of successive presidential administrations. The landmark law granted citizens the right to access all federal government information limited only by nine exemptions governing national security, private commercial or trade secrets, law enforcement, personal privacy, and other matters.[2] Despite the federal bureaucracy's resistance from the beginning, the law has served the public extraordinarily well, allowing reporters and others to reveal damning evidence of government waste, fraud, and abuse. "That act," wrote conservative *New York Times* columnist William Safire in April 1985, "I can testify, has done more to inhibit the abuse of Government power and to protect the citizen from unlawful snooping and arrogant harassment than any legislation in our lifetime."[3] Few presidential administrations have shared Safire's opinion, viewing the act as overly intrusive, and repeatedly challenging it in the halls of Congress and in the courts.

When President Lyndon B. Johnson signed the act into law on July 4, 1966, he eloquently spoke of it as demonstrating the country's commitment to an "open society in which the people's right to know is cherished and guarded."[4] According to his former press secretary Bill Moyers, however, few people realized that "LBJ had to be dragged kicking and screaming" to the signing ceremony. "He hated the very idea of the Freedom of Information Act; hated the thought of journalists rummaging in government closets; hated them challenging the official view of reality." But Johnson also harbored concerns that the law should not jeopardize national security, writing in his signing statement that "democracy works best when the people have all the information that the security of the nation permits."[5] With such words, Johnson prophesied the inevitable clash between the federal government's vast national security apparatus and citizens, journalists, researchers, and public interest groups over the public's right to know.

Most subsequent presidents have shared Johnson's view of the act. When Congress liberalized the act in 1974 following the Watergate crisis, it did so in dramatic fashion in opposition to nearly every major department and agency in the federal government and by overriding a veto by President Gerald R. Ford, who called it "unconstitutional and unworkable."[6] Although the administration of President Jimmy Carter advised agencies to construe the law more generously, the act was opposed by law enforcement, national security, and intelligence officials who argued that it compromised sensitive information to organized crime and foreign spies.[7] At the height of the Cold War and with national security an ever present concern, the Reagan administration repeatedly tried to diminish the act contending that it compromised national security secrets. These efforts produced modest changes that exempted from the law select operational and investigative files of the CIA and FBI under the 1984 CIA Information Act and the 1986 Anti-Drug Abuse Act. Moreover, an executive order gave government agencies more latitude to withhold information under the act's national security exemption.[8] In the 1990s, when national security concerns were at low tide, Clinton rolled back some of Reagan's restrictions and issued Executive Order 12958, which called for the declassification of documents after twenty-five years unless disclosure would harm national security, assist in the development of weapons of mass destruction, or identify confidential informants. Clinton also signed into law the landmark 1996 Electronic Freedom of Information Act, expanding public access to the government's electronic records. Nevertheless, he issued a 1997 executive order that extended authority to classify information as "top secret" to twenty federal officials—a power that was eventually granted to more than 1,300 "original classifiers."[9]

With the presidency of George W. Bush, the White House has returned to viewing the law through the prism of national security in an era of terrorism and an intrusion onto its executive prerogatives. The severe weakening of the nation's cornerstone sunshine law has occurred as the imperatives of national security and reassertion of executive authority have trumped the freedom of information law. The erosion of the statute has taken the form of reversing the presumption that government information should be disclosed whenever possible; encouraging agencies to withhold information under a broad and sweeping new category of "sensitive but unclassified" records; pursuing legislation to create new information categories exempt from disclosure regarding information voluntarily provided to the government by a private party and identified as "critical infrastructure information"; issuing regulations prohibiting the release of other specific kinds of information; and expanding the government's capacity to classify documents. With its concerns for national security and reasserting executive authority, the administration has moved to predicate its public information policies more on a need-to-know basis than on the public's right of access, recalling the pre-FOIA era when disclosure was at the unfettered discretion of the government.

A Predisposition for National Security and Executive Powers

It has always been difficult for the federal government to strike the proper balance between secrecy and openness, especially during wartime. Bush himself alluded to the difficulty in remarks to the American Society of Newspaper Editors in April 2005. "I've always believed in open government," he told the editors in Washington, but he added there was also "tension" between disclosure and "jeopardizing the war on terror."[10] With the 9/11 attacks and the sense of an ever present danger from within, it was perhaps inevitable the government would rush to limit information that could be used in planning another terrorist assault. Few could argue with Alane Kochems, a national security expert at the conservative Heritage Foundation in Washington, who said the government was justified in adopting new levels of secrecy immediately after 9/11 because "we didn't know what was going on with the terrorists." The question, however, was how far the government should go in regulating what Americans should know about what was being done in their name. In 1997, Senator Daniel Patrick Moynihan—the Senate's leading authority on secrecy—wrote that excessive secrecy had significant consequences for the national interest when "policy makers are not fully informed, government is not held accountable for its actions, and the public cannot engage in informed debate." The world was a dangerous place, he said, and some secrecy was "vital to save lives, bring miscreants to justice, protect national security, and engage in effective diplomacy." But Moynihan contended that the secrecy system had too often been used to "deny the public an understanding of the policymaking process, rather than for the necessary protection of intelligence activities and other highly sensitive matters."[11]

It seemed that Moynihan could have been writing about future members of the Bush administration who arrived in Washington determined to extend presidential powers and build a higher wall of confidentiality around the White House. It was no mystery to some of Bush's top aides who were longtime veterans of government that information was power and that power could be increased through controls on information. But this penchant for secrecy also reflected a belief among administration officials that they had little to learn from Congress and a lack of faith in the messiness of public debate that often leads to wise policy decisions. On assuming office in 2000, Bush officials made no secret of their intention to reverse what they contended was a decades-long erosion of presidential authority. In May 2002, the *New York Times* quoted one senior administration official as saying that there was clear "recognition within the administration that presidential authority has been eroded over the years beyond the proper constitutional separation of powers."[12] Alberto R. Gonzales, then White House Counsel, emphasized that the framers of the Constitution intended that there "be a strong presidency in order to carry out certain functions," and that Bush felt obligated to "leave the office in better shape than when he came in."[13] In speeches, moreover, Vice President Dick Cheney made clear his view that in past decades Congress had repeatedly overreached its constitutional authority by passing expansive accountability and oversight laws, impinging on presidential powers after Vietnam, Watergate, and the intelligence scandals of the 1970s and 1980s, and that this trend had to be reversed—a view that Cheney harbored since his days in the Nixon and Ford administrations.[14] No post-Watergate law was more important than the 1974 amendments to the FOIA, passed after a wave of openness swept over Washington following the government's betrayal of the public trust.

It perhaps should have been anticipated that some of Bush's closest aides would enter the White House as foes of the Freedom of Information Act and proponents of strengthening presidential authority. Two of his closest aides, Vice President Dick Cheney and Secretary of Defense Donald Rumsfeld, were longtime opponents of the information act dating to the Ford years. After Richard Nixon resigned the presidency under threat of impeachment, the new president, Gerald Ford, hired Rumsfeld to be his White House chief of staff, and Rumsfeld appointed Cheney as his deputy. Within a year, Rumsfeld became secretary of defense and Cheney replaced him as Ford's chief top aide. In his new role, Cheney came to see national security issues from the perspective of a White House that sought to keep national security and intelligence information away from public scrutiny and congressional demands for more openness.[15] In 1974, Congress passed a series of amendments strengthening the FOIA, adding important provisions speeding up responses, providing for judicial review, reducing fees, and allowing the courts to review in camera classified information to determine whether it was being properly withheld under the law's nine exemptions—changes that some critics denounced for creating an excess of openness.[16] When President Ford vetoed the amendment, he did so on the advice of his aides, including Dick Cheney and Donald Rumsfeld, and a senior Justice Department attorney, Antonin Scalia, who argued that the law unduly burdened officials and was unconstitutional.[17] While governor of Texas, Bush had also shown a proclivity for secrecy, in one case convening a private task force to propose solutions to curb air pollution and resisting efforts to make its deliberations public. When leaving office, he sent his political papers to his father's presidential library at College Station, igniting a fight over their disposition. The records were transferred to the state archives after the Texas attorney general ruled that they were subject to the state's open records law.[18]

Ashcroft and Card Memos

Even before the September 11, 2001, terrorist attacks fueled the Bush administration's efforts to close down access to information, efforts had already been underway to enforce greater government secrecy and constrict the FOIA. Vice President Cheney's early battle to keep the records of his energy task force secret reflected an administration that arrived in Washington determined to strengthen executive powers. From February to May 2001, Cheney convened a series of secret meetings to craft the administration's new energy policy for the nation.

The confidential proceedings, which largely excluded environmental and consumer groups, ironically attracted a blast of unwanted public scrutiny into the workings of the task force and demands for information about the extent that big energy companies wrote the national energy plan behind closed doors. Citing executive confidentiality, the vice president refused to release information about the workings of his task force, inviting high-profile legal and political battles from the General Accountability Office and liberal and conservative public interest groups—battles that the Bush White House eventually won.[19]

Moreover, after Ronald Reagan's presidential papers became publicly available for the first time in January 2001 under the 1978 Presidential Records Act (PRA), the White House wasted little time in delaying their release and rewriting the statute, expanding executive privilege rights of former presidents and vice presidents and extending them to their designated representatives and heirs in violation of the law. Congress passed the PRA to assert public ownership over presidential materials. The act required that all records, excepting materials relating to national security and other matters, be made publicly available twelve years after a president leaves office. When President Bush issued Executive Order 13233 on November 1, 2001, reversing the PRA's presumption of public access to the records of former presidents and vice presidents, it seemed clear that he aimed to extend his expansive view of executive powers indefinitely beyond his term of office to maximize control over the historical record of his administration.[20] In other early instances of secrecy, the White House withheld revised data on the 2000 Census that would have increased funding for California, and denied Republican congressional requests for documents concerning a thirty-year-old FBI/mob scandal. The conservative government watchdog group, Judicial Watch, complained that after taking office "President Bush and his administration moved almost immediately to ... la[y] down a stone wall of secrecy concerning government operations."[21]

At the same time, before the terrorist attacks, the Justice Department was at work on redrafting government-wide guidelines on the FOIA from the Clinton administration.[22] Attorney General John Ashcroft issued the new policy on October 12, 2001, just weeks after the 9/11 attacks on New York and Washington. The Ashcroft memorandum sent to all federal departments and agencies encouraged federal officials to reject requests for documents whenever there was a "sound legal basis" for doing so, promising that the Justice Department would defend them in court.[23] An indication that Ashcroft's policy was already in place before the 9/11 attacks came from a letter published in the *Washington Post* by a businessman who routinely filed "130 FOIA requests a year" to obtain data on government technology spending. Since April 2001, he complained, "five months before the terrorist attacks, ... agencies began blocking access to what had previously been releasable," and were charging exorbitant fees for what they were willing to disclose.[24]

The Ashcroft directive signaled a sharp reversal of policy set in 1993, when Attorney Janet Reno urged agencies to make information available whenever possible, so long as there was no "foreseeable harm" in doing so.[25] Since the Ford presidency, after Congress passed the 1974 amendments, new administrations typically outlined their interpretation of the FOIA after taking office. The Ashcroft memo recalled the Reagan administration's interpretation of the act, which replaced Carter's more permissive release policy. The Reagan administration's policy assured federal agencies that Justice Department attorneys would defend them in court for rejecting FOIA requests unless the refusal lacked a substantial legal basis, or that a defense could adversely affect the ability of other agencies to protect records.[26] Responding to criticism that the Ashcroft memorandum effectively repealed the FOIA, a representative from the Bush Justice Department downplayed such fears as exaggerated, saying that the new standard was "not such a drastic shift, as much as a change in tone."[27]

Following Ashcroft's memorandum, the administration released another directive in March 2002 by Chief of Staff Andrew Card. Unlike Ashcroft's memorandum, the Card directive stemmed directly from the 9/11 attacks with the aim of extending the attorney general's restrictive release policy to cover any unclassified information that could be exploited for terrorism. The directive ordered federal agencies and departments to withhold "sensitive but unclassified information" for national security reasons even when the FOIA exemptions did not apply. Agencies were told to review information regarding "weapons of mass destruction" and "other information that could be misused to harm the security of our nation and the safety of our people," and to report their reviews to the Office of Homeland Security within ninety days.[28]

When preparing his directive, Card solicited advice from the government's chief FOIA and classification authorities and included their guidance with his instructions. The guidance on implementing Card's memorandum urged government officials to carefully consider on a case-by-case basis the disclosure of "sensitive but unclassified information." Accordingly, any requests for this information were to be processed only in accordance with Ashcroft's memorandum by "giving full and careful consideration to all applicable FOIA exemptions." Pursuant to Executive Order 12958, the guidance instructed agencies to classify any sensitive information that was unclassified but could "reasonably be expected to assist in the development or use of weapons of mass destruction," and to reclassify such information if it had been declassified but not disclosed to the public. Issued by Clinton in 1995 to address problems with over-classification, the executive order nevertheless allowed for the classification of information for up to twenty-five years if it could foster the development or use of weapons of mass destruction.[29]

Together, the Ashcroft and Card memorandums set the tone and parameters for agencies to withhold and remove access to broad swaths of documents from public view. Critics denounced the "sensitive but unclassified information" declaration as an ambiguous but expansive concept that would give public officials license to hide any information that might be politically harmful or even embarrassing. Others argued, however, that it was "not out of line with the spirit of FOIA considering the present security concerns." Even if Card's memo and the accompanying guidance urged nondisclosure, supporters noted, it was justified "because the administration must take steps to deter the threat of terrorism."[30]

Responding to the Ashcroft memorandum, Patrick Leahy, the Senate's leading champion of open government, asked the General Accountability Office (GAO) in late February 2002 to audit the effects of the directive. Moreover, one month later, the House Government Reform Committee—then chaired by Republican conservative Dan Burton—amended its FOIA Citizen's Guide to counter Ashcroft's instruction. The amended guide declared that "[c]ontrary to the instructions issued by the Department of Justice on October 12, 2001, the standard should not be to allow the withholding of information whenever there is merely a 'sound legal basis' for doing so."[31] The GAO issued its report on the effects of Ashcroft's memorandum on August 30, 2002, finding that federal agencies—based largely on anecdotal evidence—were already falling behind in meeting the public's request for information.[32] In response to another Leahy request, the GAO issued a second study in September 2003, indicating that one-third of federal FOI officers said they were less likely to make discretionary disclosures of information, and of these, 75 percent cited the Ashcroft directive as the reason.[33] Moreover, an earlier audit of the affects of Ashcroft's memo by the National Security Archive, a public interest group in Washington, found that the government's implementation of the FOIA was already in disarray.[34] Confirming the growing chilling effect of Ashcroft's policy, a veteran Justice Department official said that "as a matter of policy, we are not advocating the making of discretionary disclosures."[35]

Reconsidering Security: Access after 9/11

Although liberals and conservatives alike noted the move toward secrecy before the terrorist attacks, the trend escalated dramatically after 9/11 as the U.S. government moved rapidly to a war footing. Alarmed federal officials concerned about publishing the country's vulnerabilities on the internet hurriedly stripped data from numerous government websites—the location and operating status of nuclear power plants, oil and chemical facilities, hydroelectric dams and other industrial sites, maps of the nation's transportation and infrastructure, information about violations of airlines and airport security, as well as a vast array of other data that could be used in the planning of another terrorist assault.[36] Before 9/11, the flood of information onto government websites stemmed largely from the 1996 Electronic Freedom of Information Act (EFOIA). Under the act, agencies set up electronic reading rooms to provide immediate and free internet access, which better regulated the flow of information to the public and lessened the administrative burden of responding to written requests.[37] When signing the act into law, President Clinton said the legislation would usher the FOIA into the information and electronic age, but few could have foreseen that government data on the internet might facilitate terrorist attacks.[38]

With the 9/11 attacks, the White House came to view the disclosure law as a critical liability in the new war on terrorism. Few disagreed on the importance of the information act in obtaining information on public safety, but the question now was whether this same data on government websites and elsewhere posed a near term or even lasting national security threat. The question became critical after the U.S. military discovered al Qaeda groups with GAO reports and government information obtained through the FOIA, a seeming indictment of the open government statute. Investigators found an array of information, including detailed maps, drawings of sensitive infrastructure sites, copies of U.S. chemical trade publications, and information on computerized water systems in caves in Afghanistan and in al Qaeda training camps.[39] Other documents showed that Osama bin Laden and his terrorist organization not only were investigating the use of nuclear, biological, and chemical weapons against the West, but that they had actually conducted preliminary experiments on animals. These unnerving discoveries were the conclusion of detailed analyses of documents found by the *Times of London* in abandoned al Qaeda houses in Kabul after the defeat of the Taliban by American and coalition forces. The documents confirmed claims by British and U.S. governments that Bin Laden was seeking ways to produce botulin poison and low-grade "dirty" nuclear devices, and went so far as to manufacture and test chemical weapons on rabbits, including cyanide gas—used by Saddam Hussein to kill thousands in Halabja in 1988.[40] Moreover, investigators found evidence of al Qaeda operatives researching ways of launching cyber attacks on U.S. power, telecommunications, and transportation facilities—assaults that former National Security Council aide Richard Clarke previously warned in 1999 could produce an "electronic Pearl Harbor."[41]

With these and other revelations, science became the leading edge of the information crackdown. In January 2002, the government began quietly withdrawing more than 6,000 technical documents concerning production of germ and chemical weapons, and began drafting a new information security policy that would result in the withdrawal of more documents. The withdrawal of these federal reports dating from the 1940s to more recent times, which were once freely sold to the public, focused on disclosures previously not considered a threat to national security. At the same time, the White House asked the American Society of Microbiology, a Washington-based professional association of germ researchers, to restrict potentially dangerous information in articles published in its eleven professional journals. One administration proposal involved eliminating sections of articles providing experimental results that other researchers would need to consult to replicate and test their validity. "That takes apart the whole foundation of science," said Ronald M. Atlas, president-elect of the society, regarding the omission of data. Abigail Salyers, the society's president, gave a more pointed response. "Terrorism feeds on fear, and fear feeds on ignorance," she said. "The best defense against anthrax or any infectious disease is information that can bolster public safety." But Tom Ridge, the director of Homeland Security, said the critics were overreacting, adding that scientists "have to remember what we're up against," referring to terrorists who sought exotic weapons with the aim of killing millions of people.[42]

Homeland Security Bill and Critical Infrastructure Information

In his address to a joint session of Congress on September 20, 2001, President Bush announced the creation of the Office of Homeland Security, a cabinet level position that would report directly to him.[43] Bush followed up his address by establishing the office by executive order on October 8 to coordinate the full range of federal agencies, as well as state and local governments with the responsibility to protect the nation.[44] Bush also issued an executive order on October 16 setting up an infrastructure board with classification authority to secure the country's computer systems and signed into law the U.S.A. Patriot Act, which included the Critical Infrastructure Protection Act of 2001. In drafting the Patriot Act, Congress aimed to "facilitate the security of the critical infrastructure of the United States, to encourage the secure disclosure and protected exchange of critical infrastructure information, to enhance the analysis, prevention, and detection of attacks on critical infrastructure, to enhance the recovery from such attacks, and for other purposes."[45]

Amid congressional skepticism regarding the ability of the proposed Homeland Security office to defend the country, Senators Joseph Lieberman and Arlen

Specter sponsored legislation to create a full-blown homeland defense agency—the Department of Homeland Defense.[46] Bush initially resisted the proposal until congressional criticism mounted regarding the failed performance of the CIA and FBI in preventing the 9/11 attacks. As congressional committees and the 9/11 Commission documented, the failure to share information, or excessive secrecy of both agencies, proved catastrophic for the country. The CIA's warnings of al Qaeda's terrorist activities dating to the mid-1990s received little attention and only limited distribution. At the same time, the FBI ignored or failed to follow up on information concerning the trail of two of the hijackers from an al Qaeda meeting in Indonesia into the United States.[47] Bowing to political pressure, Bush submitted his own proposal for the creation of the new Homeland Security Department in June 2002. Among many other things, Bush's strategy aimed to consolidate all critical infrastructure protections under the aegis of the new Homeland Security Department.[48] The bill, however, contained a single sentence that proposed creating the largest loophole in the history of the Freedom of Information Act solely on behalf of business: "Information provided voluntarily by non-Federal entities or individuals that relates to infrastructure vulnerabilities or other vulnerabilities to terrorism and is or has been in the possession of the Department shall not be subject to section 552 of title 5, United States Code [the Freedom of Information Act]."[49]

With the imperative to protect the nation's critical infrastructure systems like energy, telecommunications, agriculture, food and water systems, transportation, banking and financial services—most of which operated under private control—the administration sought to encourage companies to share information on vulnerability threats with the government. In urging this public/private partnership, Bush's proposal included sharply limiting disclosure of any vital infrastructure information that industry voluntarily shared with the government.[50] Industry pushed for a broad exemption that would also give them blanket immunity from the courts. Amid several other homeland security bills on Capitol Hill, the president's proposal soon took center stage after it was introduced in the House as H.R. 5005, the Homeland Security Act of 2002.[51] As presented in the bill and defined in the Patriot Act, the term "critical infrastructure" referred to "systems and assets, whether physical or virtual, so vital to the United States that the incapacity or destruction of such systems and assets would have a debilitating impact on security, national economic security, national public health or safety, or any combination of those matters."[52]

When the House reported the measure out of the House Select Committee on Homeland Security after hearings on the legislation, the White House's proposed exemption covering infrastructure vulnerabilities was considerably expanded to cover the sweeping protections sought by industry. Four out of the committee's nine members opposed the nondisclosure provision, asserting that it could immunize corporations from accountability or liability regarding, for example, leaks or spills of hazardous materials. The minority members advocated the complete removal of the nondisclosure provision arguing that it represented a significant retreat from government openness and accountability.[53] Nevertheless, the broad FOIA exemption aimed to allay corporate concerns by liberating industry from the disclosure requirements of local and state sunshine laws and wrapping companies in civil immunity for violations of federal security, tax, civil rights, environmental, labor, consumer protection, and health and safety laws that might surface in any information they provided. The landmark homeland security bill also imposed criminal penalties for whistleblowers—including those who leaked information about hazardous spills or other threats to public health and safety—and exempted advisory committees from the 1972 Federal Advisory Committee Act, passed by Congress to curb the influence of corporate and special interest groups on presidential and other federal advisory groups.[54]

Reflecting the concern of many, one critic said the measure would "deny to the public crucial information about hazardous materials, chemical releases, toxic spills, and other threats to health and safety—as well as vulnerabilities to threats and sabotage."[55] Critics charged that the bill's immunity provision would invite companies with something to hide to submit incriminating materials as "critical infrastructure information," putting them permanently beyond the reach of the public, the press, the state sunshine laws, the Congress, and the courts. Open government advocates also argued that the time-tested FOIA already protected against risks of harmful disclosure and that the courts had provided considerable protection to industry information. A Reagan-era executive order, moreover, required agencies to allow businesses to review FOIA requests for much of its information before releasing it.[56]

A Compromise Measure

After the House passed a homeland security bill in July 2002 with its strong secrecy infrastructure provisions, a bipartisan effort in the Senate produced an alternative measure that avoided decimating public access to industry data that would help guard public health and safety. Drafted by Senators Robert Bennett, Republican of Utah, and Democrats Carl Levin of Michigan and Patrick Leahy of Vermont, the compromise measure aimed to balance the interests of industry and the public by limiting exemptions to the FOIA only to industry information that directly related to possible terrorist attacks, as well as response and recovery efforts. Corporate data obtained by agencies other than the Department of Homeland Security would continue to be subject to freedom of information laws. Moreover, the compromise involved no civil immunity provision, no criminal penalties for government workers who disclosed information, and no blanket provision for the federal government to trump state sunshine laws.[57] The Bush administration initially endorsed the compromise and industry groups reportedly said it would encourage them to share information with the government.[58] By August 2002, when Congress took its August break, the House and Senate had produced two considerably different bills. After Republicans won majorities in both houses in the November 2002 congressional elections, however, the White House and House Republicans killed the Senate compromise, insisting on their broader secrecy provisions. Bennett argued for adding the compromise measure in the bill, but was overruled by the White House.[59]

Congress Passes the Homeland Security Act of 2002

On November 14, 2002, the House overwhelmingly passed the president's homeland security bill, 299:121. As the Senate took up Bush's sprawling 484-page bill, industry leaders seemed pleased with the blanket exemption. A spokeswoman for the American Chemistry Council stated that the nondisclosure language was a "step in the right direction."[60] But a groundswell of public interest and media groups denounced the anti-disclosure provisions that would allow almost any information provided to the new Department of Homeland Security to be hidden from public view and urged the Senate to adopt its compromise measure. Mark Tapscott, director of the conservative Heritage Foundation's Center for Media and Public Policy in Washington, D.C., said that one "need not be a Harvard law graduate to see that ... this loophole could be manipulated by clever corporate and government operators to hide endless varieties of potentially embarrassing and/or criminal information from public view."[61]

These criticisms came after months of revelations and ongoing investigations regarding some of the greatest corporate scandals in American history, involving the giant energy trading firm Enron, the very icon of corporate greed, and other major corporate debacles—events that led the public and elected officials alike to clamor for more disclosure and accountability in the corporate world. Nevertheless, the White House's congressional allies and others concerned about being tagged as weak on terrorism argued for the urgency of the blanket anti-disclosure language to encourage corporations to share security-sensitive information with the government about pipelines, railroads, dams, buildings, and other data that could provide a blueprint for planning terrorist attacks. Taking a tough law-and-order stand, Senator Dianne Feinstein, the liberal Democrat from California, declared that the FOIA "exemption will encourage private companies that operate over 85 percent of our critical infrastructure to share information about computer break-ins with law enforcement, so criminals and terrorists can be stopped before they strike again. . . ."[62]

On November 19, 2002, in one of the last acts of the 107th Congress, the Senate hurriedly voted 90:9 to approve a nearly identical version of the House bill to create a new Homeland Security Department. The House and Senate quickly ironed out their differences removing some of the most intrusive aspects of the bill, including the erstwhile proposal to create national identity cards and the plan called Operation TIPS (Terrorism Information and Prevention System)—a program that aimed to recruit "millions" of American transportation workers, postal workers, public utility employees, and others who might identify and report suspicious activities to local and federal authorities. Bush signed the Homeland Security Act into law on November 25, folding 170,000 employees from twenty-two agencies into a new cabinet-level superagency charged with defending the nation against terrorism.[63]

Nevertheless, in passing the homeland security law, Congress left unchanged the restrictive information provisions of the House bill. The act made no distinction between information that should be kept secret to protect vulnerable infrastructure and data that might be used by local governments and states to protect the public. It exempted any voluntarily submitted document stamped as "critical infrastructure," no matter how tangential its contents might be to the actual security of the facility. The provision neither obligated private companies to address their vulnerabilities, nor required Homeland Security to fix the problem. In the case of a chemical spill, the law would bar the Department of Homeland Security from releasing information without the written consent of the company that was endangering public health. The anti-disclosure provision, moreover, shielded companies from lawsuits to compel disclosure, criminalized information leaks by whistleblowers in the Homeland Security Department, overrode state and local sunshine laws, and exempted the department from the Federal Advisory Committee Act that required advisory committees to make their records and proceedings public, if nongovernmental outsiders participated in the deliberations. The department also was structured to report to the president, which immunized its policy and decision making from congressional oversight.[64] The exemption's sheer breadth, according to some critics, indicated that it was "less about national security than it [was] about protecting business interests."[65]

Bush's Presidential Signing Statement

In the rush to pass the bill, even congressional leaders most sympathetic to the White House and industry wanted to keep some oversight over the creation of a whole new class of official, domestic secrets. The final bill that President Bush signed provided for Congress and the GAO, the nonpartisan investigative arm of Congress headed by the comptroller general, to have access to domestic information received by the new Homeland Security Department, even if the public and press could not. But in a little-noticed action, Bush accompanied his signing of the homeland security bill with his own presidential signing statement aimed at negating congressional oversight and legislative intent. The signing statement asserted that the "Executive does not construe this provision to impose any independent or affirmative requirement to share such information with Congress or the Comptroller General." Bush's statement, moreover, stated that he "shall construe" the meaning of the law to give him the power to "withhold information" for reasons of national security and the deliberative process of the executive.[66]

Like many others Bush issued, the signing statement was crafted by members of the vice president's legal team who routinely reviewed pieces of legislation before they reached the president's desk, searching for provisions that were seen to impinge on presidential power. David Addington, the leading architect of the signing statements and Cheney's legal adviser and chief of staff, aimed to assert the president's right to ignore laws if they conflicted with the White House's expansive interpretation of executive powers under the Constitution. Among many constitutional scholars and others, the signing statements became one of the most controversial hallmarks of the Bush presidency, signaling a historic shift in the balance of powers away from the legislative branch to the executive. Although the framers of the Constitution distinguished between the powers of Congress and the presidency, declaring that Congress shall make all laws and the president shall see to it that the laws are faithfully executed, Bush exerted the right to carry out the laws only as he interpreted them.[67]

In March 2003, however, Senators Patrick Leahy, Carl Levin, James Jeffords, Joseph Lieberman, and Robert Byrd kept the fight alive by introducing the Restore FOIA Act. The bill's language was identical to the Senate's July 2002 compromise advanced by Senators Leahy, Bennett, and Levin.[68] The bill drew wide support from numerous media and public interest groups for balancing the needs of national security with government transparency, but died in committee.[69]

Other Exemptions and the FOIA

The erosion of the FOIA in the name of homeland security continued to gain momentum after passage of the Homeland Security Act. In the following years, the Bush administration and Republican lawmakers proposed a litany of exemptions to the open government law. While only some were enacted, the sheer number of executive actions and legislative proposals indicated a freedom of information law that was losing out to secrecy. The terrorist attacks of 9/11 prompted a necessary reexamination of U.S. information policy. Federal officials needed to prevent vital information from getting into the wrong hands. It was inevitable, however, that with the government's political impulse to control information and the White House's intent to assert executive authority that this examination would foster information restrictions that went far beyond the needs of national security. In the previous few years, the White House and federal agencies had rebuffed requests for information from Congress, public interest groups, and the press on a range of such critical issues as meetings of the vice president's energy task force, detainees arrested following 9/11, deportation hearings for detainees, implementation of the Patriot Act, weapons of mass destruction in Iraq, the FBI investigations into anthrax poisonings, and treatment of prisoners at Guantanamo Bay and Abu Ghraib. The government also had stripped data or revised its websites, recalled government publications from public availability, and placed curbs on the flow of scientific and technical information.

With Congress sanctioning or ignoring increased restrictions on access, a "massive new withholding regime" emerged surrounding information called "sensitive but unclassified." White House Chief of Staff Andrew Card originally defined the term to protect any information that could foster the development or use of weapons of mass destruction. But the vague term spawned a vast new array of ad hoc secrecy designations across numerous agencies under such terms as "sensitive homeland security information," "sensitive security information," "critical infrastructure information," "protected critical infrastructure information," "critical energy infrastructure information," "for official use only," "limited use only," and "law enforcement sensitive." The proliferation of new secrecy designations enabled the federal government to radically expand its ability to control unclassified information and put it beyond the public's reach. In 2005, OpenTheGovernment.org—one of several public interest groups that monitored government secrecy—listed some fifty such designations across the federal government, leading one secrecy critic to say it was "turning into a bigger problem than overclassification."[70]

Unlike traditional classified information that was governed by relatively uniform rules across agencies and by designated officials with classification authority, the administration's handling of restricted unclassified information lacked even minimal controls or monitoring. It was governed by a "rapidly evolving patchwork of disparate agency regulations and directives," one Democratic lawmaker observed. There were no regulations regarding which federal employees could designate documents as "sensitive but unclassified," no rules governing when or how to remove these designations, and no central office—like the Information Security Oversight Office (ISOO) that oversaw classified information—charged with monitoring these unclassified designations. The unclassified designations also had "questionable pedigrees"—neither defined by statute nor even by executive order. Despite the lessons of 9/11 surrounding the failures of intelligence agencies to share data about terrorism threats, the proliferation of pseudo-classification categories of information raised the question of whether the government's capacity to manage and share information across and within agencies had become even more problematic. Whatever the specific ramifications of this unchecked secrecy for national security, OpenTheGovernment.org believed it posed an increasing threat to government accountability and promoted "conflicts of interest by allowing those with an interest in disclosure and concealment to decide between openness and secrecy." Paul McMasters of the Freedom Forum, a nonpartisan foundation dedicated to the First Amendment, said that in a "breathtakingly short time, one of democracy's core principles, the 'right to know' for the public" was now threatening to "become a 'right to control' for government officials only."[71] Nonetheless, the Bush administration and its congressional allies moved to push through additional regulations and exemptions to the FOIA in the name of homeland security. It was not always clear whether these actions were aimed more at assuring national security, protecting business interests, or wrapping the executive in greater executive confidentiality.

A series of regulatory and legislative proposals were introduced to keep secret such matters as environmental assessments, toxic emissions, sewage systems, and risk levels at chemical plants, but none of these included provisions to make some of this information publicly available for health and safety reasons. Actions dealing with drinking water and airline travel also represented how enhanced security concerns clashed with health and safety concerns of the American public. One of the provisions of a public health and bioterrorism law passed in 2002 required that operators of water systems draft plans to address any vulnerability in case of attack or disruption. This provision was understandable enough, but critics said that citizens were prohibited from obtaining most of the information necessary for improved health and safety—a turnaround from the provisions of the 1996 Clean Water Act, which provided for annual assessments of water supply systems meant to arm the public with information necessary to push for improvements. Although water assessments continued to be performed, the new restrictions essentially transformed a program that once widely disseminated information to the public to one grounded on a strict need-to-know basis. The Federal Aviation Administration (FAA), moreover, addressed its own security concerns so vigorously that Americans could not obtain safety information once considered routine. Following the 9/11 attacks, the FAA clamped down on information on security breaches of airport security. But rather than just cutting off this information, the agency went further in sealing off records regarding enforcement actions against airlines, pilots, mechanics, and others, as well as backing away from disclosures of safety information voluntarily provided by airlines. The Transportation Security Administration also adopted new rules shutting down public access to key government information on the safety and security of all modes of transportation and setting a looser standard for withholding information.[72]

The Pentagon proposed restricting certain nonconfidential government satellite data that was often used by the news media, commercial industries in agriculture and forestry, and others studying earth sciences. Critics said that the imagery would be of little use to terrorists who would barely be able to tell the difference between an "oil tank and an ice rink."[73] Another Pentagon proposal sought a broad FOIA exemption for the Defense Intelligence Agency covering everything from human rights to historical military records, despite the lack of any evidence that current protections were inadequate for sources or methods of intelligence gathering, or that the FOIA's national security exemption was not working.[74] The director of National Intelligence proposed a plan to Congress on improving methods to share terrorism information across federal agencies, but open government advocates argued for the public's need to have some degree of access to homeland security efforts—not so detailed as to provide a blueprint for terrorists, but enough to reassure the public that government officials were taking steps to protect them and their communities.[75]

In February 2003, a Justice Department plan was leaked to the press that proposed expanding its counterterrorism powers to include approving intelligence warrants, invalidating local consent decrees that would curb spying, and prohibiting FOIA requests for information about detainees who were caught in the sweeps after 9/11. To his critics, Ashcroft represented a Big Brother figure whose expanding powers allowed him to use wiretaps, make secret decisions, shut down information, and order increased street presence to spy on American citizens. Even some of his peers complained that Ashcroft had grown too powerful, including former Republican Congressman Dick Armey, who on resigning his congressional post called Ashcroft and the Justice Department "out of control."[76] As early as November 2003, the Congressional Research Service also withdrew web access to some of its reports, a resource that scores of journalists used to inform the public about complex issues.[77] New rules also restricted access to port and maritime security information, but public interest groups said they were drawn so broad that it could include all kinds of environmental information related to ports, the coastal zone, and the maritime environment.[78] Moreover, news groups and scientific writers urged the Office of Management and Budget in 2004 to withdraw a proposal that could increase White House powers to shut down publication of scientific studies, especially those relating to environmental issues.[79]

The Bush administration also extended the power to classify documents to the secretaries of the Environmental Protection Agency, the Department of Agriculture, and the Department of Health and Human Services whose agencies were on the front lines of bioterrorism.[80] In 2003 the Bush administration won a new legislative exemption from the FOIA covering the National Security Agency's (NSA) operational files, even declassified documents. The administration claimed that performing FOIA searches required the agency to divert resources from its mission—a rationale that could have applied to any agency in the federal government.[81] The Federal Energy Regulatory Commission (FERC), moreover, became the first federal agency to formally limit the flow of information in the name of homeland security when it opted to close down public access to data on pipelines, electric transmission networks, and power plants. Citing terrorism concerns over "critical energy infrastructure information," FERC announced rules in February 2003 that would compel reviewers of such data to sign nondisclosure agreements, limit handling of disclosed information, and establish a federal critical energy infrastructure coordinator to oversee all document requests. Under the rules, the coordinator could override the FOIA. FERC Chairman Pat Wood said, "I do think it's very clear that information has become a weapon in our society, and one of the more vulnerable places for that is the very visible energy infrastructure."[82]

In December 2006, Bush signed into law a bill creating a new ultra secret biodefense agency, the Biomedical Advanced Research and Development Agency (BARDA). Operating under the Department of Health and Human Services, the bill gave the new agency super-secret status exempt from public and judicial oversight—immunity protections that not even the Pentagon or CIA enjoyed.[83] The administration also reached back in history, reclassifying public information that had long been available even to the former Soviet Union, including the number of strategic weapons in the U.S. nuclear arsenal from the Nixon era. "It would be difficult to find more dramatic examples of unjustifiable secrecy than these decisions to classify the numbers of U.S. strategic weapons," wrote William Burr, a senior analyst at the National Security Archive in Washington. A spokesman for the National Nuclear Security Administration, a part of the Energy Department, said that there was "no question that current classified nuclear weapons data was out there that we had to take back. And in today's environment, where there is a great deal of concern about rogue nations or terrorist groups getting access to nuclear weapons, this makes a lot of sense." An editorial in the *New York Times* wondered if "classifying Civil War ironclads and cannons" would be next, adding that the missile blackout was the latest symptom of a deepening government secrecy illness that had burdened the freedom of information law and was an "insult to honest history." The controversy followed another scandal after the U.S. archivist objected to a reclassifying initiative undertaken by the CIA, Air Force, and other agencies to withdraw 55,000 decades-old documents from the public record.[84]

With the drumbeat of criticism about the erosion of the FOIA rising from both sides of the aisle, the Defense Department announced in September 2006 that it was giving a grant of $1 million to the St. Mary's University Center for Terrorism Law to study possible alterations to the information act aimed at fighting terrorism. The study aimed to examine sunshine laws around the country and propose ways for limiting access to vital infrastructure information to protect the nation from another terrorist attack. "It seems like we're just losing all our freedoms in the name of homeland security, and I just wonder where the real threat is," said Randy Sanders, president of the Freedom of Information Foundation in Texas and retired editor of the *Lubbock Avalanche-Journal*. "We are not going to keep terrorists from finding out about power plants and water supplies by tightening the Freedom of Information Act."[85]

But while some of these measures conceivably had links to national security, the administration's blocking of access to important auto safety data, including information about warranty claims and consumer complaints, had nothing to do with national defense, intelligence, law enforcement, or critical infrastructure. As part of auto safety legislation stemming from critical safety flaws found in many Firestone tires used on Ford SUVs—a defect that led to 270 highway deaths—Congress ordered the industry to regularly turn over safety data to the National Highway Traffic Safety Administration. Congress did not exempt the information from the FOIA, but required disclosure to give regulators the chance of identifying defects early. The Transportation Department approved a rule in July 2003, however, allowing it to withhold data from consumers on warranty claims, child restraint systems, consumer complaints, tires, and auto dealer reports. The agency said confidentiality was necessary to prevent competitive harm to manufacturers, even though there was no evidence that releasing the data would injure the industry.[86]

Cheney vs. Executive Order 13292

On March 25, 2003, President Bush signed Executive Order 13292, a little known decree that gave what one critic said was the "greatest expansion of vice presidential power in U.S. history." It gave Cheney the same ability to classify intelligence beyond public and congressional reach as the president. "By controlling classification," said Sidney Blumenthal, a former senior adviser to President Clinton, "the vice president can control intelligence and, through that, foreign policy."[87] If nothing else, the order symbolized Cheney's co-presidency with President Bush. The order amended President Clinton's 1995 Executive Order 12958 that provided for the automatic declassification of federal agency records after twenty-five years. The new order granted the government more discretion to keep information classified indefinitely, especially if it fell within a broad new definition of "national security." The executive order facilitated the government's ability both to reclassify documents that had already been declassified and to classify what was characterized as "sensitive" material. The CIA director, moreover, was granted authority to override declassification rulings from an interagency panel. The order also expanded the list of information exemptions from future automatic declassification, including information that could assist in the development or use of weapons of mass destruction, reports concerning national security emergency preparedness, data relating to weapons systems, and any information that would impair relations between the United States and a foreign government.[88]

Moreover, Bush's order required all agencies and "any other entity within the executive branch" to report on their classification activities. More than eighty agencies collectively reported making 15.6 million decisions in 2004 to classify information, nearly double the number in 2001. But the vice president contended his office had no obligation to report on its classification decisions. Cheney and his chief of staff, David Addington, claimed that his office was not an agency and that the vice president's dual executive and legislative duties made it unique and exempt from the order, as Cheney also served as president of the Senate. Monitors of government secrecy said Cheney was flouting his own president's authority and undermining oversight of the classification system. "It's part of a larger picture of disrespect that this vice president has shown for the norms of oversight and accountability," said one critic.[89]

Indeed, it was ironic that Cheney who had been spearheading the administration's efforts to strengthen presidential authority should now be in the position of ignoring a presidential order. But a spokeswoman for Cheney said that the issue had been "thoroughly reviewed and it's been determined that the reporting requirement does not apply to [the office of the vice president], which has both legislative and executive functions." According to one critic, this statement was a "non sequitur" given that nothing in Bush's executive order excluded the vice president's office from reporting on classification decisions in carrying out its executive duties merely because it also had separate legislative functions.[90]

In January 2007, the vice president refused for the third time since 2003 to divulge his office's classification statistics to the Information Security Oversight Office (ISOO)—an obscure unit within the National Archives and Records Administration charged with making sure the executive branch protects classified information. In response, J. William Leonard, the ISOO's director, sent two letters to Cheney's chief of staff, David Addington, requesting compliance with the president's executive order but received no response. Leonard then took the extraordinary step of appealing to Attorney General Alberto Gonzales to render a legal opinion on whether the vice president was violating the order.[91]

Although the dispute centered on a relatively obscure process, it underscored the wider struggle over Cheney's mania for secrecy. Since becoming vice president, Cheney had drawn an iron veil over the workings of his office, shielding an array of information such as the participation of industry executives who helped write the administration's national energy policy, details about his privately funded travel, the names and size of his staff, even ordering the Secret Service to destroy his visitor logs. While Leonard's appeal to the attorney general languished in the Justice Department, Cheney retaliated by trying to abolish the ISOO. The standoff went public after Henry Waxman, chairman of the House Oversight and Government Reform Committee, released an eight-page letter he sent to the vice president. The letter said that after repeatedly refusing to comply with the order, the vice president's office in 2004 blocked an on-site inspection of records that other agencies of the executive branch routinely go through. "I know the vice president wants to operate with unprecedented secrecy," Waxman said in an interview. "But this is absurd. The order is designed to keep classified information safe. His argument is really that he's not part of the executive branch, so he doesn't have to comply." Indeed, the claim that the vice president's office was not an "executive entity" became fodder for late-night comedians and Democrats like Representative Rahm Emanuel who said he would introduce a proposal to suspend Cheney's financing as an executive officer. Whatever the outcome of the appeal to the attorney general, Waxman's letter accused Cheney's office of already having carried out "possible retaliation" against the oversight office. As part of an interagency review of Executive Order 12958, Cheney's office pressed both for eliminating appeals to the attorney general—the avenue pursued by Leonard—and for abolishing the Information Security Oversight Office. Both proposals were however rejected by the interagency groups charged with revising the executive order.[92]

The FOIA, Secrecy, and the Courts

As early as December 2002, just two months after Ashcroft discouraged agencies from releasing information under the FOIA, a critic observed that the new battle for government information had become "absolute trench warfare."[93] Indeed, it was in the legal arena where the administration's desire to maintain secrecy seemed to excite the most controversy. In the days following the 9/11 bombings, the federal government insisted on a rare degree of secrecy regarding the detention of more than 1,000 suspects, nearly all of them Muslim men, on charges of immigration violations or federal crimes. Others were detained on material witness warrants. On October 29, 2001, various public interest groups filed FOIA requests with the FBI, the Immigration and Naturalization Service (INS), and the Office of Information Privacy, seeking disclosure of the identities, locations of arrests, current whereabouts, nature of charges, names of attorneys, and other similar information. The groups also sought the identities of the courts that had been requested to seal their proceedings regarding each detainee. When the government, citing national security concerns, refused to provide much of the information, the groups—in one of the biggest court actions related to the 9/11 attacks—sued in federal district court on August 22, 2002.[94]

The administration responded by invoking the FOIA's exemption for law enforcement records, arguing that disclosure would disrupt a federal terrorism task force investigation. Attorney General Ashcroft said that while he was obligated by the Constitution to disclose the names of anyone arrested and charged with a criminal act, he did not have to do so in cases of those charged with immigration violations. On the eve of the hearing, the Justice Department released the names of ninety-three individuals facing criminal charges, but refused to say who they were. It also disclosed the federal charges brought against 548 other immigrant detainees as well as their country of origin. The Reporters Committee for Freedom of the Press later noted that the Justice Department had "provided no information on persons held as material witnesses; no information on those detained on state or local charges; no information on the relevant dates; no information on courts where secrecy orders had been requested; no information on the secrecy orders themselves; and no policy directives other than an INS order regarding sealing of proceedings." The disclosures only revealed partial information on those who had been detained and then released. The Justice Department made public additional information in late January 2002, including a list of each case, but the names of all the detainees except those criminally charged had been blacked out.[95]

In August 2002, Judge Gladys Kessler of the U.S. District Court for the District of Columbia ordered the administration to release the identities of the detainees and the names of their lawyers. Kessler ruled that the government failed to provide any substantial evidence of the detainees' ties to terrorism and dismissed claims that disclosing the names would interfere with its investigation. While recognizing important national security concerns, she noted that "secret arrests are a concept odious to a democratic society." Kessler stayed her order at the administration's request, allowing it to appeal her opinion.[96]

But in mid-June 2003, the Court of Appeals for the D.C. Circuit reversed the lower court's order, 2:1. In a widely anticipated ruling, the majority court accepted the administration's word that providing a list of names would give terrorist groups a composite picture of the government's investigation. The majority opinion, written by Judge David B. Sentelle joined by Judge Karen LeCraft Henderson, said that the courts should defer to the executive branch when intelligence agencies assert national security to justify government secrecy. Sentelle said that when the government officials tell the court that disclosing the names of detainees would produce harm, "it is abundantly clear that the government's top counterterrorism officials are well suited to make this predictive judgment. Conversely, the judiciary is in an extremely poor position to second-guess the executive's judgment in this area of national security."[97] Writing a blistering dissent, Judge David S. Tatel accused the majority of bowing to the Bush administration's demand to "simply trust its judgment."[98]

The majority and dissenting opinions showed the ideological divide on the nation's appeals courts and especially the D.C. Circuit, which was widely viewed as second in importance to the Supreme Court. While Judges Sentelle and Henderson were Republicans, Judge Tatel was a Democratic appointee. The majority opinion seemed to indicate a trend toward greater judicial deference to the executive on matters of terrorism and homeland security at the expense of the FOIA. By ruling that the detainees' names could be kept secret, the majority court evaded the central question of whether the disclosure of their names would impair the government's ongoing investigations. The court could have required the government to provide specifics to substantiate its national security claims through confidential court briefs, but chose instead to trust the government.[99] Attorney General Ashcroft applauded the ruling. "We are pleased the court agreed we should not give terrorists a virtual roadmap to our investigation that could allow terrorists to chart a potentially deadly detour around our efforts."[100]

The administration also carried the battle over its secret detentions to the states. With the nationwide sweep of aliens who were suspected of having ties to terrorism, the government locked up a substantial number of detainees in Pennsylvania, New York, and New Jersey. In March 2002, the New Jersey Superior Court ordered the names of federal detainees jailed in Hudson and Passaic County released under the state's open records law. The administration appealed, and in a move to bolster its case and bring the states into line, the Immigration and Naturalization Service issued interim rules aimed at prohibiting states from disclosing information on jailed detainees regardless of state open government laws. The rules were issued before the New Jersey appeals court could rule on the case. With the interim rules in place, in June 2002, the appeals court held that the new federal INS regulations trumped the state's open records law, and deferred to the administration's claims that disclosure would assist terrorist organizations. With this court victory, the INS issued final rules on January 29, 2003, requiring state and local jails to keep any information about federal detainees under wraps.[101]

FOIA and the Iraq War

Civil liberties and open government advocates fared better in battling for information regarding the treatment of detainees held by the U.S. military on foreign soil. On October 7, 2003, the ACLU invoked the FOIA for documents on the detention and treatment of prisoners in American detention centers in Iraq, Afghanistan, and Guantanamo Bay, Cuba. When the Pentagon and other agencies balked, the ACLU and its New York branch sued in federal district court in Manhattan, demanding the prompt release of the documents. In September 2004, Judge Alvin K. Hellerstein, complaining that the Bush administration "shows indifference" to the freedom of information laws, ordered the Pentagon and other agencies to produce a list of documents on the detention of prisoners at Abu Ghraib in Iraq.[102] While the FBI, the Justice Department, and the State Department began turning over thousands of pages of documents detailing mostly efforts to suppress the investigations of prisoner abuse in Iraq and the use of harsh interrogation techniques at Guantanamo, the Pentagon and the CIA proved far more resistant to releasing information.[103]

The focus of the case, however, soon shifted to dozens of photographs and videotapes documenting the Abu Ghraib prison scandal. The photographs comprised part of a larger batch turned over by Specialist Joseph M. Darby, a Reservist who exposed the abuse at Abu Ghraib by giving investigators computer disks containing photographs and videos of prisoners being abused, sexually humiliated, and threatened with dogs. A small number of the images released in spring 2004 sparked international outrage and condemnation of the U.S. military.[104] In early June 2005, Hellerstein ordered the Pentagon to release additional photographs, rejecting arguments that disclosing the images would violate the Geneva Conventions on grounds that prisoners might be identified and "further humiliated."[105] Before issuing the order, Hellerstein had already reviewed some of the Darby images in a closed session in his chambers and directed the Pentagon to redact the identifying features from the photographs of detainees and release them to the ACLU under the FOIA.[106]

Senior Pentagon officials, however, countered with compelling arguments that publicizing images regarding the abuse of detainees at Abu Ghraib would incite outrage in the Muslim world, put the lives of American soldiers and officials at risk, increase terrorist recruitment, and exacerbate "tensions between Iraqi and Afghanistan populations and U.S. and coalition forces."[107] In his opinion in September, Hellerstein refuted the military's reasoning for keeping the images secret. "My task is not to defer to our worst fears, but to interpret the law," he said. "Our nation does not surrender to blackmail," he wrote. "There is a risk that the enemy will seize upon the publicity of the photographs as a pretext for violent acts." But in a statement that went to the very heart of the FOIA, he observed that "[s]uppression of information is the surest way to cause its significance to grow and persist. Clarity and openness are the best antidotes, either to dispel criticism if not merited or, if merited, to correct such errors as may be found. These are the values FOIA was intended to advance."[108] Hellerstein stayed his order for twenty days to allow the Pentagon to appeal. Nevertheless, after many of the photographs and videotapes were posted on the internet on the website of salon.com, the government and the ACLU agreed to a stipulated dismissal. Under the terms, the government agreed to authenticate the seventy-three photographs and three videotapes that Hellerstein ordered to be released, while withholding another twenty-nine photographs and two videos.[109]

In response to another FOIA lawsuit, the Pentagon released more than 700 images of the return of American casualties to Dover Air Force Base and other military facilities, where the fallen troops received Honor Guard ceremonies. The case came after a series of FOIA requests were filed by University of Delaware Professor Ralph Begleiter with the assistance of the National Security Archive in Washington.[110] Recognizing that images define wars in the public mind, presidents since the end of Vietnam had always worried that support for their military actions would fade once the public glimpsed the remains of American soldiers arriving home in flag-draped caskets. In March 2003, the Bush administration addressed the issue on the eve of the Iraq war with a Pentagon directive banning arrival ceremonies and media coverage of deceased military personnel returning to or departing from Ramstein [Germany] airbase or the Dover [Delaware] base.[111] The military-wide policy dated to the last days of the Clinton administration, but largely went unheeded until images of caskets returning from the Afghanistan war began appearing on television broadcasts and in newspapers. Bush's critics said he was trying to limit public focus on U.S. Iraqi war fatalities, a charge the administration denied. After releasing the images, however, the Pentagon considered ending the practice of taking photographs of returning remains—a policy that produced some of the "most respectful images" regarding American casualties of war and served to inform the American public in ways in which words could not do alone.[112]

The Associated Press (AP)—the international news organization—also prevailed in a FOIA lawsuit compelling the Pentagon to release 5,000 pages of hearing transcripts of the ad hoc military tribunals of Guantanamo Bay detainees. The Bush administration insisted on concealing the identities, home countries, and other information about individuals accused of having links to the Taliban and al Qaeda. Most of the 750 detainees were captured in the 2001 American-led war that drove the Taliban from power in Afghanistan and then held incommunicado at Guantanamo Bay. In 2004, the Pentagon began holding tribunals to determine whether the detainees should be classified as enemy combatants, as well as whether they should be deprived of Geneva Convention prisoner-of-war protections and held indefinitely without charge. The AP invoked the FOIA for the hearing transcripts in November 2004. After the AP sued in federal district court, the Pentagon released heavily sanitized versions of the transcripts with all personal identifying information blacked out. The Pentagon claimed that full disclosure would constitute an unwarranted invasion of the personal privacy of the detainees and thus was exempt under the FOIA.[113]

The federal district court in Manhattan, however, rejected the administration's privacy arguments, noting that the detainees' privacy interests were "minimal" and far outweighed by the public interest in revealing "government malfeasance." The case represented another example of the government resisting the release of information about the war on terrorism. The Pentagon's privacy case diverged from the highly publicized case in 2002 in which a federal appeals court said that the administration could withhold the names of people detained within the United States for national security reasons. Because the decision appeared to cast doubt on the government's ability to use privacy as a shield to withhold information about people suspected of terrorist ties, the administration agreed to comply with the court's order in March 2006.[114]

Delays, Denials, and the Rising Backlog of FOIA Requests

The chilling effect of Ashcroft's memorandum discouraging the release of information pervaded the federal bureaucracy well after his departure in February 2005. In many cases, federal officials responded to FOIA requests with delays and denials that subverted the intention of the open government statute. In November 2003, the Justice Department initially denied a request by the People for the American Way for records about the government's legal proceedings against immigrant detainees rounded up after 9/11, saying that it would violate the detainees' privacy. In 2005, however, it said the information could be provided for a search fee of nearly $400,000. In another case, the Justice Department denied a request of a reporting team from Cox Newspapers for information about illegal aliens who had been convicted of serious crimes and then released without being deported. The agency explained that the privacy of the criminals overrode the public interest in knowing who and where they were.[115] The government's privacy argument reached absurdity when Terry Anderson, the AP journalist who was held hostage for seven years in Lebanon, was denied some of the information he sought about his captivity because it would violate the privacy rights of the kidnappers.[116] Moreover, after asking the EPA for days to learn where dangerous chemicals were leaking after the devastation of Hurricane Katrina, a reporter for the New Orleans *Times-Picayune* could not get an answer. A September 12, 2005, report by the Society of Environmental Journalists said this sort of delayed nonresponse to a FOIA request was becoming commonplace.[117]

Numerous independent studies supported this assertion. A March 2006 analysis by the AP of 250 annual FOIA reports submitted to the Justice Department between 1998 and 2005 found that many federal agencies were falling far short of the requirements of the statute, repeatedly failing to meet reporting deadlines while citizens waited ever longer for documents.[118] In July 2006, a report by the Coalition of Journalists for Open Government found that the backlog of FOIA requests pending at twenty-two agencies rose 31 percent in 2005, up from 20 percent in 2004. The coalition of thirty journalism-related groups, which tracked twenty-two cabinet-level agencies, reported that the trend was worsening with holdover requests increasing 24 percent from 2004 to 2005, compared with 11 percent from 2003 to 2004. A representative of the National Newspaper Association and the Sunshine in Government Initiative said the open government law had "become less reliable, less effective, and a less timely vehicle for informing the public of government activities and newsworthy stories."[119]

The GAO also released a study citing increasing backlogs of unprocessed requests as a major problem and found that the "number of pending requests carried over from year to year ha[d] been steadily increasing, rising to about 200,000 in fiscal year 2005—43 percent more than in 2002."[120] A study by the National Security Archive found that the federal government had twenty-eight different policies for handling "sensitive but unclassified information," resulting in unprecedented restrictions on public access. The public interest organization, which served as a valued information clearinghouse for the press and public, also was facing an unfriendly move by the CIA to rescind its search fee waiver that had long been granted to the group—a change that would potentially cost the organization hundreds of thousands of dollars.[121] The nonprofit public interest group OpenTheGovernment.org released its 2006 secrecy report card, finding that government secrecy was continuing to expand across a broad array of agencies and actions and that public use of the FOIA continued to rise as "more categories that exclude information from access are created by agencies." Among the many signs of growing secrecy, the group noted the administration's use of its unilateral authority to declare information a "state secret" at an unprecedented rate. From 2001 through 2006, the Bush administration invoked the state secrets privilege twenty-two times, as opposed to its invocation fifty-four times between 1977 and 2000. The group also reported that Bush issued as many as 132 presidential signing statements during his term of office, challenging more than 810 federal laws.[122]

The slew of studies followed President Bush's December 2005 Executive Order 13392 directing agencies to improve their administration of the law, appoint chief FOIA officers, and establish in-house FOIA centers to handle requests.[123] But Bush's order fell short of modifying Ashcroft's 2001 policy that discouraged agencies from releasing information to the public. Scott A. Hodes, a Washington-based attorney who led the FBI's Freedom of Information litigation unit from 1998 to 2002, said there was widespread disinclination to comply with the law. "It doesn't surprise me that most responses are late, and that they tend to deny a lot. Even though your higher-level administration officials will say they like FOIA, there's a general dislike of FOIA," he said.[124] Attorney General Alberto Gonzales, however, issued his own report in October 2006 on the implementation of the president's executive order on the FOIA. In sharp contrast to the many independent studies that found increasing backlogs and stonewalling of public information requests, Gonzales's lone report praised agencies for implementing the executive order "in a vigorous manner fully commensurate with the importance of this unprecedented Presidential initiative."[125]

Legislative Responses

Nonetheless, adherence to the Ashcroft directive and the Bush administration's penchant for secrecy brought the response by federal agencies to FOIA requests to a crawl, creating an outcry that finally led Bush to issue his 2005 order that appeared to endorse the values embodied in the FOIA. While Bush's language endorsed openness, his order seemed more aimed at heading off congressional action on a bipartisan open government law. Nevertheless, a number of bipartisan measures were introduced in the House and Senate to speed up the FOIA and relieve agency backlogs. In February 2005, Senators Patrick Leahy, a Democrat, and John Cornyn, a Republican, introduced a bill enabling the public to recover legal costs for challenging FOIA denials in court, extending fee waivers to freelance journalists for research and copying, and mandating agencies to establish hotline and tracking systems for requests. The bill also proposed creating a mediation system to resolve FOIA disputes. The Senate measure received support from a broad coalition of open government advocates and groups across the political spectrum, but like its House counterpart, the bill never made it to the floor.[126]

In March 2005, Cornyn and Leahy sponsored another bill proposing a commission to study backlog problems and possible improvements of agency procedures. The bill was reported favorably out of committee, but failed to receive a floor vote. The two senators, moreover, proposed a measure in May 2005 requiring future legislation to state explicitly within the text of a bill whether it contained any new exemption to the FOIA. Cornyn said the "justification for this provision is simple: Congress should not establish new secrecy provisions through secret means. If Congress is to establish a new exemption to FOIA, it should do so in the open and in the light of day."[127] The sponsors of the measure sought to address a provision in the fiscal 2006 defense authorization bill granting a broad FOIA exemption to the Defense Intelligence Agency.[128]

In addition, in May 2005, Waxman proposed a bill in the House aimed at reversing every FOIA problem incurred under the Bush administration. The measure aimed to speed up public disclosure, annul the Ashcroft memorandum, limit the exemption for critical infrastructure information, bar secret federal advisory meetings, reduce unofficial classification of information, and restore access to public records. Waxman's bill made it to committee where it languished. By late September 2006, both Senate and House versions of open government legislation were still alive, but with the November congressional elections, neither bill made it to the Senate floor or out of committee in the House.[129]

A Few Signs of Openness

In the twilight months of 2006, several actions by Congress and the White House seemed to indicate a small but countervailing trend toward more openness. With more aggressive bipartisan efforts to reassert government transparency and a president weakened by the unpopular war in Iraq, the White House seemed to begin flirting with openness. This trend accelerated after the Democrats won majorities in both houses in the November 2006 congressional elections and immediately began to demand more accountability and oversight, causing the administration to step back from its expansive interpretation of executive power. In October, Bush signed into law the 2007 Homeland Security Appropriations Act, which included provisions requiring that all documents categorized as "sensitive security information" be released after three years. The secretary of Homeland Security could continue to withhold the information, however, if there was a reason determined for doing so. Other legislation involved the Federal Funding Accountability and Transparency Act that required the administration to establish an online searchable database for grants and contracts.[130]

In a surprising move, the secrecy-prone Bush administration also enforced a December 31, 2006, midnight deadline—created in the Clinton administration— for the automatic declassification of hundreds of millions of pages of secret documents, including numerous FBI Cold War files on investigations of people suspected of being Communist sympathizers. Under Clinton's Executive Order 12958, secret documents twenty-five years or older were to lose their classified status unless agencies sought specific exemptions on secrecy grounds. Despite the exemption of large numbers of intelligence documents, the massive declassi-fication at first glance seemed to promise huge effects on public access— especially since in every successive year, millions of additional documents would be automatically declassified as they reached the twenty-five-year limit.

Nonetheless, huge obstacles stood in the way of the public actually seeing these documents; declassification was not the "same as release." Vast quantities of documents would still be withheld under the executive order's nine grounds for exemption as well as other laws that restricted their release. Moreover, the "auto-matic release" policy did not mean that documents would be rapidly released into the public domain, but instead that they would be reviewed for declassifica-tion, exemption, or referral to other agencies. The "referral to other agencies" procedure provided an enormous loophole against releasing information. A scholar writing in the *Los Angeles Times* pointed out that because "virtually all important documents involved multiple agencies," if even one agency "wanted to withhold a document, it would be withheld." Moreover, those documents deemed releasable had to be sent to the National Archives to be made publicly available, but the Archives already had a backlog of 400 million pages.[131] The executive order's promise of a flood of documents into the public domain repre-senting the nation's classified past seemed to be more chimera than reality.

Even so, in June 2007, the CIA announced that it was declassifying hun-dreds of pages of long-secret records regarding some of the intelligence agency's worst illegal abuses—the so-called "family jewels." The documents detailed a quarter-century of overseas assassination attempts, domestic spying, kidnap-ping, and infiltration of leftist groups from the 1950s to the 1970s. The reports resulted from a 1973 request from then-CIA Director James R. Schlesinger. Startled by press revelations of the CIA's involvement in Watergate, Schlesinger ordered an unprecedented examination of all operations that violated the agency's legal charter. The documents also contained revelations of break-ins and theft, the opening of private mail to and from China and the Soviet

Union, wiretaps and surveillance of journalists, and a series of "unwitting" tests on American citizens, including the use of drugs. The results of the investigation so worried Henry Kissinger that he warned President Ford that if the operations were publicly divulged it could be worse for the country than Watergate. But many of the CIA's violations were disclosed in varying detail during the congressional investigations of the 1970s that led to major intelligence reforms and increased oversight. The documents, however, promised to reveal the full contours of the intelligence abuses, providing a trove of new information to historians, journalists, and others who had long sought the materials through fruitless Freedom of Information Act requests.[132]

When it came to open government legislation, however, the White House drew the line. As the provisions of the 2006 open government bills were resurrected and sped to House passage, it met with the administration's resistance. Aided with substantial Republican support, the Democrats approved measures in March 2007 to force government agencies to be more responsive to the millions of annual FOIA requests and strengthen protection for government whistleblowers. The House also passed legislation to reverse Bush's 2001 executive order allowing presidents to keep their records under wraps. Moreover, legislation on the FOIA advanced in the Senate where it received bipartisan support. The administration, citing the president's constitutional prerogatives, struck back with veto threats if the presidential records and whistleblower bills reached Bush's desk. The House bill on the FOIA, however, went beyond the Senate version in reversing Ashcroft's policy that advised against disclosure whenever there was a sound legal basis for doing so. But the White House said it strongly opposed the House measure, contending that it would disrupt the balance between the public's right to know and the imperative to protect certain information.[133]

The actions and rhetoric of both governmental branches signaled a rapidly escalating political battle between the newly elected Democratic Congress that sought to reassert its oversight prerogatives and a White House that had from the beginning embarked on an expansion of presidential power. The Bush administration had for years waged its expansion of presidential authority by withholding information from the public, denying congressional inquiries for information, challenging the constitutionality of open government statutes in the courts, claiming authority to eavesdrop on Americans without court warrants, establishing secret prisons beyond the reach of American law or international treaties, issuing presidential signing statements to override provisions of federal laws, clamping down on leaks to the press, and pursuing other executive actions—all with the acquiescence of a muted Republican-dominated Congress that seemed more interested in retaining power and serving the interests of the party than asserting its constitutional oversight prerogatives. With the Congress having changed hands and the president weakened by the Iraq war, as well as domestic issues ranging from the firing of federal prosecutors to the warrantless surveillance program, it appeared that oversight was back in fashion.

Nonetheless, the erosion of the freedom of information law and the unchecked proliferation of secrecy designations of unclassified, public information have given the government wider latitude to hide behind veils of secrecy. As a general rule, excessive secrecy distances the government from the public and has always come at a high cost in terms of profound distrust by the American people toward their government. Americans had grown to question their government during the Cold War. Presidential administrations from Eisenhower to Reagan lied to the public about crises including the U-2 spy plane affair, the prosecution of the Vietnam War, the so-called missile gap between the Soviet Union and the United States, the Watergate affair, and the sale of weapons to Iran. As the official version of half-truths disintegrated and were replaced by a more revealing record, many Americans grew to distrust the federal government, even as Congress moved to establish greater oversight and accountability. This point was made in almost Madisonian fashion in a presidential proclamation in support of open government not long after the FOIA's 1966 enactment: "The many abuses of the security system can no longer be tolerated. Fundamental to our way of life is the belief that when information which properly belongs to the public is systematically withheld by those in power, the people soon become ignorant of their own affairs, distrustful of those who manage them, and—eventually—incapable of determining their own destinies." These words were offered in 1972 by Richard M. Nixon, whose presidency fell two years later on the sword of secrecy.[134]

Two

Overturning the Presidential Records Act

As one of his first policy moves to enforce greater secrecy and extend executive powers, on November 1, 2001, President Bush issued Executive Order 13233, which erected new barriers to obtaining access to former presidents' White House materials under the 1978 Presidential Records Act (PRA). Congress passed this cornerstone reform act following the constitutional struggle surrounding access to President Richard M. Nixon's tapes and records for the Watergate investigations and trials. The law overturned the long-running tradition of private ownership that dated to the beginning of the Republic by declaring that after January 20, 1981, the records of all presidents and vice presidents would be the property of the American people. The act allowed citizens to review all materials, including confidential communications with advisers, twelve years after a president leaves office. The act also assured that the most sensitive records relating to national security, foreign relations, financial and trade secrets, and personal privacy were exempt from disclosure.[1] While Congress passed the law to further the public's right to know, the Bush administration rewrote the act to reverse what it viewed as an unacceptable infringement onto its executive prerogatives. By doing so, the White House reversed, if not nullified, one of the key post-Watergate reform acts that aimed to make government more accountable.

In violation of the 1978 act, the Bush order authorized former presidents, vice presidents, their designated representatives or surviving family members and heirs to withhold materials in seeming perpetuity by asserting executive privilege, no matter how arbitrary the claim. Beyond radically extending executive privilege to private citizens outside the confines of the 1978 law and prior court rulings, both sitting and former presidents were given authority to indefinitely postpone public release just by withholding their permission. The order also required that a "specific need" for information be demonstrated, placed the burden on the person requesting materials to bring a lawsuit in order to challenge a denial of access, expanded the types of records exempt from disclosure, and stripped the U.S. archivist of his affirmative responsibilities under the PRA to carry out the systematic and timely release of presidential records to the public.[2] Congress passed the act to further the "public's right to know," but Bush's order inverted this presumption to a strict "need to control" basis. The Bush administration could have challenged the constitutionality of the PRA if it believed that the law violated executive privilege. Instead, the White House undertook such a sweeping rewriting of the federal statute passed by the legislative branch that critics charged that it breached the separation of powers.[3]

As a matter of law and public policy, the Bush administration seemed to have based its executive order on a selective reading of *Nixon v. Administrator of General Services*.[4] In that 1977 opinion, the Supreme Court rejected former President Richard M. Nixon's unilateral assertions of executive privilege in his bid to reclaim ownership of his presidential tapes and records after Congress seized them for the Watergate investigations and trials. The Court may have repudiated Nixon's claims of an absolute and unreviewable privilege over the materials of his presidency, but the Bush administration looked to the former president's concept of privilege to rewrite the PRA. It is perhaps one of the great ironies surrounding the troubled history of the act that Nixon, whose extreme claims of privilege failed to win back his presidential materials, became the model for later presidential attempts to undercut the law.

Like the FOIA, every administration has viewed the presidential records law with some hostility. To some extent this animosity has stemmed from the long-held view that confidentiality is vital to the constitutional operations of the White House. Presidents, however, have always viewed the raw records of their administrations with some trepidation regarding how they might determine the historical judgment of their presidencies.[5] The PRA was passed, however, to serve the interests of history, not former presidents. But unlike Nixon, who was obsessed with recording his presidential deeds for posterity to his later chagrin, the Bush administration sought from the beginning to avoid recording anything that might betray its actions to media investigations or congressional probes, or ultimately stain its legacy.

Bush telegraphed his fondness for executive secrecy even before he entered the White House. As his last act as Texas governor, Bush sent his governors papers to his father's presidential library at Texas A&M University, instead of to the state archives, putting them beyond the reach of the state's tough public information act. The attempt to federalize and bury his gubernatorial papers came after the Supreme Court's favorable ruling in the controversial Florida presidential vote recount that handed him the presidency. After a fight over their disposition, it took a ruling by Texas Attorney General John Cornyn, a Bush supporter, to make it clear that state law governed the gubernatorial papers.[6] Given the clarity of the Texas Public Information Act, the Texas attorney general could scarcely have ruled otherwise.

Bush occupied the Oval Office for only a few months before he exhibited the same suspicion of federal information laws. Asked to comment on government openness at an American Society of Newspaper Editors convention in Washington in April 2001, Bush said he was troubled by the intrusiveness of the nation's public disclosure laws—even to the point of curbing e-mail contact with his family. "I used to be an avid e-mailer, and I e-mailed to my daughters or e-mailed to my father," he said. "And I don't want those e-mails to be in the public domain, so I don't e-mail anymore, out of concern for freedom of information laws but also concern for my privacy."[7]

Bush need not have worried about e-mailing family members, however, because materials related to personal privacy are exempt under the PRA. Nonetheless, Bush's extreme sense of confidentiality extended to the official activities of his influential political adviser Karl Rove and many other executive office staffers who from the first days of the administration were using back-channel e-mail accounts to avoid the archiving function of the White House e-mail system.[8] Both Bush's statement that he no longer used e-mail out of privacy concerns and the employment of off-the-book e-mail accounts by as many as fifty-one White House staffers revealed efforts to closely guard information.

Tradition of Private Ownership

When issuing EO 13233, the Bush administration seemed to look immediately to Nixon's example for expanding privilege rights of former presidents, but the order also contained features that recalled the long-abandoned proprietary sense of early presidents. Congress passed the PRA to erase the last vestiges of this tradition by declaring that presidential records belonged to the American people. The law, however, also stemmed from a collision of two historical customs regarding executive privilege and private ownership of presidential records on the ruins of the Nixon presidency. Since the beginning of the Republic, presidents exercised both the right and power to withhold information from the other branches of government and to claim their presidential papers as private property when they left office. President George Washington set both traditions in motion by exercising the first instance of privilege and by taking his presidential papers with him on retiring from office. Washington keenly understood that his actions would set precedents for the future. On

May 5, 1789, he wrote to James Madison, "As the first of every thing, in our situation will serve to establish a precedent, it is devoutly wished on my part that these precedents may be fixed on true principles."[9]

The tradition of private ownership of presidential papers evolved separately from the custom of presidential assertions of executive privilege. While sitting presidents often asserted privilege against congressional inquiries for information in the public interest, ex-presidents exercised even greater control of their official papers after they left office, treating them as personal property. From Washington through Franklin D. Roosevelt, presidents disposed of their papers as they saw fit, purging or bequeathing them to their heirs, who in turn sold them for profit, destroyed them, or donated or sold them to one or more libraries. When George Washington left office, he had his papers packed in trunks and sent to his estate at Mt. Vernon—setting a precedent that lasted for two centuries. Noting their invaluable worth perhaps with a touch of vanity, he at one point characterized them as a "species of public property sacred in my hands."[10] Most early presidents shared Washington's view of their papers, as well as Grover Cleveland's proprietary sense that "if I desired to take [my presidential papers] into my custody I might do so with entire propriety, and if I saw fit to destroy them no one could complain."[11]

Until the Nixon administration, few questioned the right of private ownership, even after President Franklin D. Roosevelt established a new American institution—the presidential library built with private funds and operated at public expense. The new tradition of the presidential library may have dramatically increased the preservation of presidential records, but it did nothing to alter the arbitrary discretion of ex-presidents to control access to the documents of their administrations. In 1955, Congress passed the Presidential Libraries Act to enable other presidents to follow Roosevelt's example. The act established a non-mandatory system of presidential libraries, which explicitly recognized that presidential papers were the property of the chief executive. By passing this law, Congress embraced and indeed sanctified the historical tradition that presidential records remained private property. The presidential libraries system did much to encourage the preservation and early accessibility of presidential records, but the recognition of the prevailing tradition of private ownership left unresolved the problem that former presidents and their heirs could control access to—or even destroy—the records of the governmental history of the American people.[12]

Nixon's Case: Tradition Unbound

Not until the constitutional crisis surrounding Nixon and the struggle over access to his records for the Watergate investigations and trials did the customs of executive privilege and private ownership of presidential records collide and come under critical examination by the other branches of government. When Nixon resigned on August 9, 1979, under threat of impeachment, he claimed 44 million pages of presidential documents and 800 large reels of the fatal White House tapes. A month later, President Gerald Ford disclosed an agreement Nixon signed with Arthur F. Sampson, head of the General Services Administration (GSA), giving him ownership of his presidential tapes and records. The Nixon–Sampson agreement gave Nixon the right to control access to the thousands of hours of furtive tape recordings during his lifetime and to destroy any tape of his choosing after five years. After ten years, or upon his death, whichever occurred first, the remaining tapes were to be destroyed.[13] While Nixon's agreement accorded with historical precedent, it ignited a firestorm of protest from Congress, the public, and the Watergate Special Prosecutor—fearing that the former president might try to create national amnesia regarding the worst deeds of his White House years. The *Washington Post* immediately termed the agreement an "open invitation to a monumental coverup" and a giveaway that would allow Nixon "every opportunity to use the records of his presidency to obstruct justice and stonewall history."[14]

The constitutional struggle regarding access to Nixon's presidential tapes and records forced Congress to confront the question of who owned the records of the presidency and forced the judiciary to confront the limits of executive privilege. Amid the uproar surrounding the agreement, Congress passed, and Ford signed, emergency legislation nullifying the agreement in December 1974. The Presidential Recordings and Materials Preservation Act directed the GSA to seize Nixon's presidential materials to preserve them for posterity and the continuing Watergate investigations and trials. The act also directed the GSA to develop regulations governing their public access at the earliest reasonable date.[15]

In response to the congressional seizure of his presidential tapes and records, the former president sued, claiming among other things that the act transgressed the separation of powers and the president's inherent authority to assert executive privilege. Nixon lost his case on June 28, 1977, when the Supreme Court voted 7:2 to uphold Congress's constitutional right to confiscate his presidential tapes and records. In *Nixon v. Administrator of General Services*, the majority Court rejected the former president's arguments that the act violated the separation of powers as both Presidents Ford and Carter endorsed the law.[16] The majority Court also found the act to conform to the separation of powers by placing the presidential materials under the control of the U.S. archivist, an executive branch official appointed by the president.[17] The Court concluded that Nixon could be singled out for special treatment in the disposition of his records and that he must yield to the legitimate congressional aim of preserving the materials and maintaining access to them for lawful governmental and historical purposes.

Moreover, in a pivotal statement that would later bedevil the Presidential Records Act, the justices declared that the "expectation of the confidentiality of executive communications ... has always been limited and subject to erosion over time after an administration leaves office."[18] With this statement, the Court recognized for the first time the right of a former president to claim executive privilege, but failed to specify when it expired. Former presidents could exercise privilege in withholding access to their presidential materials, but it was limited and time sensitive, not absolute and indefinite as Nixon contended. Further, the Court said that an incumbent president "should not be dependent on happenstance or the whim of a prior President when he seeks access to records of past decisions that define or channel current governmental obligations. Nor should the American people's ability to reconstruct and come to terms with their history be truncated by an analysis of Presidential privilege that focuses exclusively only on the needs of the present."[19]

Although the decision rejected Nixon's constitutional claims, the separate opinions of the majority Court reflected enough ambiguity to allow future presidents—including George W. Bush—to make a selective reading of the case. The justices unanimously agreed on the fundamental importance of executive privilege to the operations of the presidency, a principle that the Court recognized for the first time in the annals of the judiciary in *United States v. Nixon* (1974). In that case, Nixon was forced to turn over sixty-four tapes to the special Watergate prosecutor—one of which implicated him in the Watergate conspiracy and destroyed his presidency. Nonetheless, the Court paid great deference to the importance of executive privilege. "The importance of this confidentiality is too plain to require further discussion," the Court said. "Human experience teaches that those who expect public dissemination of their remarks may well temper candor with a concern for appearance and for their own interests to the detriment of the decision-making process."[20]

Indeed, Justice Brennan, who authored *Nixon v. Administrator* that dismissed the former president's claims of unbounded privilege nevertheless paid deference to the vital prerogative regarding the confidential communications between high government officials. Justice White questioned whether the government could exercise any rights over a president's purely private communications despite their historical significance. Justice Stevens, concerned about the reach of the Court's decision, stressed that his verdict applied only to Nixon and not to other presidents. "The statute before the Court does not apply to all Presidents or former Presidents," he wrote. "It singles out one, by name, for special treatment. Unlike all other former Presidents in our history, he is denied custody of his own Presidential papers."[21] Justice Powell, also careful to observe the decision's narrow reach, noted the unique historical circumstances surrounding passage of the act. He wrote that Congress passed the seizure law as emergency legislation to preserve Nixon's tapes and records amid an ongoing constitutional crisis. He reiterated the Court's opinion that the seizure law was directed against a "legitimate class of one," and anticipated that "difficult constitutional questions lie ahead."[22]

The decision's significance also rested in the vigorous dissenting opinions of Chief Justice Warren E. Burger and Justice William Rehnquist who declared that it would undermine executive authority and chill future White House conferences. Justice Burger wrote that the Court's holding was a "grave repudiation of nearly 200 years of judicial precedent and historical practice," and predicted that it "may well be a ghost at future White House conferences" as presidential aides might withhold giving candid advice for fear of unwarranted disclosure.[23] Rehnquist warned that the Court's decision "countenances the power of any future Congress to seize the official papers of an outgoing president as he leaves the inaugural stand," and that it would "daily stand as a veritable sword of Damocles over every succeeding President and his advisors."[24]

Passage of the Presidential Records Act

In a sense, Justice Rehnquist's prediction proved remarkably prescient when Congress passed the 1978 Presidential Records Act, declaring public dominion over the White House materials of former presidents and vice presidents.[25] Congress acted to address the unresolved question left by the Supreme Court in *Nixon v. Administrator* regarding who should control a president's records after he leaves office. The PRA was enacted to prevent another constitutional crisis surrounding the ownership of presidential materials by declaring them to be public property and by providing for their preservation and access according to established procedures.

The terms of the act obligated the president to create and manage an adequate documentary record of his administration.[26] The PRA covered all documentary materials after January 20, 1981, produced or received by the president, his immediate staff, or any unit in the executive office whose sole function was to advise and assist the president. The new law exempted personal diaries, private political papers, and campaign records.[27] The law also exempted the most sensitive records relating to national security, foreign relations, financial and trade secrets, appointment of federal officials, personal privacy, and confidential communications with or among the president's advisers from disclosure. The 1978 law, however, declared that the automatic protection for confidential communications ran out after twelve years.

When drafting the act, Congress took note of *Nixon v. Administrator* that former presidents had an eroding right of executive privilege over their presidential communications. Congress sought to settle the matter of how long former presidents could exert privilege by allowing them to withhold materials, including confidential deliberations with advisers, for up to twelve years. Afterward, these restricted deliberative materials were to become publicly available under the terms of the FOIA. Congress believed that twelve years was ample time to protect records containing confidential deliberations with advisers and that afterward the public interest outweighed any embarrassment that might be divulged through public disclosure. In a key provision, the law made clear that "nothing in this Act shall be construed to confirm, limit, or expand any constitutionally-based privilege which may be available to an incumbent or former President."

The PRA also required the U.S. archivist to notify an ex-president when disclosure of documents might "adversely affect any rights or privileges" that he may have.[28] The National Archives subsequently issued a regulation under the dictates of the law requiring the U.S. archivist to give the former president thirty days to assert privilege against the release of documents. If the archivist denied the privilege claim, the former president was given thirty additional days to seek judicial review of the decision.[29] When passing the act, Congress sought to balance the competing interests of the public's right to know with the executive prerogative to withhold internal communications. The authors of the statute were mindful of the two Nixon Supreme Court decisions that affirmed the existence of executive privilege covering presidential materials. While *Nixon v. Administrator* recognized the right of former presidents to claim privilege, there was sparse judicial precedent regarding the scope of the prerogative. The Court asserted that a former president's privilege over his presidential records eroded with the passage of time, but this statement left the matter in utter ambiguity. The question of how much time must elapse before a former president's privilege vanished altogether, at what rate it eroded, or whether it ever disappeared at all was left unresolved.

Senator Charles Percy noted during the deliberations on the PRA that if "some future President believes that the 12-year closure period does not suffice, that President could object to the release of some document in the 13th or 14th or 20th year." The PRA, he said, did not "resolve the outcome of such legal action; the issue would be resolved by the courts."[30] Senator Percy augured the battles to come over implementation of the law. Indeed, those who drafted the law failed to see how it would shape the future struggle over the separation of powers between the executive and legislative branches, or how the Supreme Court's recognition of the existence of executive privilege for former presidents would "leave the Act in a state of constant siege by the presidency." If the drafters of the PRA believed that presidential administrations would "obsequiously obey the dictates of the Act, they were gravely mistaken, perhaps naïve."[31]

Presidential Resistance

The effort to merge and regulate the right of executive privilege of ex-presidents with the concept of public ownership met with vigorous White House resistance from the beginning. The evolution of this opposition explains to a considerable extent the nature of the Bush-Cheney administration's effort to nullify the PRA. Indeed, while the PRA may have ended the tradition of private ownership, it did nothing to prevent presidents—Republicans and Democrats—from continuing to act as if their records were private property. The Carter administration viewed the act's brief twelve-year ceiling on restricting access as deeply flawed and unconstitutional regarding the most sensitive internal White House communications. Carter's Justice Department raised this argument when the PRA was being considered. A representative of the department's Office of Legal Counsel testified that the Supreme Court clearly recognized that presidential privilege extended to confidential communications between the president and his advisers and among those advisers. "Although the justifications supporting the privilege may become less critical with the passage of time," he said, "there is no indication that it can be said to dissipate altogether after the passage of any particular period of years. An effective declaration that the privilege can be asserted for 10, 13, or 15 years but no longer must consequently be seen as of doubtful constitutionality."[32]

Against congressional efforts to pass the act, Carter's aides lobbied strenuously for a bill that would exempt his presidential papers from the law. Congress subsequently passed a modified version of the legislation that was signed by Carter as the Presidential Records Act of 1978.[33] The law exempted Carter's presidential papers, but covered those of all his presidential successors.

As the first administration to be covered by the law, the Reagan administration viewed the law's twelve-year restriction rule—the heart of the PRA—with even greater alarm. In 1985, a young lawyer in the Reagan White House wrote a memorandum to the president's counsel, Fred Fielding, who later reprised that role in the George W. Bush administration, warning that the constitutional implications of the law had to be addressed. The memorandum carried considerable significance because it framed the debate over the law and provided direction for how the White House should challenge the act. The lawyer, John Glover Roberts Jr., who twenty years later would be appointed Chief Justice of the Supreme Court by George W. Bush, wrote that the twelve-year restriction period was too brief a period and that it "might inhibit the free flow of candid advice ... within the White House." That "flow is protected by the constitutionally based doctrine of executive privilege," he said, "and a strong argument can be mounted that the statutory 12-year ceiling on restricting access is unconstitutional." Roberts averred that the act contained a key statement that "Nothing in the act shall be construed to confirm, limit, or expand any constitutionally-based privilege which may be available to an incumbent or former president." But that statement "merely frames the dispute," he said.[34]

It was unlikely, said Roberts, that any court challenge could be mounted until 2001, the year when Reagan's papers would be available for release under the act and when the case would be "legally ripe." For these reasons, he advised that the "infirmities" of the act should be "cured" before the end of the Reagan administration by taking one of two steps. The most obvious possibility was a legislative amendment, but the White House could also draft archival regulations that recognized the validity of possible executive privilege claims to block disclosure after the statutory twelve-year period.[35]

The Reagan administration never sought a legislative amendment from the Democratic-controlled Congress, but it did pursue regulatory remedies to expand the scope of presidential privilege and undercut the act. The first attempt came in 1986 when the Justice Department issued an administrative rule mandating that the U.S. archivist must bow to any claims of executive privilege by Nixon in violation of the 1974 law that allowed the ex-president's materials to be seized and made publicly available at the earliest reasonable date.[36] When Congress directed the confiscation of Nixon's tapes and records in 1974, it also ordered the National Archives to issue regulations governing their public release. The regulations quickly became a battleground, however, as Nixon, the National Archives, and Congress fought in and out of the courts over the nature of the rules. Reagan's Justice Department aimed to circumvent any such regulations by giving Nixon absolute privilege or veto power over access to his White House materials. By doing so, Justice officials sought to redefine the scope of executive privilege to accord with Nixon's lavish claims of the prerogative, which the Supreme Court already twice rejected in 1974 and 1977. The main impetus behind the directive, however, was not Nixon, but Reagan. By expanding executive privilege to suit the incumbent, the Justice Department hoped to lay the groundwork both for Reagan and the protection and courtesy of his presidential successors. Writing in the *Wall Street Journal*, historian Stanley Kutler noted that the "Reagan White House well realizes what stakes are involved in the future interpretation of the Presidential Records Act of 1978." The effort to adopt Nixon's notions of executive privilege appeared to return the issue to "square one and 1973" when one of

Nixon's lawyers flatly declared: "It's for the president alone to say what is covered by executive privilege."[37]

The Reagan administrative directive was later overturned by the U.S. Court of Appeals for the D.C. Circuit in *Public Citizen v. Burke* (1988) on grounds that the U.S. archivist was not "constitutionally compelled" to obey a former president's claim of privilege.[38] With this ruling the court reasserted the limited scope of executive privilege regarding a former president's control of his presidential materials and upheld the original intent of the PRA, a prior Supreme Court ruling, and the 1974 seizure law that directed the confiscation of Nixon's tapes and records.

Executive Order 12667

Just days before leaving office, however, the Reagan administration issued Executive Order 12667, vesting in Reagan, soon to be a private citizen, the right to exert executive privilege over his presidential records. The executive order set the procedures for asserting privilege claims by former and incumbent presidents against disclosure of presidential materials under the PRA. It created a notification process that required the U.S. archivist to give former and incumbent presidents thirty days' notice before releasing an ex-president's records. The order also required the archivist to inform the former and current presidents of any records that raised a substantial question of executive privilege. After thirty days the archivist could release the records unless the incumbent or former president claimed privilege, or unless the incumbent instructed the archivist to extend the review period. Moreover, a former president could go to the courts if the archivist denied his privilege claim subject to the authority of the incumbent president.[39]

Whether the Reagan order met White House Counsel John Roberts's definition of curing the "infirmities" of the PRA was open to question. While comporting with prior court rulings, the Reagan order ultimately relied on the incumbent president—absent a court order—to uphold a former president's privilege claim against releasing records. In the end, having failed to secure lavish Nixonion privilege rights under its 1986 administrative rule, the Reagan administration settled for a presidential order that gave a partial victory to a former president's right to exert privilege over his presidential materials.

Executive Order 13233

When George W. Bush issued his 2001 executive order rewriting the PRA, it was as if the Justice Department looked both to Roberts's 1985 memorandum advising that the law be "cured" of its "infirmities" relating to executive privilege and Reagan's subsequent 1986 directive purporting to grant unilateral privilege rights to ex-presidents. Like the Reagan directive, Bush's executive order resembled Nixon's view that former and sitting presidents should have unbounded discretion regarding disclosure of their materials. Many of the issues raised by the Bush order had already been addressed in prior court cases. But the Bush White House seemed to follow the Reagan administration's example in making a selective reading of *Nixon v. Administrator*—if not reading the dissenting opinions of Justices Burger and Rehnquist as controlling legal authority—regarding executive privilege and then devising a regulatory scheme to maximize presidential control of presidential records. It was precisely the approach recommended by John Roberts who sixteen years earlier proposed the drafting of a regulatory remedy aimed at allowing executive privilege claims to block disclosure of presidential records after the twelve-year restriction period. While not quite returning to the private proprietary claims of the early presidents of the Republic, the Bush order nevertheless asserted a constitutional proprietary claim that returned a degree of unilateral control to former presidents and their heirs.[40] The stakes were considerable since it involved whether former presidents, vice presidents, and their designated representatives or heirs—private citizens—could frustrate the letter and spirit of the PRA, congressional intent, and prior Supreme Court rulings in perpetuity.

On January 20, 2001, twelve years after Reagan invoked the PRA's twelve-year restriction rule on leaving office, the U.S. archivist—heeding the 1989 Reagan executive order—gave thirty days' notice to incumbent George W. Bush and former President Reagan of the pending release of 68,000 pages of previously privileged documents. President Reagan's representative said the former president would not invoke privilege to withhold the documents, marking the first time that privileged presidential records would be released under the PRA. When the Archives moved to release the Reagan documents, notifying the George W. Bush administration in February of their pending disclosure, White House Counsel Alberto Gonzales three times deferred their release. A Justice Department spokeswoman said the reason for the delay was to "conduct a legal review" of the documents. "We want to be sure that the Presidential Records Act is implemented correctly," she said. "We are setting precedent for future administrations."[41] But scholars and other critics accused the White House of trying to withhold documents that might be embarrassing not only to the president's father, but to other administration officials who served under Reagan. More than nine months passed beyond January 20, the date when Reagan's papers were to be released under the PRA, before Bush issued his executive order on November 1, 2001.[42] The order, entitled "Further Implementation of the Presidential Records Act," went beyond Reagan's 1986 regulatory directive to grant Nixon and all former presidents unfettered discretion over access to their presidential records, if not an attempt to return unilateral control to former chief executives and their heirs.

The Bush decree superseded Reagan's Executive Order 12667 by inventing new provisions governing executive privilege claims by former and sitting presidents and vice presidents after the twelve-year restriction period. The order reversed the fundamental principle of public access underpinning the PRA, which provided for the systematic release of records after twelve years. The decree provided that in the absence of "compelling circumstances" the incumbent president would be bound to honor any privilege claim by a former president—whether or not he agreed with it. If the former president agreed to permit access, the incumbent president could nevertheless override his wishes and keep them sealed. The order therefore provided for a double veto over disclosure; only when both the former president and incumbent president authorized access could the U.S. archivist release an ex-president's materials.[43] When drafting the act, Congress sought to assure that it would do nothing to limit or expand any constitutionally based privilege that may be exerted by an incumbent or former president. But Bush inverted this regulatory mechanism by granting ex-presidents unconditional veto power over the release of their materials regardless of the validity of the privilege claim. This grant of veto authority contravened prior court rulings by the Supreme Court and the D.C. Circuit in *Nixon v. Administrator*, *Nixon v. Freeman*, and *Public Citizen v. Burke*—all of which asserted that the U.S. archivist was not automatically bound to obey any privilege claims by a former president.[44]

While *Nixon v. Administrator* recognized a former president's right to assert privilege, it nevertheless stressed that an ex-president could not obstruct access to his presidential records merely by invoking a claim of privilege. If the Supreme Court left any doubts on this score, they should have been answered by the D.C. Circuit's opinion in *Nixon v. Freeman* and *Public Citizen v. Burke*, both regarding implementation of regulations governing access to Nixon's confiscated tapes and records.[45] In *Freeman*, the courts dismissed Nixon's arguments that researchers had to show a "particularized need" for access to his presidential materials. The court said that a former president's privilege eroded with the passage of time, that it was proper for the National Archives to disclose his materials after the requisite period of time, and that the burden for seeking judicial enforcement of a privilege claim, if administratively denied, rested with the former president.[46] As a result, *Freeman* disavowed Nixon's claims that his privilege assertions must be reflexively honored and placed the burden of proof on the former president to show how particular disclosures would violate executive privilege. The D.C. Circuit bolstered this decision in *Public Citizen v. Burke*, nullifying Reagan's 1986 directive ordering the U.S. archivist to abide by any privilege claim by former President Nixon. In that decision, the D.C. Circuit said that the Constitution did not require the U.S. archivist to defer to a former president's claim of privilege as ordered by the Reagan memorandum. There was "no reason" why the archivist was "constitutionally compelled" to bow to a former president's claim of privilege.[47] Despite these rulings, the Bush order constituted an expansion of executive privilege along Nixonion lines of an absolute discretion in violation of the clear terms of the PRA. Both the sitting president and the U.S. archivist were bound to honor any privilege claim by a former president without regard to its merit or legality.[48] In this way, the order achieved what Congress explicitly denied under the PRA. Moreover, the order seemed to breach the separation of powers doctrine by overriding key aspects of both a federal statute passed by the legislative branch and prior rulings made by the judicial branch.[49]

Under the order, former presidents and vice presidents also were given unlimited time to review access requests, allowing them to deny requests merely by withholding their permission.[50] In a protective nod to both his father who served as Reagan's vice president, and his own vice president, Dick Cheney, Bush's order invented an unprecedented vice presidential executive privilege, granting current and former vice presidents the power to withhold documents until they permitted access or a final nonappealable court order forced their disclosure.[51] Neither the PRA nor any prior court cases had ever extended the right to invoke privilege to former vice presidents. The decree also extended these constitutionally based privileges to designated representatives or surviving family members upon the death or disability of former presidents and vice presidents.[52] By considerably expanding executive privilege beyond the current president to former presidents and vice presidents, their representatives, family members, and even heirs, the decree opened the way for creating family dynasties over the history of the U.S. government. With this provision, the strong sense of propriety by ex-presidents and their heirs promised to send matters back to the nineteenth and early twentieth centuries when families and heirs capriciously ruled access to—or even destroyed—the nation's historical record. Woodrow Wilson's papers could only be seen at the discretion of his widow until her death in 1961. Family consent also governed access to the papers of Benjamin Harris until 1945 and those of William Howard Taft until 1953. In 2001 congressional hearings on Bush's executive order, constitutional scholar Jonathan Turley noted that given that a former president's claim of privilege was both "derivative and time-sensitive" under the *Nixon v. Administrator* ruling, the extension to family members showed a "breathtaking misunderstanding of the law." Moreover, under Bush's order, a president "could select any designee from a foreign citizen to a half-wit to assert privilege."[53] Nonetheless, the order required that any privilege claim must be honored precisely as claims by a former president, and that such assertions would constitute binding directives to the U.S. archivist.

The provision went beyond any attempt by Nixon to return to the old tradition of private ownership practiced by the early presidents by creating out of thin air a constitutionally based privilege that could be bequeathed to descendants as if it were a personal property right. It was this type of delegation of power that *Public Citizen v. Burke* expressly rejected.[54] If the meaning of *Burke* was not clear enough, the Supreme Court ruled long ago in 1953 that executive privilege was the province of the executive branch and could "neither be claimed nor waived by a private party."[55]

The transfer of privilege authority to family members and heirs also promised to set up a Pandora's box of endless intra-family squabbles, litigation, and delays in the release of presidential documents. More than any other provision, this part of the executive order recalled the early proprietary period when relatives and heirs committed the greatest sins against the nation's historical record. The destruction of presidential papers often stemmed from utter recklessness. Thus, relatives like George Washington Parke Curtis often acted with enormous carelessness. "I am now cutting up fragments from old letters & accounts, some of 1760 . . . to supply the call for Any thing that bears the impress of his venerated hand," he wrote. "One of my correspondents says send me only the dot of an I or the cross of a t, made by his hand, & I will be content."[56] The order also raised the possibility of legal challenges over who could exercise a former president's privilege. One only had to look at the long-running feud between the Nixon daughters who fought bitterly in and out of the courts over control of their father's presidential library and a $20 million bequest by one of Nixon's closest friends, Bebe Rebozo, that promised to bolster the struggling library's modest endowment.[57] There was ample reason to expect that intense intra-family litigation also would erupt over a bequeathed privilege.

The inheritance of privilege posed even the graver possibility that it would result in endless delays in the release of presidential documents. Such was the case with the papers of Lincoln whose son destroyed what he deemed to be of little value before depositing the rest in the Library of Congress under terms that sealed them until 1947, more than eighty years later. The John Quincy Adams papers were closed to public access until 1956, 127 years after he left office. McKinley's secretary and his son controlled access to the assassinated president's papers for more than a half a century until 1954. Bush's order once again opened the way for this possibility. After all, the order provided that "the family of the former president may designate a representative (or series or group of alternative representatives, as they in their discretion may determine) to act on the former President's behalf for purposes of the Act and this order, including with respect to the assertion of constitutionally based privileges."[58]

Finally, the order shifted the legal burden in disputes over disclosure of presidential records. Under the PRA, an ex-president who disagreed with the U.S. archivist's decision to release records had to go to court to show why his claim of privilege should be upheld. The Bush order, however, required researchers denied access to presidential records to bring suit presumably against both the current and former president. In this way, the order extended to ex-presidents the full legal protection of the current administration to uphold a claim of privilege and thereby control the records and legacy of his presidency.[59] In addition to placing the legal burden on researchers, the provision constituted a fundamental rewriting of the federal statute.

The executive order came under immediate attack from critics on both sides of the political aisle. "With a stroke of the pen ... President Bush stabbed history in the back," and "ended more than 30 years of increasing openness in government," one scholar editorialized in the *New York Times*.[60] They "would reverse an act of Congress with an executive decree," said another. "It's a real monster."[61] White House officials defended the order, saying that it would protect sensitive national security information and facilitate access to presidential documents. But historians, public interest groups, and others argued that the PRA already provided exemptions for national security documents. At a forum in Manhattan convened to discuss the Bush order, Robert A. Caro, the Pulitzer Prize–winning author of a multivolume biography of Lyndon B. Johnson, summed up some of the critical difficulties of the Bush order for researchers. "If you want to challenge the executive order, the historian must ask for specific detailed things. The Johnson Library has thirty-four million pieces of paper. Unless you've been through it, you can't possibly know what's in there."[62]

House Republicans were also among the order's sharpest critics. Representative Steven Horn of California called a hearing five days after Bush issued his executive decree. The order, said Doug Ose, another Californian, "undercuts the public's right to be fully informed about how its government operated in the past" and "greatly expands the privilege of the president in violation of the spirit and letter of the Presidential Records Act." Horn criticized the order for improperly giving "the former and incumbent presidents veto power over the release of the records." Two ranking House Democrats, Henry A. Waxman of California, and Janice D. Schakowsky of Illinois, also condemned the order. "The executive order violates the intent of Congress and keeps the public in the dark," they wrote in a letter to Bush.[63] On December 20, the White House sought to silence the complaints by announcing that nearly all the 68,000 pages of Reagan records were being released.[64]

Just weeks after the Bush administration issued its executive order, Public Citizen and several other organizations filed suit against the National Archives in the U.S. District Court for the District of Columbia seeking to block the president's executive decree. The suit also aimed to force the National Archives to fulfill its affirmative responsibilities under the PRA, including releasing the 68,000 pages of records of former President Reagan that should have been disclosed in January 2001. The suit contended that Bush's order violated the terms of the PRA and Article II of the Constitution by ceding authority to control access to presidential materials to individuals outside the executive branch and outside government and by subordinating the U.S. archivist to the binding privilege claims of private citizens, some of whom never held government office.[65]

As the suit advanced through the courts, Congress twice tried and failed to overturn the order. The first attempt came on April 1, 2002, when Representative Horn introduced legislation to nullify the Bush order. Twenty Democrats and two Republicans, including Representative Dan Burton of Indiana, the hard-line conservative chairman of the House Committee on Oversight and Government Reform, cosponsored the bill.[66] The Horn bill, however, met stiff resistance from the Bush administration, which began pressuring Republican members trying to derail the measure. In a letter from Assistant Attorney General Daniel J. Bryant to Burton, the Bush White House attacked the bill as "unnecessary and inappropriate and, more importantly, unconstitutional." Congress "lacks the authority to regulate by legislation the procedures for exercising" executive privilege.[67] The legislation to nullify the order never made it to the House floor, where leaders had little interest in embarrassing the president.[68] But in March 2003, Representative Doug Ose, a California Republican and cosponsor of the original Horn bill, took up the cause by introducing new legislation to revoke the Bush order. In his floor statement introducing the bill, Ose said that the law "would restore the public's right to know and its confidence in our government."[69] The Senate introduced its own measure in July that sought to nullify Bush's order and put back in force President Reagan's executive order governing access to presidential records.[70] Neither measure, however, was ever enacted.

As these measures were heading for dead ends in Congress, Public Citizen's lawsuit slowly made its way in the U.S. District Court in Washington. From the beginning, the Justice Department pursued a strategy to avoid the merits of the suit, arguing that the claims were not ripe, that the plaintiffs lacked standing, and that the claims were moot. When the Archives began to release the 68,000 pages of Reagan records, the government argued that the plaintiffs had not suffered any injury from the Bush order. While the plaintiffs moved for summary judgment on grounds that the order violated the PRA and proper bounds of constitutional privilege, the government filed its own motion to dismiss arguing that the suit was not ripe until a former president claimed privilege under the order and documents were actually withheld. But the order was already being applied to withhold or delay release of the 68,000 pages of records as well as all other records of former presidents and vice presidents who served after January 20, 1981—the date when the PRA went into effect—until the former office holders authorized their release.[71]

On March 24, 2004, U.S. District Court Judge Colleen Kollar-Kotelly dismissed the suit on grounds that the Reagan documents that were the subject of the litigation had already been released with the exception of eleven documents. The eleven remaining documents, the Judge said, were being properly withheld based on President Bush's assertion of privilege in concurrence with former President Reagan's representative. As a result, the suit no longer had standing. Judge Kollar-Kotelly, however, agreed to revisit her order dismissing the case after hearing arguments that the decree was still being applied to records sought by the plaintiffs. In their court papers, the plaintiffs said that the government was continuing to apply the Bush order to all new requests for release of records from the Reagan and George H. W. Bush Presidential Libraries, resulting in lengthy delays as researchers awaited authorization of former officeholders. In testimony before the 2007 congressional hearings on Bush's executive order, Scott L. Nelson, attorney for Public Citizen, said that just as the "Bush order had delayed the disclosure of tens of thousands of pages of Reagan documents after their 12-year restriction period expired in January 2001, it was also holding up the release of tens of thousands of pages of records of former President Bush whose 12-year restriction period under the PRA had expired in January 20, 2005." Approximately 57,000 pages of presidential records of Bush's father had been kept under wraps pending review under the executive order. By the end of October 2005, about half of the documents had been released with the remaining ones released in April and August 2006—eighteen months after the PRA required them to be disclosed.[72]

Throughout the more than five years of litigation, the government argued that the Bush order constituted a legitimate exercise of a president's authority to direct the U.S. archivist on matters involving the implementation of the PRA. At the same time, the government evaded the most questionable parts of the decree—the unfettered veto power it extended to former presidents to deny access, its invention of privilege rights to representatives of deceased or incapacitated former presidents and their families, and its fabrication of a vice presidential privilege. None of these principal features of the order was constitutionally based in the nature of presidential privilege or in the doctrine of the separation of powers. The government's silence on these issues seemingly indicated that it considered them to be complicating matters that could muddy their defense in the litigation. Alternatively, the government may have realized that any legislation nullifying these and other features of the order would be a constitutional exercise of Congress's power to govern the fate of presidential records—a principle underscored in *Nixon v. Administrator.*[73]

The lawsuit continued into 2007 as a newly elected Democratic Congress began a third legislative attempt to overturn the Bush order that extended secrecy to historical presidential records. In March 2007 Democratic Representative Henry A. Waxman, chairman on Oversight and Reform, and colleagues from both parties sponsored a bill to abrogate Bush's executive order on presidential records. The bill proposed re-establishing procedures to ensure the timely release of presidential documents, limit the ability of former presidents to claim privilege, and retract the authority Bush granted presidential descendents and vice presidents to withhold records. After the House overwhelmingly passed the measure to reverse Bush's executive order, the White House, citing the president's constitutional prerogatives, threatened to veto the presidential records bill.[74]

White House E-mail and the PRA

As Congress moved to extend its oversight, another controversy erupted involving the PRA with revelations of top administration aides using back-channel e-mail accounts rather than the White House e-mail system to conduct presidential business. The extensive use of nongovernment e-mail accounts surfaced with a congressional investigation of the abrupt firing of nine U.S. attorneys. In March 2007, the escalating investigation forced the Justice Department to release e-mails that showed—contrary to White House assertions—that Karl Rove, the president's influential political adviser, and Harriet Miers, the former White House counsel, may have been involved in what appeared to be politically motivated firings of the prosecutors for not serving the election-year interests of the Republican Party. The e-mails indicated that a deputy to Rove who worked in the White House Office of Political Affairs used his Republican National Committee (RNC) e-mail account to communicate about the dismissals with a top aide to Attorney General Alberto Gonzales. The revelations fanned further suspicions when administration officials admitted that thousands of e-mails to and from key White House staffers using RNC and other accounts had been deleted—potentially lost to history and beyond the reach of congressional subpoenas.[75]

The controversy involved four years' worth of missing e-mails of Rove who used RNC accounts for most of his communications. The problem dated to the beginning of the Bush administration. After the 2000 election, top political operatives who were moving into the White House, including Karl Rove, kept their campaign accounts. All e-mail was routinely deleted from the accounts after thirty days until August 2004 when the RNC ended the practice. But Rove kept deleting e-mails from his own account, obliterating his trail of communications dating before 2005. At some point in 2005, the RNC began automatically saving Rove's e-mails, eliminating his ability to delete. In addition to Rove, numerous other staffers in the executive office of the president were using the back-channel accounts, raising the specter of purposely evading the automatic archiving function of the White House e-mail system to cloak their activities from federal prosecutors, congressional oversight, and the judgment of history.[76]

Critics charged that Rove and other federal officials were using the RNC accounts to avoid oversight and the PRA. The practice triggered a congressional probe to determine whether it violated the PRA, which required the White House to maintain records, including e-mails, involving presidential decision making and deliberations. The Bush administration characterized the deleted e-mails as an "honest mistake" and said the RNC accounts were being used to avoid running afoul of the Hatch Act, which prohibits federal officials from using government resources for political activities. But critics challenged that explanation, contending that presidential appointees and staffers who work in the Executive Office of the President are exempt from some of the strictures of the law and may engage in political activity.[77]

The Bush administration's struggle with congressional investigating committees marked the latest in the remarkable saga of the White House's e-mail system. The electronic communications system was first installed in 1982 and was soon after thrust into public view after the Iran–Contra scandal broke in November 1986. Since then, every presidential administration has fought to prevent the disclosure of their e-mail communications. In November 1986, after the Iran–Contra affair began to unravel, John M. Poindexter, Reagan's national security adviser, and Oliver L. North, deleted the electronic record of their communications regarding the covert operation to sell arms to Iran and divert profits to the Contra rebels in Nicaragua. When it was discovered that backup copies had been preserved on the White House computers, the tapes were turned over to the special investigating commission led by former Senator John Tower. The e-mails enabled the Tower Commission to lay out the critical facts of the scandal—the arms sales, the diversion of cash, the Contra rebel arrangements, and the off-the-shelf logistics.[78] In the 1987 congressional hearings on

Iran–Contra, Representative Jack Brooks, a Texas Democrat, accused Poindexter of violating the PRA. The law carried no penalties, but Brooks charged that Poindexter was trying "to steal from the American People, this generation and future generations, their chance to learn what actually happened."[79] Brooks's remarks echoed throughout succeeding presidential administrations as officials sought to suppress or obliterate the trail of White House e-mails and cheat the American people of what was done in their name.

Four years later in January 1989, the outgoing Reagan White House moved to purge the entire contents of the electronic mail system. Several public interest groups sued to halt the destruction of the millions of electronic communications and to save them for posterity. Four years afterward, on January 16, 1993, a three-judge panel of the Court of Appeals for the D.C. Circuit told the departing George H. W. Bush administration that it could not erase its computer records unless the material was copied in identical form on computer backup tapes. The White House made an emergency appeal following an earlier order by the U.S. District Court that prohibited what Republicans said would be a major purging of computer-generated communications and data from the Bush and Reagan presidencies before they turned over the White House and National Security Council computer systems to Democrats. The ruling was clear enough. What seemed less clear, asked the *Washington Post*, was why the departing administration was "fighting so hard to avoid turning over these records to the office of the archivist. The natural question reasserts itself. What's in those files?"[80] It seemed the more critical question for the outgoing administration, however, was how to block Iran–Contra investigators and government watchdog groups from gaining access to the computer files.

The ruling by the appeals court ordering the preservation of backup copies offered little comfort since the computer records contained millions of e-mail messages about domestic and foreign policy initiatives—possibly including additional Iran–Contra and other embarrassing information that would be made available under the PRA after twelve years. In a frenzied effort to remedy the departing president's legal reversals, White House staffers hurried to make one last legal maneuver. On January 19, 1993, in the waning hours of his presidency, George H. W. Bush signed a deal with the U.S. archivist that gave him control over his administration's computerized records. The deal looked even worse when Don W. Wilson, the U.S. archivist, was hired as director of the George Bush Center at Texas A&M University. At issue was the preservation of 5,000 magnetic tapes, more than 140 hard drives, and one floppy disk. "That deal, made in the teeth of a law declaring that all official records are public property, was smelly on its face," said the *Washington Post*.[81] According to the Bush–Wilson agreement, George H. W. Bush could order the U.S. archivist to destroy the computer tapes and hard drives, the kind of material that proved critical to the Tower Commission's investigation of the Iran–Contra affair during the second Reagan administration. Few had any idea what could be learned from this electronic record, but the public had a right to that history and its lessons regarding how the White House made decisions on foreign and domestic policy. By aiming to establish maximum control of presidential records, the agreement raised questions about the efficacy of the then fifteen-year-old Presidential Records Act, which made the records of the presidency the property of the American people. It recalled the 1974 Nixon–Sampson agreement giving Nixon ownership of his presidential materials, including the right to destroy his secret tape recordings.

The incoming Clinton administration defended the Bush–Wilson agreement for the protection of its own historical legacy. Congress passed the PRA to prevent future presidents from repeating Nixon's efforts to claim and purge his presidential materials. In February 1995, however, a federal judge in Washington nullified the agreement as a violation of the PRA, which required presidential materials to be treated as government records, not the personal property of presidents. As the Clinton administration later faced numerous allegations of impropriety, a whistleblower claimed that officials withheld 100,000 e-mails regarding ongoing investigations. Congressional Republicans, who owned the majority, said the alleged cover-up exceeded the Watergate scandal, concluding in a House Government Reform Committee report that "the email matter can fairly be called the most significant obstruction of congressional investigations in U.S. history." The Democrats responded immediately, accusing the committee of having a "long history of making unsubstantiated allegations."[82]

The advent of government e-mail gave rise to contradictory forces, creating a much larger historical record, but producing a chilling effect on the new medium. After winning the election of 2000, incoming administration officials already seemed attuned to the accountability risks of using the White House e-mail system. They certainly knew the role that e-mails played in the investigations of the Iran–Contra and Clinton era scandals, or perhaps how the publicity surrounding Nixon's secret tape recordings led to his presidential ruin. Critics pointed out that the sheer number of staffers in the Executive Office of the President—as many as fifty-one—that were using alternate e-mail accounts belied assertions that the back-channel communications and deleted e-mails were merely an "honest mistake." Instead, the commingling of political with official executive branch communications suggested a large-scale, coordinated effort to evade the possibility of congressional probes and the PRA. It recalled a 1974 statement by Philip Buchen, counsel to President Ford, regarding the Nixon papers: "I am sure the historians will protest, but I think historians cannot complain if evidence for history is not perpetuated which shouldn't have been created in the first place."[83]

Bush's operatives might have shared Buchen's cynicism. Or perhaps they knew the Orwellian dictum: "To control the present is to control the past. To control the past is to control the future." Or maybe they recalled Nixon's 1977 televised remarks to David Frost regarding his fateful decision not to destroy his furtive tape recordings: "I brought myself down. I gave them the sword. And they stuck it [in]."[84] Indeed, several e-mails that surfaced during congressional probes seemed to substantiate suspicions of a concerted effort to evade accountability, if not the judgment of history itself. One of Karl Rove's former assistants, Susan Ralston, had been using four outside domains—all run by the RNC—plus an AOL account. At one point, she e-mailed two associates of the later indicted lobbyist Jack Abramoff that "I now have an RNC blackberry which you can use to e-mail me at any time. No security issues like my WH email." Another telling incident occurred after Abramoff sent an e-mail by accident to Ralston's White House account. On discovering his mistake, Abramoff fired off another note; "Damn it, it was not supposed to go in the White House system . . ." At the end of the day, it "looks like they were trying to avoid the [presidential] records act . . . by operating official business off the official systems," said John Podesta, who served in the Clinton administration.[85] In 2004, *U.S. News & World Report* noted in passing that many White House staffers were using web-based e-mail to evade the White House system. "I don't want my e-mail made public," confessed one White House aide to the magazine. "It's Yahoo!, baby," said another.[86] But perhaps one of the more revealing statements came from Rove himself. Responding to a question at a forum at the American Enterprise Institute in December 2001 regarding what surprised Bush the most about being president, Rove said, "I do think one of his major disappointments was that he no longer had access to e-mail, because everything is a presidential record."[87] Rove somewhat exaggerated the situation since a president's private communications with family members would be considered personal property under the PRA. But given that Rove was already making extensive use of back-channel e-mail accounts, he may have just as well been talking about himself.

In the end, Bush's executive order constituted a concerted attempt to roll back what it perceived to be an erosion of executive prerogatives since the Nixon years. Although EO 13233 seemed to be a "case of overplaying a constitutional hand" of Nixonion proportions, a Republican Congress failed to protect the historic work of a prior Congress as well as its own constitutional prerogatives.[88] In 1978, Congress made a historic commitment to further the American public's right to know about what was done in its name. Bush's executive order aborted this historic commitment in favor of returning to a form of proprietary control that recalled the sensibility of the early presidents of the Republic. Indeed, the nullifying of the PRA by executive decree seemed to be part of the administration's larger battle against the ghosts of past Democratic Congresses which sought to make the White House more transparent and accountable following the revelations of Watergate and the intelligence scandals of the 1970s.

Three

Challenging the GAO's Statutory Powers

On February 22, 2002, the General Accountability Office (GAO), the investigative arm of Congress, filed an unprecedented lawsuit in U.S. District Court in Washington over access to records from Vice President Richard B. Cheney's task force on energy policy. The case, named *Walker v. Cheney*, raised compelling statutory and constitutional questions relating to the authority of the GAO's comptroller general, and by extension, Congress, to require the vice president to provide information concerning the president's decision making on national energy policy. Each side based its arguments on fundamental constitutional concepts invoking competing theories of the proper balance of power between the legislative and executive branches, and insisted the other side was seeking to cause a revolution in separation of powers principles. But behind the façade of principled constitutional rhetoric was a power struggle between two sides, each of which sought to use the case as a means to expand its own institutional prerogatives at the expense of the other.

David M. Walker was perhaps well positioned to carry out this political and legal struggle with the vice president. As required by law, Walker's 1998 selection as comptroller general was made after ten leaders of the House and Senate submitted his name, along with a list of other candidates, to the president for consideration. From this list of candidates, the president was mandated to select a nominee—in this case Walker—who was then appointed with the consent of the Senate. With statutory powers to investigate executive actions and a fifteen-year appointment, the longest term of any position in the federal executive branch, the comptroller general had considerable latitude and independence to wage a campaign of disclosure against a vice president who refused to release information about the formulation of the administration's national energy policy.

From February to May 2001, Vice President Cheney headed up an energy task force, convening a series of meetings with representatives mostly from the energy industry, to devise a new energy policy for the nation. At the request of two ranking House Democrats, the General Accountability Office (GAO) asked for information concerning whom the task force met with. Soon after, Judicial Watch, later joined by the Sierra Club, ventured a similar request, claiming that because people who were not federal employees served as de facto members of the task force and its subgroups, the Federal Advisory Committee Act (FACA) required that its records be made public. The vice president refused to release the information, citing executive confidentiality. Given the close ties of the president and vice president to the energy industry, there seemed little doubt the records would show that the administration had predominately met with energy industry executives who significantly shaped the administration's energy policy. But the records seemed beside the point. The Bush-Cheney administration seized upon the GAO's request, which comported with the agency's numerous past investigations of executive branch activities, with a much larger purpose in mind—to reassert executive prerogatives and confidentiality that were perceived to have eroded since the Nixon administration. The case appeared indicative of the Bush administration's larger agenda upon coming into office of establishing a strong executive-centered government and rolling back decades of legislative encroachment on the prerogatives of the presidency. At the same time, the GAO seemed eager to establish legal precedent to clarify and expand its own investigative powers and oversight of the executive branch.

This particular dispute between the two branches was notable for being wholly unnecessary, even reckless. As the two branches squared off in the political and judicial arena, several executive agencies that participated in Cheney's energy task force were compelled by lawsuits filed by public interest groups to release much of the nondeliberative information the GAO was seeking and the White House was refusing to relinquish to Congress. Nonetheless, the chair of the energy task force—the vice president—and his immediate staff refused to disclose the documents in their possession. Although the release of these documents by the individual agencies should have helped to diffuse the dispute, the White House and the GAO nevertheless continued their constitutional struggle over the balance of powers. Both sides pursued the case in court, resulting in a significant institutional blow to the GAO and Congress's investigative powers of the executive branch. If the GAO was seeking clarification and expansion of its previously ambiguous powers to investigate the executive office, which often encouraged negotiated settlements when disputes arose, it received an unanticipated hit that has seemingly produced far-reaching consequences for what information the GAO can demand on behalf of Congress and how it may get it. Nevertheless, the case was ultimately decided not in the courts, but in the political arena after the Republican Party won majorities in both houses of Congress in the 2002 elections. In retrospect, it appears that the GAO's losing battle was never worth the risk, and that the vice president had lured the agency into a legal and constitutional fight as a means to erode legislative oversight. Indeed, the case marks one of the Bush administration's most significant victories not only in reasserting the prerogatives of the presidency, but also in cloaking the executive in greater secrecy.

Even before the GAO sued the vice president, however, the conservative Judicial Watch and the liberal Sierra Club brought their own actions against Cheney seeking much the same information under federal law. The public interest groups claimed that energy industry lobbyists and representatives were de facto members of the energy task force and its subgroups, a charge that Cheney denied. To decide whether the vice president should release information about the task force, a U.S. district court ordered limited discovery. But Cheney argued that for even the courts to make such a demand violated the separation of powers between the judicial and executive branches of government and posed an unwarranted intrusion into the heart of executive deliberations. As with the GAO case, the White House pursued a strategy aimed at expanding executive prerogatives by appealing its way to a U.S. Supreme Court that handed the 2000 presidential election to the Bush-Cheney administration.

Cheney's Energy Task Force

After winning the presidency in the 2000 election, President George W. Bush was in office for scarcely more than a week before facing a domestic energy crisis in California with its rolling power outages, shortages, and utility bankruptcies. Rather than heeding the pleas of California politicians to intervene in the nation's most populous and financially powerful state, the president confronted the energy crisis circuitously by forming the National Energy Policy Development Group (NEPDG) to address the nation's energy needs. On January 29, 2001, the president issued a memorandum establishing the energy task force within the Executive Office of the President to gather information and make recommendations on a national energy policy. Vice President Cheney was tasked not only with directing the group, but also with presiding over meetings and establishing subordinate groups to assist the energy task force in its work.[1] "I can't think of a better man to run it [task force] than the vice president," Bush said.[2] The president stated that the task force would examine energy shortages and draft a broad national energy policy, addressing such issues as high energy prices, reliance on foreign oil imports, and development of pipelines and power generating capacity. Although the president said that the study would examine California's electric power crisis, he stressed that the problems should be resolved by elected state officials.[3] Thus, from February to May 2001, Vice President Cheney chaired the energy panel, convening a series of meetings and soliciting the input of the energy industry to help write a new energy policy for the nation.

Even before the Bush administration publicly unveiled its national energy plan on May 17, 2001, many anticipated it would escalate the biggest debate in a generation over where America's energy supplies should come from and at what environmental cost. The plan was expected to ignite major and long-lasting battles over tapping Alaskan oil and Rocky Mountain coal and natural gas, and reviving nuclear power. For consumers and businesses, the immediate issues were whether the Bush administration's free-market philosophy could create proposals to help spur badly needed expansion in the strained energy infrastructure of refineries, pipelines, storage systems, and transmission lines. For environmental groups, the answers rested with stepped-up conservation, renewable resources, and major investment in the development of alternative energy sources. The imperative of a national energy policy carried particular urgency after the 2000 California energy crisis with its shortages, rolling brown-outs, and enormous price spikes that warned of bigger problems to come.

As chair of the energy task force, Cheney was the driving force behind nearly every aspect of the final report. The handling of the energy task force reflected Cheney's proclivity for executive confidentiality and his close ties to business, especially since the deliberations were conducted largely in secret with a high regard for industry. Ironically, Cheney's handling of the process behind closed doors attracted a blast of unwanted scrutiny as critics seized on his finances and oil industry ties in an effort to discredit the policy. Democrats and environmental groups charged that his judgment of energy issues was suspect because of his chairmanship until August 2000 of the Haliburton Company, a Dallas-based energy services firm that was expected to benefit from the administration's new energy policy. Philip E. Clapp, president of the National Environmental Trust, criticized Cheney for "seeing the [energy] problem entirely from the side of the energy producing industry that made him a millionaire, not from a consumer struggling to make ends meet." But a close aide to Cheney called the criticism an "outrage" and said Cheney's expertise in the industry was crucial to "trying to solve a problem of this magnitude."[4]

Although the plan made extensive recommendations for the use of technology to conserve energy and produce power more cleanly, the core of the report concluded the nation needed hundreds more power plants, natural gas pipelines, oil wells, and nuclear power reactors.[5] Cheney's task force included the secretaries of Energy, Interior, Treasury, Commerce, and Transportation Departments, and the head of the Environmental Protection Agency.[6] News reports of the task force's stealthy energy deliberations attracted the attention of Henry A. Waxman of California and John D. Dingell of Michigan, ranking Democrats on the House Committees on Energy and Commerce and Government Reform. On April 19, Waxman and Dingell asked the GAO to investigate the conduct and composition of the energy task force, including at minimum who served on the task force, who the task force met with, what information they provided, the location and date of each meeting, and the costs involved.[7]

The GAO thus informed the vice president's office that it was looking into the costs and practices of the National Energy Policy Development Group, which Cheney directed and which oversaw development of the energy policy. Both Waxman and Dingell asked for the inquiry to determine whether task force members or staffers had met privately with major campaign contributors. But Cheney's counsel, David S. Addington, dismissed the request, arguing there was no legal requirement to provide the information and that it appeared the GAO intended to intrude into the heart of executive deliberations. Addington attached a seven-page letter to his response from the task force's executive director, Andrew Lundquist, indicating that the NEPDG had received temporary support from five Energy Department employees and from a White House fellow. Lundquist stated the meetings "were simply forums to collect individual views rather than to bring a collective judgment to bear." Although White House officials refused to disclose the list of meetings or attendees, they provided a numerical count as to how many energy industry or corporate groups, unions, environmental groups, and others the task force met with.[8] Environmentalists nevertheless complained the process was skewed, as the vice president personally met with industry leaders, while dispatching aides to speak to the environmentalists, many of whom were grouped into one meeting. Further, while the White House publicized meetings with labor representatives, it kept sessions with industry executives and lobbyists private. Nonetheless, Cheney disputed accusations that his private meetings with industry officials who gave money to the Republican Party had compromised the work of the task force. "Just because somebody makes a campaign contribution doesn't mean that they should be denied the opportunity to express their view to government officials," he said.[9]

On June 1, 2001, however, the GAO wrote a second letter to Addington asking for information about individuals involved in the energy task force group and the "nature, purpose and attendees in connection with the meetings."[10] The letter thanked Addington for information Cheney's office had already provided, but said the GAO needed "additional information and dialog to complete our review of the energy policy development process."[11] It also noted the GAO's comptroller general, David M. Walker, had determined the inquiry was "appropriate." Addington replied on June 7 that he found Walker's decision "disappointing" and said the GAO had no legal basis for pursuing an inquiry of this scope. Cheney's counsel wrote that a request from two House members did not constitute a proper request under the statute cited by the GAO because a "committee of Congress acts by majority vote or action of the committee chairman." Nevertheless, Addington said he would try to provide requested information about the direct and indirect costs of the group "as a matter of comity between the legislative and executive branches." On June 21, Addington sent the GAO seventy-seven pages of information purportedly concerning energy task force expenditures incurred by the vice president's office. But the documents were virtually useless, largely consisting of cost figures with no corresponding explanation as to what the funds were for. In response to Addington's rebuff to the GAO, Waxman stated that "the Cheney task force's refusal to provide basic information about its interactions with nongovernmental entities and individuals raises serious questions about the access large donors have to the policy making process in the Bush administration."[12]

There appeared to be some reason for Waxman's and Dingell's concern. Nine days before George W. Bush was inaugurated, energy lobbyists met at the American Petroleum Institute (API) in Washington. Knowing they would have the ear of the White House, they drew up a wish list—looser rules for drilling on federal lands, more drilling for oil and gas in Alaska and the Gulf of Mexico, lower royalty payments for tapping offshore wells, among other suggestions. These and many other recommendations made it into Bush's energy plan. In addition, some of the key leaders of the API meeting had since been appointed to high-level positions in the new Bush administration—among them J. Steven Griles, an energy lobbyist who became second in command at the Interior Department, and Thomas Sansonetti, an energy lawyer who was named the Justice Department's top environmental attorney. The appointments of Griles and Sansonetti assured that they would assist in overseeing the policies they helped to write. *Newsweek* observed that not "since the rise of the railroads more than a century ago ha[d] a single industry placed so many foot soldiers at the top of a new administration." At the same time, it was evident that industry leaders, who had donated more than $22.5 million into GOP coffers, enjoyed constant access to the energy task force, while the environmental community received one mass meeting and was rebuffed in its efforts to meet with Cheney, a dynamic that only fueled suspicions among environmentalists and their Democratic supporters in

Congress about what was happening behind closed doors. Indeed, the appearance among environmental groups was that the nation's energy policy was being hijacked by industry insiders in secret meetings and that they were being shut out of the process altogether.[13]

Nonetheless, few expected the GAO's Comptroller General David M. Walker would become one of the Bush administration's leading antagonists. Before becoming the director of the GAO, Walker had been invited by George H. W. Bush to volunteer in his 1980 campaign for president, was a delegate to the Republican National Convention, worked in Ronald Reagan's Labor Department, and won his job at the GAO with the support of Senate GOP leader Trent Lott. Despite his impeccable Republican credentials, in 1998 President Bill Clinton appointed Walker to a fifteen-year term to run the agency. When Clinton nominated him, Walker switched from Republican to Independent and saw himself as beholden to neither party. Now as the comptroller general, Walker began leading a high-profile, high-stakes battle to force Cheney to release records detailing administration deliberations on energy policy. Confronted by Cheney's intransigence, in August 2001 Walker threatened to sue the administration in federal court. "This is not a situation where the vice president is resisting the congressmen," Walker stated. "He's now resisting the GAO. And his attorneys are engaged in a broad-based, frontal assault on our statutory authority. We cannot let that stand." Bombast aside, with such words Walker began setting the stage for a public showdown between the executive and legislative branches. In Walker's view, his quest had gone far beyond where it began the previous spring when Waxman and Dingell demanded that Cheney release the information. The issue now had been wholly transformed into a defense of the GAO's very reason for being. Walker further considered the battle not to be "about ideology or party, but about openness and the Constitution." Walker said he had done everything he could to avoid a confrontation. To reach an accommodation, GAO lawyers spoke with White House attorneys, and Walker himself called the vice president on July 30 in a futile effort to find a solution to the impasse.[14] Walker gave little credence to the White House's arguments that meeting the GAO's demands would violate the confidentiality of executive deliberations.[15]

By the mere threat of a lawsuit against the White House, Walker had already elevated the confrontation to unprecedented levels. Indeed, the GAO had never before challenged the executive so directly since its creation by Congress in 1921. Although Walker insisted he was not looking for a showdown with Cheney, he nevertheless seemed to see the confrontation as a chance to expand the GAO's investigative powers and oversight of the executive branch. On July 18, Walker pressed for disclosure of the documents by issuing a demand letter to Cheney as chair of the energy task group. The letter again requested any information concerning the date and location of the meetings, the persons present, the purpose and agenda, meeting minutes or notes, how the vice president and others determined who would be participants, and the associated costs. Anticipating a statutory and constitutional showdown, on August 2, Cheney sent letters to both houses of Congress discussing the task force records dispute. The vice president's letter asserted the GAO was exceeding its lawful authority and sought to unconstitutionally interfere with the executive branch. Shortly afterward on August 17, the GAO exercised its statutory powers by issuing a formal report to the president, the vice president, the leaders of the House and Senate, the director of the Office of Management and Budget, and the attorney general, informing them of the dispute over the energy task force records and demanding the release of the documents according to law. In the report, the agency said it had "ample authority to conduct this review," and said it may go to court to get the documents if they were not provided within twenty days according to the 1980 law that gave the GAO authority to initiate judicial action in support of its requests. Further, in an attempt at compromise and as a matter of comity, the agency noted it had offered to "scale back" its demand for deliberative information, including meeting minutes and notes and information presented by nongovernment participants, even though it was legally entitled to the documents. Nevertheless, the GAO continued to insist on information detailing who attended the energy task force's meetings, who was hired, who was consulted, and what was the policy cost.[16]

Under the 1980 GAO statute, the administration could have quickly ended Walker's crusade by officially declaring that any disclosure would substantially impair government operations.[17] But the White House saw opportunity in a possible legal case and had a much larger purpose in mind. According to an article in the *Washington Post,* congressional sources viewed the White House's adamant stance to be a reflection of its desire to reclaim the powers of executive privilege that had been squandered with the various investigations under the Clinton administration, including those dealing with the Monica S. Lewinsky matter and the case of former Agriculture Secretary Mike Espy.[18] The administration's intent, however, was considerably more ambitious. Not only did the White House seek to use the case to help restore the powers of the presidency that had been eroded under the Clinton administration, but more important, to roll back Congress's relentless thirty-year encroachment on the executive branch since the Nixon era. Thus, at least initially, both sides appeared to see opportunity in escalating the confrontation with the aim of expanding their own powers at the expense of the other under the guise of principle.

In early September 2001 Walker said he would decide by the end of the month whether to sue the executive branch, which would be a first in the agency's eighty-year history. Nevertheless, with the September 11 terrorist attacks on New York and Washington, Walker decided to delay his decision. As Walker was deliberating on whether to sue the White House, the Natural Resources Defense Council (NRDC) filed suit on December 11, 2001, in federal court to force the Department of Energy to produce documents concerning the development of the Bush administration's energy policy. The group initially requested the information months earlier in April under the Freedom of Information Act (FOIA), but the administration denied the request on the grounds that the Cheney task force was not a federal agency and therefore not subject to the FOIA. Nevertheless, since the task force included the heads of various federal agencies directly subject to FOIA, the NRDC decided to sue the Energy Department, which held the most documents. The environmental group also sued the Energy Department because it was not permitted under law to sue the White House.

The left-leaning environmental group joined the conservative watchdog organization Judicial Watch in an effort to gain access to information that both groups believed should be public. Judicial Watch filed its own suit in May against the Energy Department and other agencies, and in July against the National Energy Policy Development Group chaired by Cheney, demanding the administration release records on who met with the task force and when. Both groups decided to lay siege to the administration at a time when the GAO had opted to delay its own legal challenge for the records. Moreover, because energy legislation was pending in the House, the groups sought to understand who had a role in shaping it. According to the organizations, the administration's effort to withhold the records was part of a larger pattern of secrecy and an abuse of executive power. One of NRDC's attorneys, Sharon Buccino, stated the "public has a right to know who's trying to buy government policy. We've waited long enough. So we're going to court to get it."[19]

The Enron Connection

But the GAO's confrontation with the administration assumed new prominence with the collapse and numerous investigations of the energy trading company, Enron Corporation, which had ties to the Bush White House. Enron's huge trading losses stemming from massive corporate fraud led it to file for bankruptcy on December 2, 2001. The spectacular corporate bankruptcy of the giant energy trading firm fueled demands and elevated the political stakes for information about the secret meetings of the energy task force. The *New York Times* questioned "how could the Houston-based energy company, ranked seventh on the Fortune 500 list of America's largest companies, and often touted as one of its most innovative, fail so unexpectedly, wiping out $60 billion in shareholder value?" In the halls of Congress, calls for an inquiry into the largest corporate demise in American history came from both sides of the aisle, although Democrats had added incentive to pursue the investigation for political gain.[20]

Enron's collapse proved to be an embarrassment to the Bush White House. After all, no company had more generously supported President Bush throughout his political career than Enron. The Bush family's ties to the firm and its chairman, Ken Lay, went as far back as 1980 when Bush the elder made his first run for the presidency. During that campaign, Lay provided funds to the elder Bush after he won the Iowa caucuses. After becoming vice president following his lost bid for the White House, President Ronald Reagan tasked him with chairing the administration's task force on government deregulation. In one of its biggest deregulatory moves, the Reagan administration pushed through the lifting of federal controls on natural gas markets, a move that Lay strongly favored. Beginning when Bush the younger entered the 1993 Texas governor's race through his 2000 presidential bid, Lay and Enron had become his biggest campaign contributors. In the 2000 election alone, Lay's personal donations exceeded $275,000 to the Republican National Committee while Enron's contributions to the party totaled more than $1.1 million.[21]

But Enron's association with the White House went further than President George W. Bush. The new president named Marc Racicot, the former governor of Montana and Enron lobbyist, to lead the Republican National Committee. Larry Lindsey was on Enron's payroll, earning $100,000 in consulting fees before becoming Bush's chief economic adviser. Bush chose Robert Zoellic, who served on an Enron advisory council, as U.S. trade representative. Thomas White, Bush's secretary of the army, served as chairman of Enron Energy Services while it was involved in market manipulation and price-gouging during the California crisis. Beyond these ties, the Bush-Cheney administration granted Lay and Enron unprecedented access, producing results for the giant energy trading firm in the energy panel's final report. The report, for example, proposed the creation of a national electricity grid, a project that would have greatly facilitated the company's trading of electric power in all regions of the country. It recommended speeding up pipeline construction, a move that would have helped Enron expand its already considerable capacity as one of the world's largest pipeline companies. The report also noted the California energy crisis and the imperative to increase both energy efficiency and domestic natural gas production.[22]

With news of the Enron collapse, Representative Henry Waxman, the administration's chief antagonist over the energy policy task force records, wasted little time in demanding information from the White House about its ties to the disgraced energy firm. On January 8, 2002, he publicly released his correspondence with Addington, the vice president's counsel, indicating that Cheney or his aides met six times with Enron representatives in 2001, including a session two months before the energy company made the largest corporate bankruptcy in American history. The meetings continued after the White House released the energy policy that Cheney's task force had developed. Five of the meetings were with Cheney aides; the other occurred between the vice president and Kenneth L. Lay, Enron's chairman. Addington wrote, however, that Cheney and Lay "discussed energy policy matters, including the energy crisis in California, and did not discuss information concerning the financial position of the Enron Corporation."[23] The administration's confession of its meetings with Enron officials signaled a tactical retreat as pressure mounted to fully disclose its ties to the energy firm. By releasing Addington's letter to the press, Waxman sought both to reveal the Houston-based company's longtime personal and financial ties to Bush and to indicate the corrupt firm's undue influence over the administration's new energy policy. Waxman said the letter "show[ed] that the access provided to Enron far exceeded the access provided by the White House to other parties interested in energy policy."[24]

Waxman's accusation received added, if unexpected, support when *Newsweek* disclosed that the White House had not been fully forthcoming in its contacts with Enron. The news magazine reported that on March 29, 2001, Cheney's top energy assistant, Andrew Lundquist, met with members of the Clean Power Group, a coalition funded by five power companies, including Enron. The coalition sought the replacement of environmental regulations with a plan that would enable industries to trade pollution credits among themselves. If adopted, the plan stood to earn Enron hundreds of millions of dollars. The meeting was arranged by Brad Card, the coalition's lobbyist and brother of White House Chief of Staff Andrew Card. When questioned about this omission, a White House aide responded that Lundquist had no recollection that Enron was part of the group—a statement that directly contradicted a Brad Card associate, who said he had made it clear to Lundquist that Enron was a coalition member. Cheney spokeswoman Mary Matalin said that it did not matter, since the proposal never made it into the energy plan. "Who cares if there were a hundred meetings?" she said. Despite Matalin's flippant dismissal of the matter, the Justice Department intervened with an order for the administration to preserve any documents related to Enron.[25]

The growing publicity surrounding the administration's contacts with Enron, together with Cheney's meeting with Lay, elevated demands by the GAO for documents on the workings of the energy task force. But press secretary Ari

Fleischer said releasing the documents to the GAO would undermine executive privilege and the candor of people who meet with administration officials. He further dismissed a congressional report stating that seventeen provisions in the administration's energy policy appeared to benefit Enron as a "partisan waste of taxpayer money." To Waxman and other Democrats, however, the administration's decision to withhold documents smacked of a cover-up.[26]

On January 22, 2002, in light of Congress's upcoming consideration of establishing a national energy policy, four Senate Democratic chairmen of powerful committees urged the GAO to continue its investigation of the NEPDG to determine who helped shape the administration's energy plan.[27] As a result, GAO Comptroller General David Walker again demanded the White House turn over the documents, this time issuing an ultimatum that "unless we get the information or we're in the middle of intense negotiations, I'm not going to sit on this much longer."[28] Walker's ultimatum further escalated a battle with the White House at a time when the administration faced questions from various directions about its ties to Enron. Democratic lawmakers sought to know whether Enron had undue influence in the administration because of campaign donations, a criticism the White House rejected. Nonetheless, the Enron connection loomed ever more ominously for the Bush administration. At the same time when Walker issued his ultimatum to the White House for the documents of the energy task force, former Enron executives publicly disclosed that a top Bush campaign adviser, Edward Gillespie, served as the company's key conduit to the administration. Enron paid Gillespie $525,000 in 2001 for lobbying that included the energy task force and economic stimulus legislation with tax provisions that would have benefited the corporation. In addition, Judicial Watch announced that it was filing a complaint with the Federal Election Commission to determine whether Karl Rove, Bush's top campaign adviser, arranged for an Enron consulting contract for strategist Ralph Reed, instead of paying him from campaign funds. The White House and Reed denied the allegation, made by an anonymous source in the *New York Times*, that Reed's contract was arranged to keep his allegiance to Bush during the early days of the Texas governor's presidential bid.[29]

As part of his continuing campaign for the administration's energy task force documents, Waxman released additional papers indicating the White House altered its final report to benefit Enron by calling for a boost in energy production in India. Waxman's aides said that Enron officials met with the energy task force before the administration issued its final report. The change was made at about the same time the White House was trying to aid Enron in India. The company was in a dispute with the Indian government over its Dboal project, a gas-fueled power plant. As efforts to resolve the dispute foundered, Enron sought $2.3 billion from India for its interest in the plant. Cheney twice met with Indian officials and Bush was scheduled to discuss the matter under a campaign coordinated by the National Security Council. The administration's final energy policy called for the "secretaries of state and energy to work with India's Ministry of Petroleum and Natural Gas to help maximize its domestic oil and gas production." Although the energy task force's March 30, 2001, draft report made no mention of this provision, it appeared in the final report after Cheney met with Enron Chairman Kenneth Lay on April 17, 2001.[30]

Despite these revelations of close ties with the giant energy firm, the White House remained fixed in refusing to give up the energy task force records. The continuing standoff was shaping up as the highest profile court fight between Congress and the White House since Watergate. Cheney rejected the demand for information in broad constitutional terms, professing a desire to restore presidential power to a level not seen since the Nixon administration. "I have repeatedly seen an erosion of the powers and the ability of the president of the United States to do his job," he said. The vice president said it was "wrong" for past administrations to have bowed to congressional demands. "We are weaker today as an institution because of the unwise compromises that have been made over the last 30 to 35 years," Cheney said to ABC News.[31] Cheney attributed the threatened lawsuit to efforts to tar the administration with the Enron scandal by Democrats, particularly Representative Henry Waxman. Nonetheless, on *Fox News Sunday*, the vice president said what was "really at stake here is the ability of the president and the vice president to solicit advice from anybody they want in confidence . . . without having to make it available to a member of Congress."[32]

The administration's willingness to fight a high-profile legal battle with Congress surprised even some legal experts sympathetic to preserving executive power. Bruce Fein, a lawyer who had served in the Nixon and Reagan Justice Departments, believed there was a "possibility" the administration could win a case against the GAO, but he said it would be a "pyrrhic victory." He believed a court victory would only prompt congressional committees to issue subpoenas for the information, and the damage inflicted on the administration's public image and integrity would be irreparable. It would give the appearance of a cover-up, similar to the last such legal battle when President Nixon in 1974 won a case against a Senate committee that was seeking information related to campaign contributions and executive actions.[33] Indeed, the Bush administration was already facing a growing public relations problem on the Enron situation. According to a CBS–*New York Times* poll taken in January 2002, 67 percent of Americans surveyed believed the administration was either hiding something or lying about its relationship with Enron. Pressing the offense,

Senate Democratic Majority Leader Thomas A. Daschle said on CBS's *Face the Nation* that the GAO was on "solid ground in demanding these records be turned over. The American people have a right to know what the facts are." But Cheney said the issue of Enron was not about the administration. "What it's really about is whether or not laws were broken or laws need to be changed with respect to the functioning of a major corporation."[34] As the confrontation between the GAO and the vice president intensified, some Republicans threatened to block any lawsuit by Congress's investigative arm. Senator Orrin Hatch from Utah, the senior Republican on the Senate Judiciary Committee, said the GAO should not be "trying to impose disclosure on internal White House meetings to determine policy." House Majority Leader Dick Armey of Texas said he and Speaker Dennis Hastert of Illinois planned on speaking to the agency. Senator Arlen Specter of Pennsylvania commented that he would be investigating to see whether the GAO would be overstepping its authority by suing the administration. "My concerns are that it would encroach upon the deliberative process and make it impossible for the vice president at the direction of the president to make a recommendation," Specter said.[35]

Cheney's refusal to release the documents on the grounds that it would set a dangerous precedent in making it impossible for future presidents to receive "unvarnished" advice represented the administration's most dramatic attempt after two years in office to resurrect a greater wall of privacy around the executive branch. The effort followed the White House's attempts to delay the release of the Reagan presidential papers, its refusal to disclose Justice Department records to Congress, and a general intolerance of leaks to the press.[36] But critics and independent analysts disputed Cheney's position on the documents, noting that while the administration has a right to withhold information dealing with national security, any meetings with private industry or lobbyists for the purpose of developing national policy should be disclosed. The prospect of a White House victory in the case worried some observers since it would likely strengthen the hand of the executive branch in determining what should be kept secret. "What's bizarre is not just that the executive branch has staked out a fairly extreme separation-of-powers point of view, but they seem to be looking for a fight to pick," said Peter Shane, a professor of law and public policy at Ohio State. "Unless they're covering something up, this is an odd thing to go to the mat over."[37]

In many ways, the standoff between the GAO and the White House was reminiscent of First Lady Hillary Rodham Clinton's task force on health care, created in 1993 to develop proposals for reforming the U.S. health care system. When Hillary Clinton refused to turn over documents about the task force's secret meetings, conservatives and Republicans raised a storm of public criticism.[38]

Mrs. Clinton eventually backed down, but it was in part because of these retreats by the executive branch that Cheney claimed he was taking such an unyielding stand. Cheney made little secret that he aimed to reverse an erosion of executive branch authority that had occurred over decades, with Congress increasingly emboldened to demand information from presidents who acquiesced under political pressure. While the U.S. Supreme Court has ruled in the past that the executive branch has the right to withhold certain types of documents, it also has held that such a privilege must be balanced with Congress's right to know. As a result, the Court compelled former President Nixon to turn over his White House tapes during the Watergate scandal since the material was relevant to a criminal investigation. Indeed, in most past legal battles involving an administration's effort to withhold information, the courts have favored the party seeking disclosure. "In our democratic system, the balance generally favors openness of information," said Mark Rozell, a professor of public policy at George Mason University. The relevant law in this case was the Federal Advisory Committee Act, which requires all policy meetings with outside advisers to be open and to avoid the appearance of deals being made with lobbyists behind closed doors. Nonetheless, Cheney remained wedded to the purpose of reversing Congress's erosion of the prerogatives of the presidency. According to Larry Klayman, head of Judicial Watch, Cheney's position represented "an old-world view of government, that people should not ask questions."[39]

The GAO had already tried to accommodate the White House by scaling back its demands for the minutes and notes of energy task force meetings, stating that it only wanted information related to the identities of the people in the meetings and the date, subject, location, and cost of each meeting. Nonetheless, this move made little headway with a White House that made it exceedingly clear the administration was ready to mount a high-level and protracted legal fight. On February 21, the eve of the filing of the GAO lawsuit, the White House disclosed it would be represented in its battle against the GAO by Solicitor General Theodore B. Olson, the government's top litigator, and by Robert D. McCallum Jr., the assistant attorney general in charge of the Justice Department's Civil Division. A senior White House official told the *Washington Post* that the top lawyers were selected to remove "any question about how seriously we take this principle" of protecting the confidentiality of executive deliberations and advice.[40] The White House threatened that if it failed to win the case, it would seek to have the statute empowering the GAO declared unconstitutional—an action that, if successful, would considerably curtail the legislative branch's oversight of the executive branch. The White House's willingness to escalate a battle of interpretations of a congressional statute into a constitutional test of the power of the presidency indicated it was willing to sustain a legal battle that could take months, if not years to resolve. Nevertheless, by assuming this uncompromising stance, the administration was taking a political risk in keeping its ties to Enron, the largest political benefactor of Bush, in the news.

The GAO Files Suit

On February 22, the GAO filed its suit against the Bush administration, an unprecedented legal action growing out of a ten-month standoff between the executive and legislative branches of government.[41] The lawsuit, filed in U.S. District Court in Washington, was named *Walker v. Cheney*. In a written statement the GAO said, "we take this step reluctantly. Nevertheless, given GAO's responsibility to Congress and the American people, we have no other choice."[42] Officials involved in the dispute predicted the lawsuit would end up in the Supreme Court if the two sides were unable to reach a compromise. At issue was the law giving the U.S. comptroller general power to investigate all matters related to the receipt, disbursement, and use of public money. The White House maintained the GAO was limited to investigating the cost of government activities while the GAO took a broader view. "If that in fact were true there would be nothing in this White House, including any activity by the president or vice president, that would not be subject to investigation by the GAO," an administration aide said in an article in the *Washington Post*, which was assiduously following the case. "That would be an unconstitutional infringement on the powers of the presidency."[43] Also at issue was the GAO's contention that Cheney, in his role as head of an interagency task force, was not protected by the normal constitutional powers of the vice president. But the White House argued that Cheney was acting in his capacity as vice president, not head of a task force.

The GAO's legal action against the White House joined three private lawsuits filed by the conservative watchdog group Judicial Watch and the environmental groups Sierra Club and Natural Resources Defense Council (NRDC). But while those groups sought information under the Federal Advisory Committees Act and the FOIA, the GAO believed its authority as a congressional entity gave it more clout. The GAO's lawsuit argued that federal law "broadly authorizes GAO to investigate all matters relating to the use of public funds" and "confers broad authority on GAO to evaluate federal government programs and activities." The suit noted that for decades the GAO had monitored and investigated a myriad of executive branch activities. "During that period, the executive branch has complied with countless GAO requests for information." The lawsuit said that at times there have been disputes between the executive branch, including the White House and the GAO concerning the scope of a particular request. Nonetheless, "until the instant dispute, accommodations have generally been reached, and GAO has never been forced to file suit to obtain access to records." The complaint claimed that despite the reasonable accommodations the comptroller general made, the vice president refused to provide records that the head of the GAO was statutorily entitled to inspect. The lawsuit named Cheney both as the official who served as the chair of the task force and in his official capacity as the vice president.[44]

Although the White House carefully refrained from invoking a claim of executive privilege in the case, its lawyers contended that Cheney was covered under the same executive privilege as the president. This assertion was a highly questionable, if not revealing, supposition since the Constitution does not vest executive authority in the vice president, but rather relegates his office to legislative matters. The assertion seemed indicative of a conception of Vice President Cheney as a co-executive in the White House with the full privileges of the president. Nonetheless, in response to the lawsuit, senior administration officials said they welcomed the GAO's legal action and expressed confidence that the White House would prevail. "There is an important principle here," Alberto Gonzales, the White House counsel, said in an interview. "We view this as a matter of statutory construction. Does the GAO have the authority under the governing statutes to conduct this kind of investigation of the vice president and his advisers? We do not believe the statute provides that kind of authority."[45] In Congress, Henry A. Waxman and John D. Dingell, both of whom sought the documents in April 2001, applauded the filing of the lawsuit. "It is unfortunate that the vice president doesn't believe the American people or Congress has a right to know who's influencing public policy," Dingell said. "Thankfully, the GAO is not afraid to stand by its principles and fight to ensure the American public knows the truth." Waxman said it was "remarkable and sad" that the accounting office was forced to take legal action to get access to the information. "Everyone in our government—even the vice president— should be accountable to the American people, and I hope the White House will reconsider their unjustifiable insistence on secrecy," Waxman said. "Revealing the names of lobbyists and campaign contributors may be unpleasant to the vice president, but, as previous administrations have learned, avoiding embarrassment isn't a constitutional protection."[46]

Private Litigants Win Release of Documents

Despite the considerable fanfare surrounding the filing of the GAO's lawsuit, the focus quickly shifted back to the private litigants. On February 28, 2002, one week following the GAO's legal action, Federal Judge Gladys Kessler of the U.S. District Court in Washington ordered the Bush administration's Energy Department to turn over 7,500 pages of documents pertaining to Cheney's energy task force, a decision that made public for the first time detailed information about the influence of industry executives and others over the White House's energy policy. The court order, in response to the suit by NRDC, represented a significant setback to the Bush administration, which cited confidentiality of executive branch discussions for not releasing the documents. The order required the Energy Department to disclose documents revealing the contacts between outside groups and numerous department staffers working on Cheney's inter-agency task force. The NRDC predicted it would receive most of the information sought by the GAO, which could defuse the battle between Congress and the executive branch. The judge declared that "there can be little question that the Department of Energy has been woefully tardy" in responding to the NRDC's FOIA request and that the information requested by the plaintiffs was of "extraordinary public interest," especially since "the terrible events of September 11, 2001." The NRDC had filed its suit in December 2001 after eight months of requests for the information produced only thirty-three documents—a release the court order called "virtually meaningless."[47]

Despite the judge's order, it remained unclear how much the Energy Department would release. The judge gave the Energy Department discretion to postpone some releases and to make claims to withhold others. Although the documents to be released appeared to include nothing related to the task force's deliberations, the NRDC believed the information would substantiate that the Bush administration met secretly with industry officials who had too much influence over shaping the new energy policy. If this proved to be the case, NRDC senior attorney Jon Devine said the administration would have violated the Federal Advisory Committee Act, which requires that such meetings be open to the public, that detailed minutes be kept, and that membership be balanced. The public did not have the same level of access to the task force that big business did, Devine said. "Justice is finally served," said Sharon Buccino, NRDC lawyer. "This is going to expose the Bush energy plan for what it is— payback to polluters."[48]

On the same day that Judge Kessler issued her court order on the NRDC case, Judicial Watch appeared in a pair of hearings in U.S. District Court in Washington. In both hearings, judges thwarted the administration's attempts to avoid identifying business executives who met with Cheney's group. "I assume the government is stalling," U.S. District Court Judge Emmet Sullivan said at a hearing on a lawsuit demanding the release of task force documents. Sullivan reluctantly gave the administration seven days to file written arguments on why the Cheney task force should be allowed to withhold documents. At the other hearing, Justice Department lawyers argued that the Judicial Watch lawsuit, seeking documents from all federal agencies that were members of Cheney's task force, should be dismissed. U.S. District Court Judge Paul Friedman scoffed that the case should be thrown out. "So what! This is just gamesmanship," Friedman said. After nine months, he said, the Bush administration had turned over almost no documents and was withholding tens of thousands of pages from public scrutiny.[49] Thus, while one federal judge had ordered the Energy Department to release its documents on Cheney's task force, another judge indicated he would rule similarly on documents held by nine U.S. agencies.

During a visit to Des Moines, Iowa, Bush told reporters he was not concerned about documents being released by agencies under the FOIA but remained adamant against releasing details of meetings between Cheney and industry executives. "I receive advice and in order for people to give me that advice that information ought not to be public," Bush said. "And therefore, when the GAO overstepped its bounds to try to get advice given to the vice president and me, we resisted." The intention of the White House to keep the deliberations of its energy task force meetings shrouded in secrecy, even as thousands of related documents were poised for release, appeared to reveal a grand irony—that almost everything the GAO was suing for was about to be made a matter of public record.[50] But the prospect of other federal agencies releasing documents appeared to have little effect either on the White House's campaign to fight the GAO to reassert certain prerogatives of the presidency or on the GAO's ambitions to set a legal precedent for greater oversight of the executive. Stephen Hess, a senior fellow at the Brookings Institution, observed that since the White House had "already lost the political war, they may as well stay in there and see if they can win the philosophical war."[51] It would have seemed, however, that the pending release of the documents would have convinced one side or the other in the constitutional showdown to give up the fight.

The White House's fight against the GAO began to concern some Capitol Hill Republicans who supported the administration publicly but were growing more worried about the case. Echoing growing sentiment among Republicans, one congressional aide noted that "obviously the other court cases are strengthening the GAO case. From a political point of view, the White House should have given up the records a while ago. But they are fighting over principle, and the final arbiter of principles is the judiciary."[52] Indeed, the administration's continuing refusal to release the documents to the GAO began to isolate the White House politically and damage its credibility on energy issues. By this time, it was clear that energy industry officials, including some from Enron, the very icon of corporate greed, had influence over the task force's deliberations. From the information that had already been made available, it appeared that energy firms that made big financial contributions to the Bush campaign had a strong hand in shaping the administration's energy policy. But the *Milwaukee Journal Sentinel* asked why any of this information needed to be kept secret and said that industry influence should have been expected. "If you're putting together a campaign against terrorists, you better check with soldiers. And if you're putting together a campaign to meet the energy challenges of the future and wean America from its reliance on foreign oil, you'd better make use of the expertise found in the energy industry. So what? Why keep any of this secret?"[53] Indeed, industry executives pointed out that they had met routinely in the past with White House officials, even during Democratic administrations, and that it was no secret within the industry which corporations had met with Cheney's task force. Some industry officials complained that Cheney's refusal to be more open was tarnishing the industry's image.

In early March 2002, in response to Judicial Watch's FOIA lawsuit against nine executive branch agencies, Judge Friedman ordered the release of thousands of additional energy task force documents and rejected the Bush administration's attempts to have the case dismissed on technical grounds.[54] The court's ruling went beyond Judge Kessler's order in support of NRDC in setting a timeline for releasing the documents and in demanding an explanation why certain documents were being publicly withheld. One of the more recalcitrant agencies, the EPA, had been withholding more than 19,000 pages, citing a "deliberative process" exemption under the FOIA. Friedman's court order mandated the documents must be released to Judicial Watch by March 25, with others disclosed by May 3. The lawsuit complemented Judicial Watch's second lawsuit, before Judge Emmet Sullivan, against Vice President Cheney and the energy task force under the open meetings law known as the Federal Advisory Committee Act. "The stone wall is beginning to crumble. The court's ruling is a victory for openness of government," said Judicial Watch Chairman and general counsel Larry Klayman.[55]

The release of the documents under the court orders on behalf of Judicial Watch and NRDC provided the first glimpse into the behind-the-scenes efforts that shaped the administration's energy policy. The 11,000 pages of heavily redacted documents from the Energy Department bolstered the contention of Democratic lawmakers and environmental groups that the Bush administration relied almost exclusively on the advice of executives from utility companies and producers of oil, gas, coal, and nuclear energy while the energy task force drafted recommendations that would vastly increase energy production. Most of the corporations that met with Energy Secretary Spencer Abraham were large contributors of unregulated soft money to the Republican Party during the

2000 election campaign. Despite the Energy Department disclosure, the agency continued to fight to keep another 15,000 documents secret on the grounds of privacy, security, and other reasons. At the same time, large portions had been deleted from documents released not only by the Energy Department, but also by the EPA, the Agriculture Department, and the White House's Office of Management and Budget (OMB). Trent Duffy, OMB's spokesman, would not explain the deletions to the press beyond saying the "items that were part of the deliberative process were redacted." In addition, most of the attachments were missing and in many cases documents were withheld except for the subject line. The agencies also withheld thousands of other documents entirely, prompting the public interest groups that won the release of the documents to threaten to return to court.[56]

Nonetheless, the documents released were most revelatory of Abraham's meetings with big business. Between February 14 and April 26, 2001, the energy secretary met with executives from such groups as the National Association of Manufacturers, the Independent Petroleum Association of America, and the Nuclear Energy Institute. Top executives of Westinghouse Electric Corporation, Duke Power, Entergy, Exelon Corporation, UtiliCorp United, American Coal Company, and many others also met with Abraham.[57] Among the documents released was a letter from the Alliance of Automobile Manufacturers favoring tax credits for hybrid-fuel cells and fuel-cell vehicles and other incentives for fuel efficiency that were included in the energy task force report. Another company—Citgo—urged the White House to "exercise federal authority to prevent" states from implementing separate fuel standards. As a result, the Bush energy plan directed the EPA to work with states to eliminate them. An Energy Department e-mail indicated close collaboration with industry by showing that Texaco offered to help promote Bush's energy policy. In addition, the Southern Co., the largest provider of electric power in the Southeast, urged reform of EPA's new source review program, then being used to compel utilities and refineries to spend billions of dollars on antipollution equipment. According to the Center for Public Integrity, Southern had donated $1.8 million to Republicans and contributed $100,000 for Bush's presidential inauguration.[58]

Amid these revelations, the administration denied charges that it rebuffed efforts by environmental groups to meet with the energy task force. The Energy Department said that environmental groups did not respond to its request for advice, and the administration claimed to have held at least one major discussion with ten environmental groups in late March 2001, prior to releasing its energy policy. The Energy Department, moreover, released a chart indicating Cheney's task force had adopted nine NRDC recommendations, which NRDC attorney Sharon Buccino called "an outright lie."[59]

Meanwhile, Senate Democrats continued their offensive against the White House over the mounting Enron scandal and the collapsed energy firm's ties to the Bush-Cheney administration. On May 23, 2002, a Senate panel voted 9:8 on strict party lines to deliver two subpoenas to the offices of the president and vice president for records of all communications since 1992 between White House officials and Enron concerning the company's dealings with eight federal agencies. The vote came out of the Senate Governmental Affairs Committee's investigation of Enron and its connections to the Bush administration. The subpoenas also called for information about contacts between Enron and the White House regarding the shaping of the administration's national energy policy, covering much the same ground as the lawsuits filed by the GAO and the two public interest groups against the vice president. The subpoenas came the year after the Democrats took control of the Senate and after they accused the White House of resisting earlier requests for information. Joseph Lieberman, chairman of the Governmental Affairs Committee, accused the administration of "stonewalling," but Senator Thad Cochran, Republican of Mississippi, suggested that the subpoenas were a politically motivated fishing expedition intended to smear the White House.[60]

On the same day that Lieberman issued the subpoenas, the White House released a seven-page document, listing at least nineteen meetings between the White House and Enron officials including five meetings with Cheney's energy task force and at least half a dozen telephone calls. The document, which was not a legal response to the subpoenas and which aides to Lieberman found to be wholly inadequate, showed a glimpse of the extent of Enron's access to many people in the Bush administration with specific requests or seeking to discuss such topics as electricity policies, tax credits for wind power, the California energy crisis, and legislation governing power plant pollutants. The document showed several contacts already disclosed—including the April 17, 2001, half-hour meeting between Lay and Cheney in which they discussed energy policy and the California energy crisis. The document also listed phone calls Lay made to Bush chief political adviser Karl Rove recommending twenty-one people for jobs in the administration, three of whom were appointed, as well as calls made to other senior officials seeking help amidst Enron's collapse in late 2001.[61] Lay also attended numerous White House functions in 2001, including President Bush's inauguration, the Easter Egg Roll, T-ball games, speeches, and social events. With these revelations, the *Columbus Dispatch* of Columbus, Ohio, wondered, "what else Lay was doing and who else he was talking to each time he called or visited the White House."[62]

These disclosures came soon after internal documents were released detailing how the energy trading firm bled hundreds of millions of dollars from

California during the state's power crisis. By utilizing secret ploys with nicknames like "Death Star" and "Ricochet," Enron insiders milked California regulators out of vast sums of money, sometimes by overloading the state with more electricity than it could handle, then collecting a penalty fee of $750 per megawatt hour for not shipping more. Other times, Enron shipped power out of California, only to bring it back to evade price caps on in-state electricity. The manipulation of the energy markets sent California power costs skyrocketing from $44 per megawatt hour at the start of 2000 to $292 by year's end, causing brownouts and leaving "The Golden State" in desperate straits. After the revelations of Enron's massive bankruptcy and manipulations of energy markets became news, the accounting firm Arthur Andersen went on trial on criminal charges of helping Enron hide $500 million of debt in fraudulent partnerships. Swindled Enron employees, who were ruined after the firm's savings plan collapsed because it invested primarily in Enron stock, also filed a lawsuit charging various banks and lawyers in aiding and abetting Arthur Andersen and Enron executives in an elaborate scheme to hide Enron's enormous debts.[63] The *Charleston Gazette* predicted that Enron would "enter the history books as a grotesque example of duplicity in American business," but lamented that most Americans were "paying little attention to the scandal … because the machinations are almost too complicated to comprehend."[64]

FACA Case before U.S. District Court for the District of Columbia

On July 11, 2002, U.S. District Court Judge Emmet Sullivan issued his written order and opinion allowing the Sierra Club and Judicial Watch to proceed with their suits challenging the Bush administration's attempts to keep Cheney task force meetings with industry executives secret.[65] The opinion followed his oral ruling on May 23, rebuffing the administration's motion to dismiss the lawsuits and was notable in recognizing the administration's executive-centered concept of the federal government. Sullivan's opinion called "troubling" the administration's argument that the two groups should not be allowed to sue for documents about the task force under the Federal Advisory Committee Act. According to Sullivan, by the Bush administration's reasoning, any action by Congress or the Judiciary that intrudes on the president's ability to recommend legislation to Congress or get advice from Cabinet members in any way would necessarily violate the Constitution. Such a "thing would eviscerate the understanding of checks and balances between the three branches of government on which our constitutional order depends," the opinion said. "The fact that the government may want to advocate a new theory of executive authority and the separation of powers is its prerogative. It cannot, however, cloak what is tantamount to an aggrandizement of executive power with the legitimacy of precedent where none exists."[66] Sullivan criticized the Justice Department lawyers defending the Cheney task force for mischaracterizing a minority opinion in a Supreme Court case as if it were controlling legal authority that should result in the dismissal of the lawsuits. Sullivan was referring to the case, *Nixon v. Administrator of General Services* (1977), in which former President Richard M. Nixon lost his constitutional bid to reclaim ownership of his presidential materials after they were seized by an act of Congress for the continuing Watergate trials and investigations. It seemed peculiar that the administration's lawyers would use dissenting opinions in this case, written by Chief Justice Warren Burger and Justice William Rehnquist, as an underpinning rationale for its defense, especially since the majority Court rejected Nixon's extreme concept of executive privilege.[67]

In response to Sullivan's written opinion, a Justice Department lawyer said the administration would consider all of its options and would issue a counterproposal. In a hearing in August, however, Sullivan scarcely liked what he heard. Although some of the federal agencies involved in the task force had been ordered to turn over thousands of pages of documents, the Bush administration balked at Sullivan's July 11 order that it begin providing more detailed membership information, including White House records. Sullivan was exasperated with the government's claim that executive privilege and the Administrative Procedures Act shielded such information from public disclosure. "We are able through a sworn declaration to say that the law was followed," said Shannen Coffin, the Justice Department lawyer presenting the government's case. "The plaintiffs should then come forward and suggest something that questions that presumption of regularity." But Sullivan dismissed this position, which echoed a similar government position in the NRDC lawsuit. "Your position seems to be, 'the government wins because the government says this is what happened, and no one can ask what happened,'" Sullivan said. "Discovery is going forward in this case." David Bookbinder, senior attorney for the Sierra Club, and Judicial Watch Chairman Larry Klayman described the ruling as a clear victory. "The administration's arrogance can be amazing," Bookbinder said. "We want to see all these documents, and then we'll be able to tell what else we need."[68]

Cheney v. GAO in Court

As the private litigants pursued their case against the administration, the GAO's suit made its way through the federal judicial system. On September 28, 2002, lawyers for the GAO and Cheney clashed before a federal judge with both sides claiming irreparable harm by a ruling against them as the historic showdown between the two branches of government got underway. As Judge John D. Bates of the federal district court realized, the lawsuit raised a fundamental constitutional question concerning whether a vice president could ignore a request for information by the GAO, acting on behalf of Congress, without the president exercising executive privilege. The case also continued to threaten to tarnish the White House since the dispute made it difficult for the administration to distance itself from the scandal of the Enron Corporation, in which executives met with Cheney and other task force members seven times in 2001.

Carter Phillips, the outside attorney representing the GAO, argued that if the administration won the case it would cripple the GAO's ability to carry out its fundamental responsibilities. "The executive branch is asking the court to deal blows ... that would be extremely damaging or fatal to the GAO's ability" to investigate the executive branch, said Phillips. "It would have an extraordinary sweeping effect and would significantly halt Congress's use of the GAO to conduct nonpartisan investigations." Phillips argued that Title 31, the legislation delineating the powers of the GAO, allowed the comptroller general to "investigate all matters related to the receipt, disbursement and use of public money." He also contended that the law gives the comptroller general the right to obtain all "information the comptroller requires about the duties, powers, activities, organization and financial transactions" of the agency under investigation.[69] The GAO's legal brief stated the executive branch had complied with "countless" GAO requests for similar information, including records on the White House China Permanent Normal Trade Relations Working Group and White House records that involved an investigation of alleged vandalism by the outgoing Clinton administration.

But Paul Clement, the principal deputy solicitor general, representing Cheney, countered the agency had no legal standing to sue the vice president and was overstepping its authority in seeking information on executive deliberations. "No court that I am aware of has ever ordered the executive branch to turn over a document to a Congressional agent," Clement argued. "This is unprecedented. It would allow a revolution in the separation of powers."[70] Clement warned that if the administration was ordered to release the information, there would be no end to similar lawsuits filed by the GAO against the executive branch. There were other means that Congress could have used to obtain the documents, said Clement, including a subpoena sent by the House Governmental Affairs Committee on which served Representatives Waxman and Dingell—the two Democratic lawmakers who requested the GAO investigation of the vice president's energy task force. Clement was joined at the defense table by the solicitor general, Theodore B. Olson, who was known to seldom attend arguments at the district court level. Olson's presence indicated the significance of the case to both Cheney and Bush, who proclaimed that disclosure of the information would severely hinder the executive branch's ability to solicit the advice of outside experts.

Thus, the matter of how much privacy the Bush White House should have resided with Federal U.S. District Court Judge John Bates, who had been in office less than a year before becoming subjected to the powerful crosscurrents of an unprecedented lawsuit brought by the investigating arm of Congress against the vice president. Leading critics of the White House saw Bates's political connections—an appointee of President Bush with many friends in the administration—as an ominous sign. At the same time, Bates's background seemed to give the GAO some grounds for hope. In 1977, as a deputy to White House prosecutor Kenneth W. Starr, Bates compelled the release of White House documents in a case before the Supreme Court. Nonetheless, the two cases were different. Bates's win before the Supreme Court was an attorney–client privilege case involving notes of then First Lady Hillary Rodham Clinton's conversations with government lawyers concerning her former law firm's billing records. The Walker case, however, rested on the GAO's statutory authority to sue the executive branch.

But the similarities between the two cases were strong as well. In both cases, the White House argued that disclosure of presidential deliberations would produce a chilling effect on advisers and hinder presidential decision making. In both cases, the White House claimed that its opponents were on fishing expeditions and that the matter should be handled in the legislature, rather than in the courts. In both cases, the White House also decided not to invoke executive privilege, perhaps mindful of the image of Watergate and the prospect of raising a host of unresolved constitutional issues. In the immediate case, it was unclear whether Cheney could assert the presidential prerogative of executive privilege since the vice president has no constitutionally assigned executive function. Under the Constitution, the vice president's role is legislative in nature—to preside over and break ties in the Senate. In addition, at no time did the GAO request information about the deliberations of Cheney's energy task force group, but only for the names of participants in the meetings and for other non-deliberative information. As a result, it was not clear whether an assertion of executive privilege, even if it did apply, could extend beyond the content of the discussions to cover information about who was involved in the meetings. Thus, there was no advantage for the vice president to assert a dubious claim of executive privilege in order to withhold information from Congress. Such a privilege claim only would have immensely complicated and weakened the administration's case.[71] Given Bates's involvement in the Clinton case, it was thus not readily apparent which way he would decide the GAO lawsuit.

The ruling involving fundamental constitutional issues was not long in coming. On December 9, 2002, Bates threw out the case against Vice President Cheney over the formulation of the administration's energy policy.[72] Bates found that the GAO, which conducted hundreds of investigations into governmental affairs each year, did not have sufficient standing to sue the vice president. "The case ... engenders a struggle between the political branches that is historically unprecedented and that transcends both the specific information sought and the political identity of the legislative and executive branch players involved," Bates wrote in dismissing the suit. Bates grounded his decision in the vice president's core arguments premised on existing Rehnquist court precedents. The vice president's argument relied heavily on *Raines v. Byrd*, which addressed whether six members of Congress could sue under the Line Item Veto Act of 1996. Although the statute expressly provided for congressional members to bring action if they were adversely affected by the act, the Court held that no such standing existed. The Court found that the congressional members who filed suit had no constitutional standing as they sustained no personal injury, that any claim that Congress itself suffered an institutional injury was a mere abstraction, and that Congress could have pursued other remedies, including repealing the law. Moreover, the Court stressed that the congressional plaintiffs received no authorization to represent their respective houses of Congress in the lawsuit and that both houses opposed the suit. Cheney's lawyers contended the 1980 statute providing the GAO judicial enforcement powers was similarly unconstitutional under the Raines precedent and asked that the case be dismissed with prejudice for lack of standing.

Siding with the vice president and adopting the *Raines* criteria, Bates held the court had to conduct an especially rigorous standing inquiry given the core separation of powers questions at issue. As a result, Bates found that the suit against the vice president did not establish a sufficient personal injury to Walker to merit standing since his interest in the dispute was "solely institutional, relating exclusively to his duties in his official capacity as Comptroller General." Further, Bates said that neither had Walker suffered sufficient institutional injury because he was not an independent constitutional actor and had no freestanding institutional injury of his own to assert. Nor was there sufficient institutional injury to Congress to merit standing, said Bates, beyond a mere "abstract dilution of institutional legislative power," which was too "vague and amorphous to confer standing." Bates said that Congress had undertaken no effort to obtain the documents at issue, that no committee had requested the documents, that no congressional subpoena had been issued, and that an injury to any congressional right to information thus remained "wholly conjectural or hypothetical." Bates therefore found it of "some importance" that "like the plaintiffs in *Raines*, the Comptroller General here has not been expressly authorized by Congress to represent its interests in this lawsuit." Indeed, said Bates, this "case, in which neither a House of Congress nor any congressional committee has issued a subpoena for the disputed information … is not the setting for such unprecedented judicial action."[73] The decision marked a significant legal triumph for the Bush White House, which seized upon the case as a vehicle for reversing what it saw as a generation of congressional encroachment on the prerogatives of the executive branch. At the same time, the decision was a blow against congressional oversight of governmental affairs. The ruling was in direct conflict with a 1980 law that gave the GAO the authority to sue.

The decision, which followed the script of the administration's core arguments, had the unavoidable patina of a political judgment. A Republican judge who had been an appointee of the Bush-Cheney administration had seemingly returned the favor to the White House. Beyond the appearance of a politically based ruling, some were concerned that the ruling had potentially far-reaching consequences for Congress's investigative agency. If left to stand, the opinion would be "definitely precedent-setting," said Susan Low Bloch, a professor of constitutional law at Georgetown University Law Center. "It will make it a lot more difficult for the GAO to even negotiate for documents."[74] Waxman and Dingell both assailed the opinion. A "Republican judge has decided that, once in office, Bush and Cheney can operate in complete secrecy with no oversight by Congress," Waxman said.[75] In a written statement, Comptroller General David Walker, head of the GAO, said he was "very disappointed" by the ruling. "We are in the process of reviewing and analyzing the decision to fully understand the bases for it and its potential implications," Walker said. "We will consider whether or not to appeal after we have completed this review and consulted with congressional leadership on a bipartisan basis."[76]

The GAO Drops Suit against the White House

The calculus of the clash between the executive and legislative branches of government over the case changed dramatically with the November 2002 elections. Under heavy political pressure from Republicans after they won majorities in both houses of Congress, the GAO capitulated and dropped the suit, ending a dispute between the two branches that spanned nearly two years. On February 7, 2003, the GAO announced that it was terminating its lawsuit against the vice president, a decision that scholars said would significantly weaken the legislature's ability to check executive power. The GAO said it would not appeal Judge Bates's federal court ruling that denied the GAO's right to force Cheney to turn over information about which individuals and groups met with the Bush administration's energy task force. The decision, which was hailed by the White House and condemned by Democrats and advocates of open government, was made despite the GAO's earlier concerns that accepting defeat would cripple its ability to investigate the executive branch. Whatever the precise long-term consequences of the GAO's defeat, many lawyers interpreted it as eviscerating the agency's ability to use the courts to enforce its demands for executive branch information.[77]

Although the White House praised Walker's decision for terminating the suit, Representative Waxman, who was one of the lawmakers who requested the investigation, said Walker's move not only was "very disappointing," but represented a "tremendous setback for open government." Perhaps most revealing of the GAO's emasculation was Walker's own statement that he "hope[d] the administration will do the right thing and fulfill its obligations when it comes to disclosures to GAO, the Congress, and the public." Indeed, the GAO, uncertain of the ramifications of its own decision to drop the suit under political pressure, now appeared to be reduced to mere hoping for executive branch compliance with its requests. Sharon Buccino, the NRDC lawyer pressing one of the private suits against the administration, commented that the GAO's abandonment of the case meant that Congress's hands were "seriously tied" in overseeing the executive. "If the GAO does not have the right to go to court to enforce compliance with its requests for information, then there is no incentive for the executive or agencies to comply."[78]

In terminating the suit against Vice President Cheney, Walker issued a public statement that said that "despite GAO's conviction that the district court's decision was incorrect, further pursuit of the [energy task force] information would require investment of significant time and resources over several years." Walker's reasoning, however, hardly accounted for his own understanding of this fact when he initially sued the vice president. Further, that a federal appeal would take time and investment of significant resources was a routine situation in any federal appeals case. The appeal would have posed critically important issues concerning the balance of powers between the government's legislative and executive branches, a point that Walker emphasized when he filed the lawsuit and that Judge Bates purposely evaded by dismissing the suit without addressing its merits. Moreover, Walker said that Judge Bates's decision was "confined to the unique circumstances of this particular case and does not preclude the GAO from filing suit on a different matter involving different facts and circumstances in the future."[79] But this position contradicted the GAO's position in court, which argued that Cheney's position, if accepted, would decimate the agency's ability to obtain information from the executive branch under any circumstances. Indeed, Thomas E. Mann, a senior fellow in government studies at the Brookings Institution, saw the decision as having major implications. "President Bush and Vice President Cheney have an extreme and relentless executive-centered conception of American government and it plays out every day, and there are dozens of fronts in this effort to strengthen the presidency," he said. "Power naturally gravitates to the presidency in times of uncertainty, but people are going to question putting all of our trust in an unfettered president."[80]

Walker's public statement also stressed that his decision came only after "extensive outreach with congressional leadership and others concerning various policy matters and the potential ramifications of the court's decision." Walker evidently tried but failed to win the support of the new Republican congressional leadership on behalf of the lawsuit. GOP leaders, however, wanted to stem any further embarrassing revelations of the vice president's ties to the energy industry, including Enron, from a court-ordered release of documents. It is also possible that they were concerned that the GAO would ultimately lose its case before the Supreme Court, resulting in a further diminution of Congress's investigative powers.

Indeed, from the beginning the vice president's sweeping attacks on the constitutionality of the GAO's request indicated a much larger agenda at stake. Cheney's unyielding stance together with his arguments that the comptroller general was seeking a revolution in the separation of powers pointed the way toward a showdown before the Supreme Court with the intent of expanding executive prerogatives and diminishing legislative authority. The vice president and his government lawyers were aiming to build a case from the start to take to the same Supreme Court that both handed the 2000 presidential election to the Bush-Cheney administration and that since 1995 had been incrementally limiting congressional power. Commenting on the Walker case in October 2002, former Nixon counsel and FindLaw commentator John W. Dean noted that in the "noble name of federalism, the Supreme Court, under Chief Justice William Rehnquist, [has been] on the warpath against Congress." Not since the days of Republican Chief Justices William Howard Taft and Charles Evan Hughes, said Dean, had the Supreme Court been more hostile toward congressional power.[81] In the cases that came before the Court, the majority of the justices, including Rehnquist, Scalia, Thomas, Kennedy, and O'Connor, issued opinions aimed at limiting congressional authority under the Commerce Clause and the Fourteenth Amendment, the two primary constitutional bases permitting Congress to initiate nationwide actions.[82] Attuned to the nature of these opinions, the White House purposely played to the Court's anti-congressional sentiments. Accordingly, in their court papers, the vice president's lawyers drew heavily on the Rehnquist Court's anti-congressional opinions hoping to roll back the investigative powers of Congress. As a result, even if Walker had won his case at the appellate level, his chances of success before the Supreme Court were problematic at best.

Theoretically, Walker, who President Clinton appointed to a fifteen-year term, could have continued the suit for the energy task force documents and his larger quest both to defend the agency's statutory authority to sue for access to information and to strengthen the GAO's investigative powers and oversight of the executive branch. But he would have confronted considerable political hostility and isolation, which would have hindered the agency's ability to function. With the Republicans in control of the White House and Congress after the 2002 elections, the GAO found itself in a losing position no matter which way it turned. Walker evidently found the political risks too high to appeal the Bates decision after receiving threats of reprisals from Republican lawmakers. In a meeting with Republican Senator Ted Stevens, chairman of the powerful Appropriations Committee, Walker was allegedly warned to drop the suit upon threat of having the GAO's budget cut.[83] To placate the Republicans further, Walker indicated he would voluntarily withdraw the GAO's authority to litigate without the express imprimatur of at least one full committee. In a letter informing Waxman about the GAO's decision not to appeal, Walker wrote that "given the district court's decision, and other considerations, as a matter of procedural prudence, I believe it would be appropriate to have an affirmative statement of support from at least one full committee with jurisdiction over any records access matter prior to any future court action by GAO."[84] By "other considerations," Walker may have been referring to GOP pressure to drop the suit.

Walker's statement indicated the GAO would live within the confines of the Bates opinion. Accordingly, having sacrificed its independence, the GAO would pursue court actions to enforce its rights to information only with the blessing of the majority party that controlled Congress's oversight committees. As a result, it was unlikely that the GAO would be willing to pursue important or controversial assignments either on its own—as it had done in the past—or at the behest of minority party committee members. Nor was the agency likely to confront the White House over access matters without strong congressional support. In this new era, the majority would dictate GAO action, while the minority party would have no say in initiating investigations.

In the end, Walker was facing a situation in which he already suffered a court defeat at the hands of a Republican judge with ties to the Bush-Cheney administration, was under political pressure to drop the suit under threat of budget cuts to the GAO, and was looking at the prospect of ultimately arguing the case before a conservative Supreme Court whose majority members were intent on circumscribing congressional power. Given these odds, Walker and his attorneys may have figured that it was better to affect a strategic retreat and reserve the GAO's fight over its judicial authority for another day under more favorable circumstances.

With some justification and despite his lost cause, Henry Waxman accused the Republicans of "breathtaking" hypocrisy. During the Clinton years, congressional committees—at the initiation of Republicans—spent over $15 million investigating the White House. They demanded and compelled the disclosure of internal White House memos, e-mails, phone records, even lists of guests at White House movie showings; they initiated numerous GAO investigations ranging from Clinton's Health Care Task Force to his working group on China Permanent Normal Trade Relations; and they subpoenaed top administrative officials to testify about advice given to the president. By Cheney's own standards, the intrusion onto the prerogatives of the presidency was extraordinary. Nonetheless, before the television cameras, in the newspapers, and in the halls of Congress, Republican leaders with a rhetorical flourish said it was the public's right to know and congressional oversight that were paramount. Now that "President Bush and Vice President Cheney are in office," said Waxman, "suddenly these priorities have changed. Oversight is no longer a priority. In fact, it's something to be avoided at all costs, including sacrificing the independence of the GAO. Even when GAO asks for the most basic information—what private interests met with a White House task force—the answer is that GAO is not entitled to ask these questions."[85]

Whatever the politics of the matter, the implications of the GAO's decision not to appeal may be far-reaching. If the *Walker* decision is interpreted broadly, the GAO may no longer be armed with judicial enforcement powers to compel or leverage the release of information from either the White House or executive branch agencies. In the past, the GAO's investigative authority and independence has been critical for congressional oversight. Since its creation in 1921, Congress has increasingly relied on the agency to monitor and oversee an executive branch that underwent enormous expansion in size and power. With an administration seemingly determined to veil its actions behind new screens of secrecy and expand the prerogatives of the presidency, the Bush administration was eager to provoke a fight that would cripple the GAO's oversight function. Walker said that his decision to terminate the lawsuit would have little effect on the agency's daily operations, which involves primarily the auditing and evaluation of government programs. But the irony of this statement was hard to miss given that his initial ambitions in the case were to expand the agency's investigative and oversight powers of the executive.

It remains to be seen whether the Bates decision will be interpreted as applying only to the specifics of the Walker case with little or no impact on future court actions, as Walker said after the court's decision, or whether it will be read more broadly precluding suits against the vice president and president. The latter case would not necessarily prohibit the GAO from bringing suit against executive agencies which are the focus of the vast majority of its reviews and investigations. Nevertheless, if Bates's rigorous standing requirements are extended to executive branch agencies, it would strip the GAO of its judicial enforcement powers altogether. After all, Bates singled out Walker in his opinion, not Cheney. He concluded that as a delegated agent of Congress, Walker had "no personal stake" in the dispute and consequently no constitutional standing to sue, despite the GAO's statutory authority to bring court actions. Under this reasoning, it would seem no comptroller general would ever have a sufficient personal stake to meet standing requirements—not even in a case brought against the head of an agency. If sustained in the future, Bates's reasoning means that executive branch officials would be able to refuse a GAO request for information and the agency would be able to do nothing about it. Further, Bates's denial that the GAO had any standing to enforce its delegated authority on behalf of Congress by extension raised the question of whether a congressional committee as a delegated agent of Congress also had any constitutional standing. By not appealing the decision, Walker may have affected a strategic retreat, but he also left a need to clarify the parameters of Congress's delegated oversight and investigative authority, an issue only the Supreme Court could ultimately decide.[86]

Should it turn out that the GAO has no standing to enforce its information requests, the 1980 law expressly granting statutory authority to pursue court actions, which has proved effective countless times in the past by prompting negotiation and compromise for release of information, would be nothing but a dead statute. It would largely return the agency to where it was before 1980 when the White House and executive branch agencies frequently stonewalled GAO requests for information to which it had the right of access by law. Congress addressed this problem by passing legislation authorizing the comptroller general to pursue court actions to compel the disclosure of documents from the executive branch in cases in which it failed to comply with a request for information.[87] By granting the GAO the power to sue, Congress believed that over time it would minimize, if not eliminate, access problems. Congress also made clear that the agency's newly granted judicial authority could be used against the president and his principal advisers. The Senate report concerning the statute, for example, stated that "with regard to enforcement actions at the Presidential level, certifications provided for under section 102(d)(3) of the bill are intended to authorize the President and the Director of the Office of Management and Budget to preclude a suit by the Comptroller General against the

President and his principal advisers and assistants, and against those units within the Executive Office of the President whose sole function is to advise and assist the President, for information which would not be available under the Freedom of Information Act."[88] With this passage, the executive branch fully understood Congress's intent to authorize judicial actions for access to White House documents. As a matter of compromise, Congress gave the White House the power to prohibit disclosure through a certification process if it deemed that release of information would impair government operations. The 1980 act was introduced just months after two GAO access disputes with the White House, a fact noted by Congress in passing the statute.

The 1980 law reflected Congress's strong institutional interest in seeing that the GAO remained a "principal means by which the legislative branch conducts oversight of Executive Branch programs and expenditures." The Senate report concerning the General Accounting Act of 1980, the bill granting GAO judicial enforcement authority, stressed that since the agency's 1921 creation, Congress by necessity became more reliant on GAO assistance in fulfilling its oversight and legislative responsibilities. The report noted that the GAO "not only provides Congress with essential information about Federal programs, but uniquely, exercises statutory authority to participate directly in the oversight process as an independent congressional entity." Since its establishment, the broad array of emerging problems and the complex economic, social, military, and political issues that confronted Congress led to an expansion of GAO's responsibilities from traditional finance and accounting activities to assessments of the effectiveness of executive agencies. By passing a series of measures, including the Budget and Accounting Procedures Act of 1950, the Legislative Reorganization Act of 1946 and 1970, and the Congressional Budget and Impoundment Control Act of 1974, Congress made "mandatory, explicit, and emphatic the requirement for GAO to assess the efficiency, economy, and effectiveness of program operation by the Executive Branch."[89] By law, it could launch investigations or evaluations on its own initiative or at the request of a congressional committee or subcommittee, or member of Congress.[90] But it was this explicit congressional recognition of the GAO's independent status with delegated authority to conduct autonomous investigations, including making stand-alone requests for information from the executive branch, which came under sweeping attack by the vice president's lawyers and which drew little support from a Republican-controlled Congress that seemingly viewed the GAO's lawsuit at the behest of two ranking House Democrats as an attack on the Bush-Cheney administration.

To be sure, the vast majority of the GAO's audits and reviews of federal programs are unlikely to be affected by Bates's ruling. Indeed, the GAO's hundreds of annual investigations meet with little agency resistance and enjoy broad bipartisan support from congressional committee and subcommittee members who are intent on exercising their oversight prerogatives. In addition, under its decentralized system of semiautonomous committees, Congress employs many other means to obtain information on executive activities in order to hold agencies accountable. These methods may comprise committee and subcommittee hearings and investigations, agency reporting requirements, confirmation hearings, casework, authorization and appropriation processes, informal communications between committee members and staffers with agency officials, and data provided by private interest groups, lobbyists, constituents, and others with a stake in the outcome of federal programs. Further, oversight committees may rely on data analysis from other legislative support agencies, including the Congressional Research Service, and the Congressional Budget Office. With this arsenal of oversight powers, Congress may make the lives of executive officials difficult if they prove unresponsive to demands for information, programmatic improvement, or reform. Because Congress has ultimate authority to create or abolish bureaucracies, expand or diminish their powers and responsibilities, increase or decrease their staffs and budgets, and determine the parameters of what they do, agency officials have political incentive to cooperate with congressional oversight committees that control their authorization and budgets.[91]

These methods, however, are fraught with partisanship and may be of little use during times when the majority party owns both the White House and Congress. Initiating contempt proceedings, for example, or passing program cuts requires getting a majority of Congress or at least one House to initiate action. Further, the majority party in Congress controls the political agenda. In the immediate case in which the Republicans controlled both chambers, the minority party—the Democrats—could not schedule congressional hearings, require testimony, issue subpoenas, demand a special counsel, or evidently now rely on the GAO to acquire information from the White House. Few committee chairmen of either party have much inclination to use these means to investigate a president who is the leader of their own party. Moreover, the executive branch is unlikely to readily entertain calls by the opposition party to appoint special counsels to investigate itself if presidential stakes are involved. Indeed, the Justice Department had declined several calls by Democrats to appoint special counsels to investigate Republican conduct—including, for example, campaign contributions to Republicans by Westar Energy, a Kansas utility seeking regulatory exemptions, or whether there were conflicts of interest in the administration's inquiry into Enron's collapse. Neither had the Democrats been able to convene hearings on White House policy and other issues of concern, leaving them to "demand answers through press releases, op-ed articles and open letters, hoping for new coverage" and public pressure. With few exceptions, most notably the Senate Intelligence Committee's investigation of American intelligence failures in Iraq and the special 9/11 Commission—both of which were set up in response to enormous political and public pressure—Republicans had avoided holding hearings that might embarrass the president, a contrast to the forty subpoenas, three investigative hearings, and the appointment of five special counsels that congressional Republican leaders directed against the Clinton White House by the end of his first term alone. To a large extent, in matters of oversight, partisans on both sides of the aisle had switched sides. Democrats like Waxman who decried the investigations of the Clinton White House now complained of lacking the means through the GAO and other ways to obtain information from the Bush-Cheney administration. Republicans like House Majority Leader Tom DeLay, who defended the Clinton-era inquiries, dismissed calls for investigations and hearings as nothing more than "politics of personal destruction."[92]

As the final act in the long-running battle with the Bush-Cheney administration, the GAO released its report on April 12, 2003, on Cheney's energy task force. According to the report, the White House collaborated closely with corporations in developing its energy policy but repeatedly refused to give congressional investigators details about the closed-door meetings. The GAO's report stated that Energy Secretary Spencer Abraham held private discussions concerning the formulation of the energy policy with chief executive officers of oil, chemical, natural gas, electricity, nuclear, and coal companies, among others. Further, while the energy task force led by Vice President Cheney actively sought outside advice primarily from petroleum, coal, nuclear, natural gas, and electricity representatives and lobbyists, it pursued limited input from academic experts, environmentalists, and policy groups. The report noted that none of the task force meetings were open to the public and participants told GAO investigators they could not recollect whether official rosters or minutes were kept. The GAO said its report was incomplete because of administration intransigence. Although the Energy Department had already been compelled by a lawsuit by the National Resources Defense Council to release e-mails, letters, and calendars that revealed heavy corporate influence, the GAO report provided the first comprehensive look at the extent to which the White House relied on corporate advisers and used secrecy to develop its policy.

In an interview, Walker said the battle over the task force records called into question the existence of a "reasonable degree of transparency and an appropriate degree of accountability in government." He said the energy investigation standoff was the first time since he was appointed comptroller general in November

1998 that the GAO was stonewalled. "The Congress and the American people had the right to know the limited amount of information we were seeking," Walker said. The report bolstered Democratic contentions that the Bush-Cheney energy policy was filled with special favors for the administration's corporate allies and donors. Senator Joseph Lieberman, a Democratic presidential candidate who joined the request for the GAO investigation when he was chairman of the Senate Governmental Affairs Committee, said voters should be informed about the extent of corporate influence in writing the nation's new energy policy. "They will never know the full truth because the White House chose to stonewall instead of cooperate with investigators," Lieberman said. The White House's only comment on the report came from Cheney's spokeswoman, who said she hoped that "everyone will now focus as strongly as the administration has on the substance of meeting America's energy needs."[93]

Vice President Cheney's battle to keep information about the energy task force secret reflected an administration that arrived in Washington determined to strengthen executive authority. The vice president's intransigence also exemplified the administration's wide-ranging opportunism in search for cases with which to roll back legislative oversight. Indeed, the White House could have immediately protected the information from disclosure and ended the dispute with the GAO by merely certifying that the release of the documents would impair government operations. Instead, the vice president lured the GAO, which appeared to have had its own ambitions to expand its prerogatives at the expense of the executive, into a statutory and constitutional fight with the aim of diminishing Congress's oversight and investigative powers of the presidency. Cheney's victory in the case marked a significant triumph in reasserting the prerogatives of the presidency, although it still remains to be seen how the Judge Bates decision will play out in the future.

Four

Defeating the Federal Advisory
Committee Act

Cheney's victory over the GAO had little effect on the Sierra Club and Judicial Watch, which had filed their own lawsuits against the vice president seeking much the same information on the workings of the energy task force. The case that began with a pedestrian discovery request in two consolidated civil suits moved quickly to the U.S. Supreme Court. The suit against the vice president was similar to the GAO's, involving separation of powers issues and whether Cheney could keep information about his energy task force's meetings secret. Both the Sierra Club and Judicial Watch claimed that the task force violated the 1972 Federal Advisory Committee Act (FACA), requiring that its activities and records be open to the public if nonfederal individuals participated. The plaintiffs argued that energy industry representatives and lobbyists who were major donors and political allies of the administration were so integral to the task force's deliberations that they comprised de facto members of the group, a charge that Cheney denied. The vice president claimed that the task force was exempt from the FACA's requirements because it was made up exclusively of senior Bush administration officials. He argued that requests for information intruded into the heart of executive deliberations and that to make even a preliminary disclosure would violate the constitutional separation of powers between the executive and judicial branches. A key to the administration's strategy involved taking the case to the same Supreme Court that gave the 2000 presidential election to George W. Bush, betting that the majority of justices would be more sympathetic to executive confidentiality than to open government.

Congress passed FACA to curb the domination of government advisory groups by special interests and their unaccountable influence over public policy. The key features of the open meetings law are straightforward. The law requires that committees set up by the president or federal agencies to provide advice generally must conduct their business in public. Under the statute, presidential and other federal advisory committees that include nongovernmental participants must publicly announce their meetings, hold their meetings in public, take minutes of the meetings, and allow for differing views to be represented. The act also allows for public access to minutes and other records, reports, and transcripts, but exempts open access to information that is classified or deals with national security. Committees composed entirely of federal officials and employees are exempt from the statute, however. The act was passed with the best of intentions for promoting open government, but in the end, executive confidentiality trumped open government in the courts, handing the Bush-Cheney administration another important victory in building a higher wall of secrecy around the White House.

Like its fight with the GAO, the White House invited the lawsuits filed by the Sierra Club and Judicial Watch—a fight triggered by the vice president's refusal to release information about the role that energy industry executives and lobbyists played in shaping the nation's energy policy. Both public interest groups sued the vice president before the GAO initiated its own highly publicized and unprecedented lawsuit against Cheney and the energy task force seeking much the same information on behalf of Congress. In response to the secrecy surrounding the task force meetings, on April 19, 2001, Judicial Watch filed FOIA requests with eight federal agencies seeking information on the task force and its deliberations and communications with outside parties and between task force members. When the administration proved unresponsive to Judicial Watch's FOIA requests, the group sued on May 9, 2001, to compel compliance with the open records law. The group then wrote a June 25 letter to the vice president requesting copies of minutes and other documents under the disclosure provisions of both FACA and FOIA. On July 16, 2001, the conservative government watchdog organization sued again—this time under FACA— after the vice president's office refused its request, stating that the energy task force was not covered under either statute.[1] On January 25, 2002, the Sierra Club joined the fray, filing suit in federal district court against the vice president, the energy task force, and various agency officials under FACA, the open meetings statute.[2] The group's lawsuit was nearly identical to Judicial Watch's, seeking information on the energy task force's confidential deliberations.

The lawsuits against the vice president under the open meetings law was enlivened by the massive collapse and corporate fraud of Enron, the giant energy trading firm that had close ties to the Bush administration, and the release of thousands of pages of internal documents in March 2002 by the administration's energy department. Following Enron's demise, the public interest groups sought to discover to what extent the disgraced energy firm and its chairman, Ken Lay, influenced the administration's energy plan. In an effort to quickly disassociate itself with Lay, the White House admitted that it had met with Lay several times in 2001, but that there were no discussions concerning the financial condition of Enron.

Besides the embarrassing association with Lay, the administration was compelled to release thousands of documents in March 2002 in response to long-running FOIA lawsuits filed by the National Resources Defense Council, the environmental group, and Judicial Watch. The heavily redacted documents provided a glimpse of the extent of influence wielded by energy lobbyists over the writing of the White House's national energy report. A review by the *New York Times* of documents disclosed to the NRDC revealed that several recommendations from energy lobbyists were written directly into the White House's national energy report and into an executive order signed by President Bush. The documents showed, for example, that the American Petroleum Institute submitted a proposal to the Energy Department on March 20, 2001, suggesting that the president issue an executive order requiring that federal officials consider the impact on energy supplies before they issue regulations. Two months later, the president issued an executive order incorporating the trade group's proposal after the task force recommended it. In another example, a lobbyist from the Southern Company, one of the country's largest utilities and a contributor of $1.8 million to Republicans, sent an e-mail message to a senior Energy Department official suggesting a revision of the Clean Air Act with the aim of weakening enforcement actions against large utility companies, including the Southern Company. The policy recommendation was subsequently adopted in the national energy policy.[3] The task force also adopted a recommendation by the Alliance of Automobile Manufacturers, which noted in a report to the Energy Department on March 22, 2001, that fuel economy standards were an ineffective policy. Instead of calling for new fuel efficiency standards, the energy task force recommended only that the new standards receive further study.[4] As a result of these revelations, John H. Adams, president of the NRDC, said at a news conference that "Big Energy companies all but held the pencil for the White House task force as government officials wrote a plan calling for billions of dollars in corporate subsidies, and the wholesale elimination of key health and environmental safeguards."[5] Indeed, with these kinds of revelations and the enormity of the unfolding Enron scandal, the public interest groups seemed to step up their case against the vice president to discover who the national energy task force met with and to what extent they wrote the administration's national energy policy.

The case involving the open meetings statute was being overseen at the trial level by Judge Emmet Sullivan of the U.S. District Court for the District of

Columbia. A highly respected jurist with a reputation for fairness, Sullivan had risen through the judiciary with the bipartisan support of the Reagan, George H. W. Bush, and Clinton administrations. On July 11, 2002, Judge Sullivan ordered Cheney and others to disclose non-privileged documents on the composition of the energy task force and any of its subgroups to determine whether it was covered by the federal open meetings statute. In issuing his opinion, Sullivan acknowledged important separation of powers issues and the question of whether the application of the FACA to the energy task force would interfere with the president's constitutionally protected ability to receive confidential advice from his advisers. Indeed, Cheney's lawyers contended that even for the courts to require discovery to determine the constitutional issues would be a violation of presidential prerogatives. Sullivan, however, found these arguments unpersuasive, saying that they flew in the face of "precedent that has developed separation of powers doctrine as a fact-intensive, case-by-case analysis of the specific nature of the intrusion into the President's performance of his constitutional duties." Sullivan concluded that any resolution in the case as to the constitutional issues of the separation of powers and interference with a president's ability to receive candid advice was premature since discovery had yet to take place to establish the factual record. According to Sullivan, an examination of the factual record was necessary to determine whether and to what extent private individuals participated in the work of the task force and its subgroups and whether Sierra Club and Judicial Watch had any factual basis for their claims. Moreover, the judge did not give free rein to the groups to initiate unlimited discovery, but said that any discovery would be tightly limited. He chastised the government for a consistent pattern of misconstruing precedent and wrote that the vice president and codefendants were seeking a ruling from him that "would eviscerate the understanding of checks and balances between the three branches of government on which our constitutional order depends."[6]

The vice president refused to comply with Sullivan's order to produce non-privileged documents, saying it was a matter of principle to protect the ability of presidents to receive unvarnished advice. Rob Perks, a spokesman for the National Resources Defense Council, disagreed, stating that it was a question of how secret the administration could be. "What do they have to hide, and why are they hiding it?"[7] Rather than directly contesting Sullivan's discovery order, the vice president's lawyers attempted to preempt the ruling by petitioning the U.S. Circuit Court of Appeals for the District of Columbia in the middle of the case, first to a three-judge panel, which rejected Cheney's claims, and then to the full circuit court of appeals. In seeking to cancel Sullivan's order, Cheney's lawyers took the unusual step of filing a writ of mandamus, a rarely granted order reserved for drastic and extraordinary cases involving preventing a court from acting illegally or abusing its official power of discretion. With few exceptions, the courts refuse to consider appeals of discovery orders before actual trial proceedings because they would prove too disruptive to the judicial process. The administration, however, argued for an exception, claiming that discovery in this case would violate the Constitution by interfering with a president's essential functions of seeking advice and developing legislation.[8] Like much about the litigation and issues surrounding the vice president's energy task force, the courts split along partisan lines. On the three-judge panel, Judges Harry Edwards, a Carter appointee, and David Tatel, a Clinton appointee, rejected Cheney's appeal, while Judge Raymond Randolph, appointed by George H. W. Bush, dissented in favor of the vice president's claim that discovery was inappropriate and that the case should be dismissed.

The 2:1 ruling by the panel of judges of the court of appeals affirmed Sullivan's order seeking documents that would reveal the composition of the task force that the vice president assembled more than two years earlier. Judge Tatel said that Cheney had failed to show that any disclosure would result in irreparable harm if the lower court was allowed to proceed with limited discovery. Tatel wrote that the administration was free to invoke executive privilege if it believed information needed to be protected, but to grant wholesale immunity would undermine the judicial process. "Were we to hold that the Constitution protects the President and Vice President from ever having to invoke executive privilege, we would have transformed executive privilege from a doctrine designed to protect presidential communications into virtual immunity from suit," Tatel wrote. In his dissenting opinion, Judge Randolph criticized the majority's opinion as troubling. "For the Judiciary to permit this sort of discovery strikes me as a violation of the separation of powers," he said. Randolph argued that there was little in the law that provided any guidance as to what qualifies a person as a member of a presidential committee—an issue that would require the court to go to great lengths to make such a determination.[9] Moreover, Randolph argued that as "applied to committees the President establishes to give him advice, FACA has for many years teetered on the edge of constitutionality. This decision pushes it over."[10] As a result of the panel's majority opinion, the vice president appealed to the full circuit of the court of appeals, which also spurned his petition. Cheney then appealed to the Supreme Court, even though no federal judge had yet to hold a trial on the merits of the issues.

Before the Supreme Court

On December 15, 2003, the Supreme Court agreed to hear arguments from the Bush-Cheney administration about why it should not be ordered to release documents disclosing the identities of participants in the vice president's energy task force. More than two years after the task force had concluded its work and disbanded, the White House continued to guard the secrecy of its operation, including the names of energy industry representatives who played a significant role in shaping the administration's national energy policy. The administration was facing a court order to turn over limited non-privileged information and a decision by the court of appeals refusing to overturn that order. The fundamental question before the Supreme Court was whether the vice president must submit to pretrial discovery, which would allow the federal district court to determine whether the task force was covered under the FACA. In its petition to the Supreme Court, the government argued that any construction of the FACA that would permit discovery of the vice president and other presidential advisers would violate fundamental principles of the separation of powers. As a result, the court orders were far from ordinary discovery orders since they would "subject the President to intrusive and distracting discovery every time he seeks advice from his closest advisors." Further, "they would open the way for judicial supervision of internal Executive Branch deliberations."[11] Both "legislative power and judicial power cannot extend to compelling the vice president to disclose ... the details of the process by which a president obtains information and advice from the vice president," said Theodore B. Olson, the Justice Department's top litigator. Olson's appeal suggested that the Court should either narrow the reach of the Federal Advisory Committee Act or rule it unconstitutional for infringing on a core executive function.[12]

There were two notable precedents relating to this case—one involving a criminal investigation and the other a private lawsuit over an "unofficial act" by the president. The Watergate scandal led to a precedent-setting Supreme Court ruling that made clear that presidents were not immune from court orders in a criminal case. In *U.S. v. Nixon*, President Richard M. Nixon was being investigated for conspiring to cover up his administration's role in the break-ins at the headquarters of the Democratic National Committee. The special prosecutor issued a subpoena for previously secret tapes that the president recorded in the Oval Office, but Nixon asserted executive privilege to block the order. The Supreme Court ruled unanimously, however, that the president must comply with the judicial order in a criminal case. Nixon resigned shortly afterward. In the other case, President Clinton was sued by Paula Jones over alleged sexual harassment that she claimed occurred three years earlier when he was governor of Arkansas. In an effort to delay the lawsuit until after he left the White House, his lawyers argued before the Supreme Court that the chief executive had "temporary immunity" from answering lawsuits. They argued that presidents were absolutely immune from being sued for their "official actions." But the Supreme Court issued another unanimous decision, rejecting the president's claims and ruling that the current president had no constitutional shield against lawsuits that stem from his "unofficial acts." The ruling allowed for questioning Clinton under oath and led to his impeachment in the House of Representatives. In Cheney's appeal, however, Olson cited *U.S. v. Nixon* as establishing the principle that presidents and vice presidents could challenge court orders without fear of being held in contempt. Compelling Cheney to comply with the discovery order was clearly at odds with the Nixon case, not to mention the separation of powers established by the Constitution, Olson argued.[13]

In a decision ten years earlier, however, a similar effort to obtain information concerning the health care task force headed up by Hillary Clinton when she was first lady, the U.S. District of Columbia Circuit Court of Appeals held that formal membership limited to federal officials did not necessarily entitle a task force to exemption if other individuals acting as advisers or consultants participated to the extent of being de facto members. In urging the justices to reject the vice president's appeal, Judicial Watch said that through repeated appeals, the administration had "succeeded splendidly in delaying the advancement of this case," while the task force's proposals were being presented to Congress. "This transparent strategy of running out the clock should not be tolerated," Judicial Watch said.[14] "We're hoping at the end of this process the court is going to remind the vice president that he's not above the law," said Sierra Club lawyer David Bookbinder. But a Justice Department spokesman said that the case tests "issues critical to the effective functioning of the presidency," and that it was important that the "president's constitutional authority to gather candid advice from his advisers be respected."[15]

The Court's decision to hear the case came as the White House was gearing up for the 2004 presidential campaign. Setting up a high-stakes clash over the Bush-Cheney concept of executive powers, the Court agreed without comment to hear the administration's appeal that both the district court's order for limited discovery and the federal appeals court's ruling not to block that order threatened substantial interference with vital executive branch functions. The case, moreover, held political stakes in the upcoming presidential election. If the Court ruled against Cheney, the documents might provide more ammunition to critics who claimed that the White House was paying off big campaign contributors, ensuring them billions in subsidies and environmental giveaways. "This is an extraordinary situation where the Bush administration is going to the Supreme Court to make sure that meetings that Ken Lay had in the White House aren't made available to the public," alleged Tom Fitton of Judicial Watch. "That is what this is about; fear of political embarrassment."[16] But political sensitivity and partisanship also surrounded the litigation itself: among the federal judges who ruled on the merits of the case, those appointed by Democratic presidents consistently decided against Cheney, while those appointed by Republican presidents consistently ruled in his favor. Thus, the question of whether a court order for limited discovery was a violation of the separation of powers rested with the more conservative Supreme Court whose majority of members had been appointed by Republican presidents.

Across the country, many editorial writers looked to the Supreme Court to side with government openness, criticizing the Bush-Cheney White House for excessive and unwarranted secrecy. The *St. Petersburg Times* said the administration was "one of the most secretive in history," denouncing Cheney's position as "an open-ended recipe for unaccountable government." The *Austin American Statesman* noted that if the Supreme Court ruled for Cheney, "then the founding idea that the government's power derives from the people" would be "diminished." The *Albuquerque Journal* called governing from behind closed doors "wrong" and observed that the Court's ruling would be "eagerly awaited by proponents of open government regardless of political affiliation." The *Arizona Daily Star* denounced the vice president's position as "supreme folly," while the *Palm Beach Post* said that if "Hillary Clinton couldn't use a task force to make health-care policy in secret, Dick Cheney can't use one to make energy policy secret." When the Supreme Court agreed to hear the Cheney case, the *Washington Post* said it was a "banner week for government secrecy," citing also the government's classification of documents provided to the 9/11 commission—criticized by chairman and former New Jersey governor Tom Kean as unnecessary—and actions to keep more Pentagon information out of the public domain. Typifying the sentiment of many others, the *Los Angeles Times* wondered: "Why, in a democracy, is there so much resistance to public scrutiny of the workings of our government? Why does the White House apparently believe that national energy policy is like growing mushrooms—best done in the dark?" The hard-hitting editorial speculated that the "documents would reveal that the shortsighted and dangerous policies crafted behind closed doors by the energy task force were simply an effort to guarantee big campaign contributors an adequate return on their investment. How else to describe an energy bill that has been described by [Senator John] McCain as stemming from a philosophy of 'no lobbyist left behind.'"[17]

Justice Scalia's Controversy

The lawsuit against the vice president was plunged into new controversy after the *Los Angeles Times* broke the story that on January 5, 2004, Justice

Antonin Scalia accompanied Vice President Cheney on a duck-hunting vacation on Air Force Two to Southern Louisiana. The vacation was hosted by Wallace Carline, president of an energy services company. The trip, coming just three weeks after the Court agreed to hear the vice president's appeal, created the public appearance of a conflict of interest and blatant favoritism. "Frankly, I'm puzzled by it," said Senator Patrick J. Leahy, the ranking Democrat on the Judiciary Committee. "He has to know that with similar tactics, in any state in the country, a state Supreme Court Justice would have to recuse himself. It's Law School 101." Senator Orrin G. Hatch, Republican of Utah and chairman of the Judiciary Committee, however, declined to respond to the question of a conflict of interest, but said in a prepared statement that he had confidence that Scalia would do "the proper thing."[18]

Nonetheless, the trip provoked a chorus of denunciation from Democratic politicians and editorial writers across the country, excoriating Scalia for compromising the public's confidence in the Court and calling for his recusal. Senators Leahy and Lieberman wrote to Chief Justice William H. Rehnquist, questioning the ethics of Scalia spending extended time in a social setting with the vice president after the Court agreed to hear the case involving Cheney as a defendant. The letter asked what procedures were in place for justices to recuse themselves or whether a justice could be removed if ethical issues arose. Rehnquist answered that ethical situations were covered by federal laws that govern judicial conduct, but that the Supreme Court had no formal procedure for reviewing a decision by a justice in an individual case and that it was up to each individual justice to decide whether it was proper to hear a case. David Bookbinder, the Washington legal director for Sierra Club, said the trip had raised to "another level" questions of whether Justice Scalia could fairly decide a case involving the vice president.[19]

Many of the nation's editorial writers agreed. Ranging from polite to sarcastic, newspapers across the country called on Justice Scalia to step aside in the interest of promoting public confidence in the Court's integrity. The *Seattle Post-Intelligencer* delicately wrote that "no matter how much integrity can be presumed of public officials, the appearance of bias on Scalia's part is unavoidable," while the *Houston Chronicle* stated bluntly that in "this case, Scalia's impartiality is not only in question, but in tatters." *Newsday* said the justice had been "hopelessly compromised," and that it was nothing less than "Scalia's reputation and the court's credibility" that were at stake. The *Denver Post* wrote that the "high court's reputation and credibility of the federal judicial system" were "much higher than one man's pride." Scalia should step down from the energy task force case, said the *Columbus Dispatch*, because justices of the "nation's highest court should act in a manner that inspires public confidence that their decisions are being rendered without even the appearance of bias." The *Cincinnati Enquirer* quipped that Scalia's "participation would be an embarrassment," while the *Chicago Tribune* warned that the justice risked "being part of what many Americans will view as a tainted decision." The sarcasm of the *Buffalo News* was emblematic of many liberal editorial writers across the country: "The continuing, obstinate refusal of Supreme Court Justice Antonin Scalia to recuse himself from a case involving his hunting buddy, Vice President Cheney, illuminates one of the great truths about many of today's conservatives in high office: They will do what they want when they want and they don't give a hoot what anyone thinks about it. The arrogance is breathtaking." Editorial writers also criticized Scalia for accepting a gift from the vice president in the form of a free trip for himself, his son, and his son-in-law. The question of accepting the gift was aptly summed up by the *Los Angeles Times*: "It's bad enough that Scalia went hunting with the vice president, who has a case before him. It's worse, as several legal experts have noted, that the trip was at the expense, in effect, of the vice president."[20]

From the beginning, however, Scalia defended his duck-hunting trip with the vice president. Writing to the *Los Angeles Times* after that newspaper first broke the story, Justice Scalia said that "social contacts with high-level executive branch officials (including cabinet officers) have never been thought improper for judges who may have before them cases in which those people are involved in their official capacity, as opposed to their personal capacity." In February 2004, the conservative justice told a gathering at Amherst College in response to a question from a member in the audience that there was nothing improper about the trip and nothing about the case that made it a conflict for him. "It's acceptable practice to socialize with executive branch officials when there are not personal claims against them," he said. "That's all I'm going to say for now. Quack, quack."[21]

With the justice under enormous criticism from the national press and becoming fodder for late-night comedians, the Sierra Club, one of the two plaintiffs suing the vice president for access to energy task force documents, filed a motion with the Supreme Court calling on Justice Scalia to remove himself. The Sierra Club said that Scalia's conduct undermined the integrity of the judicial system, noting that "8 out of 10 newspapers with the largest circulation in the United States, 14 of the largest 20, and 20 of the 30 largest have called on Justice Scalia to step aside." Because the "American public, as reflected in the nation's newspaper editorials, has unanimously concluded that there is an appearance of favoritism, any objective observer would be compelled to conclude that Justice Scalia's impartiality has been questioned," said the group. According to the group, these facts more than satisfied any judicial requirements, mandating "recusal merely when a Justice's impartiality might reasonably be questioned."[22] The Court rebuffed the motion, however, referring the matter to Justice Scalia in "accordance with its historic practice."[23]

But a combative Scalia, known for his tough talk on and off the bench, refused demands that he remove himself from the energy task force case, which involved his friend Vice President Cheney. In an unprecedented twenty-one page memorandum bristling with defiance, Scalia said his duck-hunting trip was nothing more than a routine social interaction and that his recusal would be required if his impartiality might be reasonably questioned. "Why would that result follow," he wrote, "from my being in a sizeable group of persons, in a hunting camp with the vice president, where I never hunted with him in the same blind or had other opportunity for private conversation?" Given the circumstances of the trip, Scalia wrote, the only possible reason for recusal would be his friendship with Cheney. "A rule that required members of this court to remove themselves from cases in which the official actions of friends were at issue would be utterly disabling," he wrote. He said that he and Cheney had been friends since their time in the Ford administration. "While friendship is a ground for recusal of a justice where the personal fortune or the personal freedom of the friend is at issue, it has traditionally not been a ground for recusal where official action is at issue." Writing with a candidness for which he was well known, Scalia said that "many justices have reached this court precisely because they were friends of the incumbent president or other senior officials." Scalia argued that throughout American history justices have socialized with high-ranking government officials and that as recently as Christmas 2003, other justices attended a social gathering at the vice president's home.[24]

Aside from the appearance of a conflict of interest, Scalia may have had a point. Jeffrey Rosen, professor of law at George Washington University, noted that throughout the twentieth century justices sometimes socialized with executive officials who had cases before them. "These relationships reflected a complicated dance, as newly appointed justices often navigated the transition from political underling to social equal," said Rosen. "Some justices had the character and independence to manage the transition well; others did not and their reputations were ruined as a result." But as the Supreme Court increasingly ventured into the political arena in the postwar era, social interaction between justices and the executive branch became more cautious as Washington assumed a more polarized and legalized climate. This wariness increased exponentially after Watergate, which further altered the "relationship among the justices, the president, the press and the public." As a result, Scalia may have been correct in recalling historical examples of social interaction between justices and politicians, but he appeared to be asking that "he and his colleagues be judged by standards of a vanishing era."[25]

Besides revealing the often clubby relationships among decision-makers in Washington, Scalia's memo stood as one of several recent actions that cast the justice in news headlines and made him the target of late-night comedians. Scalia's sometimes controversial outspokenness both on and off the bench distinguished him from the other justices since he had been appointed to the Court by President Reagan. In 1996, the Harvard Law graduate and inveterate Washington insider attracted news with his speech urging Christians to stand behind their traditional beliefs: "We must pray for the courage to endure the scorn of the sophisticated world." In February 2004, he mocked a court decision that permitted states to provide scholarships for secular study but that excluded theology students. "What next? Will we deny priests and nuns their prescription-drug benefits on the ground that taxpayers' freedom of conscience forbids medicating the clergy at public expense?" His blunt talk, however, sometimes ricocheted to his own detriment. In a case involving the constitutionality of the Pledge of Allegiance, his public comments caused him to step down from adjudicating the dispute. A U.S. appeals court had rendered a decision that a public school policy requiring students to recite the words from the pledge, "one nation under God," violated the First Amendment. After Scalia appeared to criticize that decision in a speech in Fredericksburg, Virginia, in 2003, the atheist father who brought the case asked Scalia to step down. Scalia complied and thereafter in the Cheney case cited the episode as evidence that he will step aside from a case only when "I have said or done something" that warrants it.[26]

Scalia's refusal to recuse himself did little to quiet his critics, who now turned their attention to how his participation would influence the outcome of the case. The New York Times editorialized that "if the court decides this case, which has implications for the Bush-Cheney re-election campaign, by 5 to 4, with Justice Scalia casting the deciding vote, it will bring back memories of Bush v. Gore. And it will further harm the reputation of a court whose authority has already derived from its claim to be a legal body, not a political one."[27]

The Supreme Court's Decision

On April 27, 2004, at the start of lively arguments before the Supreme Court, Solicitor General Theodore Olson, the Bush administration's lead government attorney, said that the case was about the separation of powers. He framed the case as a fundamental test of executive power, arguing that to compel disclosure of confidential records would intrude on a president's authority to receive candid advice. In his brief to the Court, Olson said that upholding the rulings of the lower courts would "convert FACA into a mechanism for intrusive and unconstitutional interference with core Executive Branch functions." As a result, by ordering the discovery of selected task force records to test the allegations raised in the lawsuits, the judge would be invading the exclusive domain of the executive branch in violation of the Constitution's mandated separation of powers. "The important separation of powers questions in this case are neither premature nor stale," said Olson. "And the discovery ordered [by Judge Sullivan] was not some preliminary step on the way to a possible separation of powers violation, but a significant violation in itself."[28] The public interest groups argued that the vice president's energy task force records would show whether the energy industry received special access and favors. In his brief, Alan Morrison, the lawyer for the Sierra Club, argued that "not only would production of such records not be burdensome, but they could readily be redacted to delete any arguably deliberative or otherwise privileged information." Washington lawyer Paul Orfanedes, representing Judicial Watch, said that the group was only seeking information needed to determine whether private individuals were on the task force. The group characterized the limited discovery order by the lower courts as minimal, arguing that it would not disrupt the separation of powers of the branches of government.[29] The case came amid election-year politics as Democrats sought to highlight Cheney's resistance to releasing the records as part of the Republican administration's overall pattern of shrouding its activities in secrecy and doling out special favors to big corporate donors.

A host of public interest organizations, professional associations, and media groups filed "friends of the court" briefs in support of the lawsuit by Sierra Club and Judicial Watch. Five public interest organizations together with four library groups and the nation's leading archival association filed a joint brief urging the Court to reject the government's claim that it should have the right to exercise the public's business in secret.[30] "The administration is fanatically resistant to oversight and public accountability," said People For the American Way Foundation President Ralph G. Neas.

The Reporters Committee for the Freedom of the Press, the American Society of Newspaper Editors, and the Society of Professional Journalists said their interest in the case stemmed from wanting to preserve the uninhibited exchange of information and access to federal government records and that open government laws such as the Freedom of Information Act and FACA were of vital importance to an informed citizenry. In their brief, the media groups argued that the vice president's interpretation of the "doctrine of separation of powers and executive privilege not only totally ignores the doctrine of checks and balances, but would render FACA ineffective and useless." Indeed, this point was precisely the aim of the vice president. Just as Cheney had won a significant victory over the GAO, effectively creating a higher wall of secrecy around the executive branch, the vice president now was seeking to eviscerate an important open government law. The media groups said that if the vice president had his way, "all the government would have to do to hide the activities of an advisory committee from the news media and the public would be to associate it with upper-level executive officials, and no court could even look behind that assertion into the actual workings of the committee."[31]

The vice president's lawyers premised their arguments, however, on the necessity for the executive branch to be immune from even the slightest interference with executive power, a point that the Supreme Court emphatically rejected in the landmark 1974 case *United States v. Nixon*. In that case, the Supreme Court rejected President Richard Nixon's broad assertions of absolute executive immunity from judicial review, which resembled Vice President Cheney's claims in the immediate case. In response to being served with a subpoena in a criminal proceeding to produce White House tapes and records, Nixon attempted to quash the subpoena by arguing that it stood as an unconstitutional judicial violation of executive privilege. The Court rejected Nixon's assertions that the judiciary did not have the constitutional authority to review a claim of executive privilege, holding that this prerogative was not absolute and was subject to balancing against other interests. "[N]either the doctrine of separation of powers, nor the need for confidentiality of high-level communications, without more, can sustain an absolute, unqualified Presidential privilege of immunity from judicial process under all circumstances," the Court said. Further, the Court said that absent a "claim of need to protect military, diplomatic, or sensitive national security interests, we find it difficult to accept the argument that even the very important interest in confidentiality of Presidential communications is significantly diminished by production of such material for in camera inspection with all the protection that a district court will be obliged to provide." The Court, however, was dealing with the criminal matter of Watergate, and thus did not address the balance between executive privilege and the need for relevant evidence in a civil suit. Nonetheless, the principle had been firmly established that executive prerogatives are not absolute and must be weighed against other interests.[32]

The Court reaffirmed this principle in subsequent cases, including *Nixon v. Administrator of General Services*. Here, Nixon sued claiming separation of powers and executive privilege to nullify congressional passage of the Presidential Recordings and Materials Preservation Act, which directed the General Services Administration to seize the former president's tapes and records for the continuing Watergate trials and investigations and to make them available to the public at the earliest reasonable date. The Court recognized the critical importance of the case, involving whether and to what extent the legislative branch could intrude on the constitutional prerogatives of the presidency. But the Court weighed the extent of congressional intrusion into the executive's constitutional prerogatives against the overriding aims of Congress to preserve the Nixon materials for legitimate governmental, judicial, and historical reasons.[33] In *Morrison v. Olson*, the Court again rejected the idea that any infringement on executive authority by the legislature or judiciary violated the separation of powers.

At the start of the proceedings, the *New York Times* had published an editorial, stating that Cheney stood on "weak legal ground, as both the trial court and the United States Court of Appeals for the District of Columbia have ruled." The *Times* said that the case involved "substantial issues about the degree to which a vice president can claim to be above the law."[34] Nonetheless, on June 24, 2004, the Supreme Court refused to order Cheney to release the records of his 2001 energy task force, but kept the case alive by sending it back to the court of appeals with instruction to give more deference to the administration's weighty separation of powers objections, which challenged the lower court's constitutional authority to order a limited inquiry into the task force. By sending the case back to the court of appeals, the Supreme Court's 7:2 ruling assured that none of the documents presumably implicating Cheney's close ties to energy officials who significantly shaped the administration's energy plan would be released before the November 2004 presidential election. The ruling, moreover, seemed to assure more federal litigation over the propriety of executive confidentiality and spared the administration the embarrassment of an election-year dispute between the White House, the courts, and the two watchdog groups seeking public disclosure of the energy task force documents. The conservative *Wall Street Journal* editorialized that the "best that can be said of the Supreme Court's decision ... is that it deprives the Democrats of a bogus campaign issue," and agreed with Judge James Buckley's opinion in the Clinton health care task force case nearly a decade earlier that "FACA should be declared unconstitutional as an intrusion on the President's right to take advice his own way."[35]

The majority opinion, written by Justice Anthony Kennedy, agreed with the administration's arguments that private deliberations among the president, vice president, and their close advisers must be given special consideration—a principle arising from the constitutional presidential prerogative of executive privilege. Nonetheless, the Court said the administration still needed to prove the specifics of its case in the lower courts. "All courts should be mindful of the burdens imposed on the Executive Branch in any future proceedings," Justice Kennedy wrote. "Special considerations applicable to the president and the vice president suggest that the courts should be sensitive to requests by the government" in such appeals. The majority Court also criticized the sweeping request for documents by Sierra Club and Judicial Watch as "unbounded in scope" and "anything but appropriate." Justices Clarence Thomas and Antonin Scalia, who enlivened the case with his much publicized duck-hunting trip with the vice president, voted with the majority but issued a separate opinion that the U.S. District Court, which initially heard the case, "clearly exceeded its authority" and that the appeals court judgment should be reversed.[36]

In sending the case back to the court of appeals with instructions to reexamine the issues, the majority Court made clear that it rejected the appeals court's initial reasoning that the Bush-Cheney administration must first invoke executive privilege in order to deny the documents request. The Court said that the appeals court "labored under the mistaken assumption that the assertion of executive privilege is a necessary precondition to the government's separation-of-powers objections."[37] The administration's critics found the Court's acceptance of the Bush administration's executive immunity argument—that there need not be an assertion of privilege to deny the discovery request by the U.S. District Court—to be perhaps the most troubling aspect of the ruling. With this one line, the Court averred that the separation of powers doctrine allowed the administration the inherent right to withhold information from members of the public and from the court in a noncriminal case without having to assert privilege.[38]

Indeed, the opinion revealed a Court evidently sympathetic to White House needs for executive immunity from certain kinds of litigation. The Court's insistence that executive privilege claims must be presumptively honored lest it invite distracting and "vexatious litigation" seemed to run counter to presidential experience. After all, aside from compelling Nixon to divulge incriminating tapes to the special Watergate prosecutor, the courts denied President Clinton immunity from Paula Jones's sexual harassment lawsuit. Clinton submitted to questioning under oath by the Office of Independent Counsel, and the Iran–Contra scandal involved the testimony of President Reagan. None of these distractions were seen to have seriously disabled the presidency.[39] But in the majority opinion—speaking to the Nixon tapes case—Justice Kennedy wrote that during Watergate an intrusion on internal White House deliberations was justified to produce information for a criminal case. As such, there was no comparison between criminal subpoena requests in the Nixon case and the interests by outside groups seeking information about what went on in Cheney's meetings.[40] In rendering its decision, the Court seemed to indicate that the vice president was worthy of the right to invoke presidential privileges and immunities concerning civil suits. Indeed, the opinion was notable for referring to the president and vice president interchangeably regarding presidential prerogatives, laying the groundwork for future vice presidents to assert a distinct vice presidential immunity from legal proceedings under the Constitution's separation of powers doctrine.[41]

At least initially, there were differing interpretations as to the meaning of the Court's opinion. The Sierra Club's David Bookbinder saw some grounds for optimism. "The Supreme Court was pretty clear in rejecting the Bush administration's argument that they should stop the case and throw us out of court." While acknowledging that the request for documents was very broad, Bookbinder said the Supreme Court's message was that they were going to get something. "Are we going to get shut out? The answer from the Supreme Court is no."[42] Tom Fitton, president of Judicial Watch, said the Court's opinion suggested that the majority of justices had rejected the administration's argument that the White House should be shielded by the federal disclosure law. Sanjay Narayan, an attorney for Sierra Club, agreed. "The vice president wanted this case gone, but the court has left the door open for the public to learn who formulated the administration's dangerous energy policy," she said.[43] Nonetheless, C. Boyden Gray, White House counsel under the first President Bush, said the decision was "a significant victory for Cheney, but it's obviously not an ultimate resolution."[44] Professor John Duffy, an expert on administrative law at George Washington University Law School and a former law clerk to Associate Justice Antonin Scalia, saw matters more optimistically for the vice president. "This is a big victory" for Cheney and government lawyers, he said. "They won almost all they had asked the court for." Duffy called the Court's criticism of the plaintiff's request for documents "extraordinary." If the "appeals court judges follow the instructions and certainly the hints of the Supreme Court, then the government will win almost everything it wants" when the case is reargued in the court of appeals, Duffy said.[45] For Democrats who viewed the Bush-Cheney administration as secretive and the close friend of corporate interests, the Court's decision provided little comfort, especially after the GAO's own defeat against the vice president over access to much of the same information. A spokesman for Senator John Kerry, the presumptive Democratic presidential candidate, wasted little time in denouncing the Court's opinion: "The Nixon legacy of secrecy is alive and well in the Bush White House. Americans shouldn't have to rely on court orders to learn what special-interest lobbyists are writing White House policies."[46] Critics of the decision could possibly take solace in the dissenting opinions of Justices Ruth Bader Ginsberg and David H. Souter, who accused government lawyers of unwillingness to propose any accommodation with the plaintiffs concerning a narrower request for documents. Ginsberg criticized the "government's failure to heed the court's instructions" in the federal district court where the controversy began. They said the lower court should be given the latitude to consider what documents should be available through discovery.[47] Although the Court's decision bought the administration more time, if it lost again in the appeals court, the White House could still return to the Supreme Court in another extended round before knowing whether it must release information related to Cheney's energy task force.

But on May 10, 2005, the same federal appeals court that previously ordered Cheney to turn over the names of energy industry officials who met with the energy task force, this time threw out the lawsuit against the vice president, ruling that he was free to meet in secret with industry lobbyists in 2001 while drafting the administration's energy policy. The ruling ended the four-year legal battle over Cheney's refusal to disclose information about the task force—one that involved the Supreme Court and drew unflattering attention to Justice Antonin Scalia. The unanimous ruling by the court's eight judges signaled a major legal and political victory for the White House, further bolstering the president's power to deliberate and seek advice in secret from influential lobbyists without having to disclose details to the public. Although the court evaded the question of whether FACA constitutionally applied to presidential committees, it said that separation of powers considerations had an important bearing on the proper interpretation of the statute. The court therefore kept its ruling within narrow parameters in determining whether the statute, strictly interpreted, infringed on the autonomy of the executive branch to receive confidential communications. The court agreed with the administration's contention that compelling the White House to produce documents about its internal policy discussions would violate the president's constitutional powers. Writing for the appeals court, Judge A. Raymond Randolph—the lone dissenter in the earlier D.C. Circuit ruling in the Cheney case—said that "the president must be free to seek confidential information from many sources, both inside the government and outside."[48]

Despite the contention by Judicial Watch and Sierra Club that it was necessary to examine the minutes of task force meetings and other records in order to determine whether the vice president had violated the open meetings law, the court disagreed. According to the court, the groups had failed to prove that individuals other than federal officials were de facto members of the energy task force under the court's admittedly narrow definition of the open meetings statute. Outsiders were not task force members, said Randolph, because they had no right to vote or veto policy recommendations to the president. "The outsider might make an important presentation, he might be persuasive, the information he provides might affect the committee's judgment. But having neither a vote nor a veto over the advice the committee renders to the President, he is no more a member of the committee than the aides who accompany

Congressmen or cabinet officers to committee meetings," said the court. The vice president therefore had the right to create an advisory body whose internal communications would remain confidential, so long as the right to vote or veto was not later extended to non-federal participants.[49]

The court's decision hinged on accepting at face value, without examination or discovery, the assertions of two senior administration officials who said energy officials were not task force members. Randolph noted that Karen Knutson, one of Cheney's deputy assistants for domestic policy, said in her affidavit that industry officials participated in smaller stakeholder meetings, but that these "were simply forums to collect individual views rather than to bring a collective judgment to bear." The court therefore concluded that the "only individuals the President named to the task force were federal officials; only federal officials signed the final report."[50] But one observer noted that the court's ruling created an "absurd standard," requiring the public interest groups to prove their assertions while being denied the right of discovery to establish their claims. "It's impossible to establish that industry substantially participated in these meetings, if you deny them basic discovery needed to show those facts," said Jonathan Turley, a George Washington University professor of constitutional and environmental law. It was notable that during the Clinton administration, the same appeals court gave the 1972 statute broader reading, saying that it applied to the health care policy task force led by First Lady Hillary Rodham Clinton. Then, the court said outside participants in a White House advisory group were de facto members, and the public had the right to know about the meetings. Tom Fitton, president of Judicial Watch, denounced the ruling as "without any basis in the text of the open meetings law and contrary to the intent of the law." David Bookbinder, the lead attorney for the Sierra Club, saw the ruling as a double blow. "As a policy matter, we see the Bush administration has succeeded in its effort to keep secret how industry crafted the administration's energy policy," Bookbinder said. "As a legal matter, it's a defeat for efforts to have open government and for the public to know how their elected officials are conducting business." But a senior vice presidential adviser disagreed, saying that what "this court decision does is to preserve the confidentiality of internal deliberations among the president and his advisors that the Constitution protects as essential and wise to informed decision making."[51]

FACA's Defeat

In the end, the court interpreted the Federal Advisory Committee Act in a way that gave the White House sweeping authority to set up policy groups, provide access to influential outsiders who have a stake in the outcome of policy decisions, and carry on such proceedings behind closed doors without having to disclose details. There was irony in the court's ruling. Although the court insisted on strictly construing the law, it spun an opinion that had no basis in the text of the statute and ignored the fundamental intent of Congress. Indeed, the court's ruling, which defined for the first time "participation" in an advisory committee as meaning having the power to vote or veto, reinterpreted the law's intent in favor of executive prerogatives. Enacted in 1972 to curb the unrestrained growth, influence, and abuse of government advisory committees by special interest groups, the decision appeared to return matters back to where industry could play an influential or dominant participatory role in the public process with official government sanction and with the public left out in the cold. The appeals court said that "Congress could not have meant that participation in committee meetings or activities, even influential participation, would be enough to make someone a member of the committee."[52]

But contrary to the court's statement, influential participation on advisory committees by outside interests is precisely what Congress had in mind when passing the 1972 open meetings law. In enacting the statute, Congress was worried about the growth and domination of advisory committees by special interest groups and their invisible, often unreviewable, influential role on government policy. In hearings before the House and Senate, Congress found this phenomenon a potential danger to its own constitutional powers and sought to enact fundamental rules of public accountability by regulating and counteracting the confidential role of private interests on advisory committees in explicitly or implicitly setting government policy. In public hearings held by the Senate Subcommittee on Intergovernmental Relations in 1971, Chairman Lee Metcalf, the primary author of the Senate bill to open up federal advisory committees to public scrutiny, set the theme of the inquiry:

> What we are dealing with, in these hearings, goes to the bedrock of Government decision making. Information is an important commodity in this capital. Those who get information to policymakers, or get information from them, can benefit their cause ... And decision makers who get information from special interest groups who are not subject to rebuttal because opposing interests do not know about meetings—and could not get in the door if they did—may not make tempered judgments. We are looking at two fundamentals, disclosure and counsel, the rights of people to find out what is going on and, if they want, to do something about it.[53]

On introducing his own bill in the Senate, Charles H. Percy of Illinois added that there was the "belief that these committees do not adequately and fairly represent the public interest, that they may be biased toward a point of view or interest, and that their proceedings are unnecessarily closed to the public."[54] During the Senate hearings, William Ruckelshaus, administrator of the Environmental Protection Agency, observed that some advisory committees were reaching decisions from a "quiet spot" beyond public view and neglecting any obligation to justify their decisions to other officials or to the public.[55] In hearings on amendments to FACA in 1989, Senator Heinz of Pennsylvania recalled that prior to the open meeting statute, the "interested public often couldn't even find out about the activities of a committee supposedly representing their views to the Federal Government."[56]

The Senate hearings on the growth and influence of federal advisory committees involving outside interests were complemented by a broad-scale review on the House side by the Legal and Monetary Affairs Subcommittee of the Committee on Government Operations in November 1971. The hearings were chaired by Congressman John S. Monagan, who described the system of advisory committees as a "fifth arm of the Government," existing alongside the executive, legislative, judicial, and regulatory arms. "There is a growing awareness," said Monagan, "that an invitation to advise can ... confer the power to regulate and legislate."[57] Under questioning, Frank C. Carlucci, associate director of Organization and Management Systems of the Office of Management and Budget—which opposed legislation regulating advisory committees on behalf of the Nixon administration—admitted that the influence of special interests on advisory committees was a "serious problem" and that he did not know "how to deal with it."[58]

Also appearing before the House committee, Senator Metcalf summarized the findings of his own extensive Senate committee hearings, which documented a situation of undue influence by special interest representatives serving on presidential and other federal advisory committees. Of particular concern, said Metcalf, was the influence of industrial advisory committees, which had emerged as a new factor to be reckoned with in government and whose operating procedures were "frightening in their anti-democratic implications." Such committees neither opened their sessions to the public or press, nor did they keep detailed transcripts of their discussions for public scrutiny. Under this hidden system of quasi-governmental or nongovernmental advisory committees, Metcalf said, the government had made a practice of designating which interests would be officially entrenched within the halls of the executive branch, and these interests, through advisory groups, had become an "official and key part of the policy making process." Metcalf stated that his own hearings of the Senate Subcommittee on Intergovernmental Relations had "uncovered conflict of interest, potential anti-trust abuse, use of the cloak of Federal authority to promote special interests, creation of bad advice clothed in secrecy, and arbitrary and capricious denial of the public with legitimate interests to be heard." Moreover, a 1972 House report noted that "testimony . . . pointed out the danger of allowing special interest groups to exercise undue influence upon the Government through the dominance of advisory committees which deal with matters in which they have vested interests."[59]

Based on the findings of both the House and Senate, Congress believed that it was essential that advisory committees—including those advising the president and other executive branch officials—be diversified and open to public participation and scrutiny. By enacting FACA, Congress aimed to strip away the veil of self-interest and secrecy, opening up the advisory process to public accountability and participation. The law provided that commissions or advisory committees "established or utilized by the President" be open to the public; that records, reports, transcripts, minutes, working papers, studies, agenda, and other such documents be kept and made available for public inspection; that committee membership be "fairly balanced in terms of points of view represented"; and that advisory committees not be "inappropriately influenced by the appointing authority or by any special interest."[60] Congress exempted national security matters from the statute as well as committees that were composed wholly of full-time or permanent part-time federal government officers or employees. Although the Nixon administration tried to preempt the law's passage by having the Office of Management and Budget draft a directive governing advisory committees, Congress believed the executive branch was unsuited to the task of overseeing committee operations.[61] Moreover, neither during congressional consideration of the statute nor afterwards did the Nixon administration, known for its secrecy and assertions of privilege, seek to contest the act on constitutional grounds; it evidently did not see the open disclosure law as an intrusion onto core executive functions.

In 1971, Senator Metcalf, speaking on behalf of the Senate Subcommittee on Intergovernmental Relations, put the issue succinctly: "Do we want the government to be open to all, or do we want it closed to all but elite industrialists? Do we want information to freely flow through the government and society for all to critically examine, or do we want it hoarded and concealed by advisory committees until after decisions are foisted upon the public?"[62] Both Cheney and ultimately the courts were unambiguous on these questions. Against the clear meaning and purpose of FACA, passed by Congress during another era and under differing political circumstances, the courts held that the executive had an inherent and unreviewable right to confidentiality concerning the influential participation of powerful outside interests on a presidential advisory panel and regarding a domestic matter of extraordinary public interest. Although stopping short of declaring the law unconstitutional, the full court of appeals all but rendered the statute meaningless, or at least subject to White House discretion. By equating participation, "even influential participation," on an advisory committee with having explicit veto or voting rights—a factor never considered by Congress and not included in the text of the law—the court's decision ran counter to the statute's legislative history and intent to curb privileged access and outside influence by private interest groups over public policy.

Nonetheless, the defeat of FACA has meant another loss for congressional power and oversight and another victory for the expansion of executive authority under the Bush-Cheney administration. As with the battle with the GAO, the White House steadfastly refused to invoke executive privilege to prevent disclosure in order to establish the executive's inherent constitutional authority against what it views as unwarranted demands for information. Similarly, the administration followed a strategy aimed at appealing its way to the conservative U.S. Supreme Court, which had delivered a deferential ruling on behalf of the White House in this case. Indeed, underpinning the Court's decision was an important distinction between executive privilege and executive powers. While executive privilege is the prerogative that permits a president to withhold confidential information concerning his executive duties, executive powers comprise those powers assigned exclusively by the Constitution to the president rather than to the legislative or judicial branches.

Throughout the FACA case, the White House refused to invoke executive privilege, which would have prevented disclosure but triggered judicial review of the claim. Instead, the vice president's lawyers averred that in carrying out his constitutional duties, the vice president had the right to withhold documents relating to the discharge of those duties and that it was outside the ambit of the judiciary to even review that decision. In matters involving international affairs, which fall exclusively within the domain of the presidency, the executive may restrict information from public disclosure without invoking privilege or being subject to lawsuits. Indeed, Cheney's aim was to extend this prerogative to the domestic arena, establishing immunity from judicial intervention concerning public demands for executive information. In the past, an administration would have to claim privilege in the midst of a lawsuit if it wanted to withhold information on domestic matters and take its chances with judicial review as the courts decided whether the claim had any legitimacy. In the FACA case, the district court and the court of appeals had ruled that since the energy task force involved a domestic matter, it was incumbent on the White House to invoke executive privilege and submit limited non-deliberative documents to the courts for review. But the Supreme Court disagreed, stating that the court of appeals labored under the erroneous assumption that a claim of executive privilege was a necessary precondition to the administration's separation of powers objections. In other words, the Supreme Court handed the administration an opinion that seemed to say that the White House may withhold documents when members of the public seek it under federal law if an administration wishes to do so, even when it concerns matters of a domestic nature.[63]

Thirty years earlier in the case *United States v. Nixon*, the Supreme Court rejected Richard Nixon's assertions of a non-reviewable, absolute right of executive privilege as the rationale for refusing to turn over his White House tapes to the Watergate special prosecutor. Although the Court explicitly recognized for the first time the existence of executive privilege as being fundamental to the operations of the executive, it said that it was the province of the judiciary to say "what the law is." As a result, the Court overrode Nixon's claim of privilege, compelling him to turn over the secret tape recordings for the Watergate investigations. It was perhaps ironic that the Court now seemed to have bowed to executive power and reached the opposite conclusion concerning an administration's right to withhold documents. Nonetheless, the Court made the critical distinction between the Nixon case, which involved criminal matters of presidential conduct, and the FACA case, which involved a civil suit.

When the Supreme Court handed the case to the full circuit court of appeals, however, it did so with instructions that all but sealed the fate of the case in favor of the vice president. Had the full court of appeals ruled against Cheney, it seemed a foregone conclusion that the administration would have spurned any order for disclosure, opting to appeal once again to a Supreme Court whose majority of justices were sympathetic to the vice president's arguments on behalf of executive powers.

Postscript

In November 2005, a dispute erupted between Democrats and Republicans when several oil executives testified at a Senate hearing that they did not "participate" in the vice president's energy task force. The question was raised by Democratic Senator Frank Lautenberg of New Jersey, who asked the chief executives of ExxonMobil, ConocoPhillips, Chevron, Shell Oil, and BP America whether they or representatives of their companies participated in meetings with Cheney's energy task force. Despite their denials, an internal White House document obtained by the *Washington Post* showed that in 2001, officials from ExxonMobil, Conoco (before its merger with Shell), Shell Oil, and BP America met in the White House complex with Cheney's aides who were drafting the administration's national energy policy, parts of which became law. Although Chevron was not listed in the document, the General Accountability Office found that Chevron was one of several companies that gave detailed energy policy recommendations to the task force.[64]

Soon after the hearing, a spokeswoman for the GOP staff of the Senate Energy and Natural Resources Committee, one of two panels that convened the hearings, said that its lawyers had reached a preliminary conclusion that the executives appeared to be telling the truth based on the circuit court's definition of what constituted "participation" on the task force. "What we simply determined," said the spokeswoman, "was that the definition of 'participation' was something litigated, and what the court concluded was that attending meetings, even making presentations, did not rise to the level of fully participating." Lautenberg, however, asked the Justice Department to look into the matter, stating that the "White House went to great lengths to keep these meetings secret, and now oil executives may be lying to Congress about their role in the Cheney task force." The executives, however, were not under oath when they testified and therefore were not vulnerable to charges of perjury—an offense that may result in being fined or imprisoned for up to five years for making false, fictitious, or fraudulent statements to Congress. According to the source who leaked the information, the document was based on records kept by the Secret Service of people admitted to the White House complex. The anonymous source said most of the meetings occurred with Energy Secretary Andrew Lundquist and Cheney aide Karen Knutson.[65] As might be expected with the Republican control of the White House and both houses of Congress, Lautenberg's call for an investigation into the veracity of statements given by energy industry executives fell on deaf ears.

Five

Subverting the Federal Intelligence Surveillance Act

The White House's attempt to invalidate the 1978 Federal Intelligence Surveillance Act (FISA) has perhaps represented the sharpest expression yet of its efforts to expand the scope of executive power and secrecy. Like the other landmark accountability laws passed by former Democratic Congresses in the post-Watergate era, the administration has sought to override the surveillance law as an infringement on its executive powers. Although FISA was never meant to promote open government, it was passed to make the executive branch and its security apparatus more accountable. When the National Security Agency (NSA) was established in 1952, it faced few legal constraints on its power to spy on Americans. Then came the intelligence-gathering abuses of the Nixon years, when the NSA and FBI spied on civil rights and anti–Vietnam War activists. Following extensive hearings on these abuses, in 1978 Congress passed FISA, which required the NSA and FBI to obtain a warrant any time they sought to monitor communications inside the country. Before doing so, however, the law required that the NSA establish probable cause that the target of electronic surveillance is a foreign power or an agent of a foreign power.[1]

Congress passed the new law to check unrestrained executive power by establishing the FISA court, an eleven-member secret panel that could grant government authority to wiretap Americans after a showing of probable cause. The Bush administration has argued that the FISA process was too cumbersome to wiretap terrorists. But in the post-9/11 era, Congress showed its readiness to meet national security threats by extending the time that the executive could eavesdrop without a warrant from forty-eight to seventy-two hours. In passing the 1978 law, Congress acted to circumscribe any claim of inherent presidential authority and provided that FISA serve as the "exclusive means" by which surveillance could be carried out.[2]

But in the fevered atmosphere following the September 2001 attacks, President Bush declined to pursue these exclusive means and instead unilaterally and secretly authorized the NSA to eavesdrop on American citizens and others on American soil. Critics charged that the Terrorist Surveillance Program—as the administration called it—violated the clear language of the Foreign Intelligence Surveillance Act, the landmark statute that was enacted with the approval of President Jimmy Carter and that had been amended many times since. The surveillance program appeared to breach the law's prohibition on statutorily unauthorized eavesdropping as well as the act's provision that it constituted the "exclusive means" by which domestic spying could be lawfully conducted for foreign intelligence purposes.[3] Nevertheless, Bush claimed to have the inherent constitutional as well as implied congressional authority to engage in warrantless domestic spying. Under a 2002 presidential order, Bush authorized the intelligence agency to hunt for terrorist activity by monitoring international telephone calls and e-mail messages of thousands of people inside the United States without warrants. The massive surveillance operation—ensnaring tens of thousands of Americans—was conducted for three years before the *New York Times* broke the story of the secret program on December 16, 2005, igniting a firestorm of controversy from numerous critics across the political spectrum.[4]

On December 17, 2005, the day after the *Times* reported the story, Bush went on the political offensive after acknowledging that the government had been conducting secret, domestic wiretapping. In summing up his warrantless surveillance program, Bush declared that "if you're talking to a member of al Qaeda, we want to know why."[5] While civil liberties groups, Democratic lawmakers, and some Republicans called for an immediate inquiry into the eavesdropping program as an illegal intrusion on the privacy rights of innocent Americans, conservatives attacked the disclosure of classified information as an illegal act, demanding an investigation and prosecution of those who leaked the information. The Bush administration wasted little time in opening up a wide-ranging criminal investigation into the circumstances surrounding the disclosure of the highly classified surveillance program and laying the groundwork for a grand jury inquiry that could lead to criminal charges. The investigation progressed as the debate about the eavesdropping raged in and out of Congress.[6]

Nonetheless, after initiating the secret program on July 17, 2003, the Bush administration informed the four leaders of the intelligence committees about the surveillance program, swearing them to secrecy. But in an assertion of executive power, the White House kept Congress as a whole in the dark, neither consulting nor asking it to amend FISA to give the president the surveillance powers he sought. The briefing concerned Senator Jay Rockefeller, the ranking member on the Senate Intelligence Committee, enough that he wrote a letter to Cheney. Rockefeller complained that the surveillance program recalled the Total Awareness Program—a massive data-mining plan designed by the Pentagon to monitor Americans' credit card transactions, website visits, bank transactions, travel records, and other databases. For critics, the Pentagon's total awareness scheme, led by Iran-Contra figure John Poindexter, represented the ultimate invasion of privacy, leading Congress to kill the program. The administration extended this secrecy to rebuffing requests from the Senate Judiciary Committee for its classified legal opinions on Bush's domestic spying program as it swiftly moved to hold its first hearing on the matter in early February 2006. While the administration vigorously defended the legality and necessity of its surveillance program, Republican Senator Arlen Specter, who chaired the judiciary committee, declared that the operation "violates FISA—there's no doubt about that." He also questioned why the administration did not go to Congress or the intelligence court to seek changes in the surveillance law before launching the secret program after the September 11 attacks.[7]

The Legal and Constitutional Debate

Within days of the uproar over the *Times* story, the administration quickly advanced its legal arguments for the NSA program on statutory and constitutional grounds—first in a December 22, 2005, letter to the House and Senate intelligence committees, and then just weeks later on January 19, 2006, with a lengthier White Paper to Congress.[8] In both documents, the Justice Department said that the president possessed the inherent constitutional authority as commander in chief to order warrantless surveillance on American soil, and that these Article II powers were "supplemented" by statutory authority under Congress's emergency Authorization to Use Military Force (AUMF) in Afghanistan. Passed seven days after the attacks, the AUMF authorized the president to "use all necessary and appropriate force against those nations, organizations, or persons he determines planned, authorized, committed, or aided the terrorist attacks of September 11, 2001 . . . in order to prevent any future acts of international terrorism against the United States."[9] The administration claimed that the AUMF "clearly contemplated action" within the United States and that the Supreme Court's ruling in *Hamdi v. Rumsfeld* strongly supported this reading of the force authorization statute.[10] In *Hamdi*, the Court addressed the scope of the AUMF, concluding that it implicitly authorized the military detention of enemy combatants as a "fundamental incident of waging war." Drawing on longstanding principles of warfare, the Court construed that such detentions were covered under the "necessary and appropriate force" language authorized by Congress. While the force authorization statute said nothing about detaining enemy combatants, a plurality of five justices nevertheless found that it was congressionally sanctioned. In the same way, the administration said that the AUMF's "expansive language" implicitly covered the gathering of surveillance intelligence on American soil—even without court orders—as a longstanding and fundamental incident to waging war.[11] That the force resolution did not explicitly authorize the conduct of warrantless surveillance was immaterial. The purpose of the AUMF was for "Congress to sanction and support the military response to the devastating terrorist attacks"; it was never meant to "catalog every specific aspect of the use of forces it was authorizing and every potential preexisting statutory limitation on the Executive Branch."[12]

The administration, moreover, insisted that because the AUMF statutorily authorized the NSA's activities, the surveillance program must be read to accord with the surveillance law. To read it any other way would be to raise serious constitutional questions involving whether FISA's restrictions impeded the president's constitutionally assigned duties as commander in chief.[13] The administration argued that the principle of constitutional avoidance should come into play to avoid infringing on the president's Article II powers under the Constitution. One constitutional scholar noted, however, that the ramifications of this argument were considerable since it essentially "urged the adoption of a new and entirely unprecedented principle that would declare unconstitutional all legislation that prevents the president from doing anything he considers useful in defending the country."[14] Nonetheless, the administration also contended that the surveillance program was consistent with the Fourth Amendment against unreasonable searches and seizures. According to the administration, the Supreme Court had long recognized that "special needs" sometimes exist that justify venturing beyond the warrant requirement. In the midst of an armed conflict in which terrorists had already launched a catastrophic attack inside the United States, the administration argued that the gathering of critical intelligence fit squarely within the "special needs" exception to the law's warrant requirement.[15]

In response to the administration's legal arguments, on January 5, 2006, the non-partisan Congressional Research Service (CRS) released a report analyzing the constitutional and statutory issues surrounding the NSA program. Initiated at the request of several congressional members, the report cast doubt on the administration's arguments aimed at justifying its secret and warrantless surveillance program. The CRS pointed out that Congress expressly intended the 1978 law to be the "exclusive means" by which electronic surveillance was to be conducted, and refuted the administration's claim of an inherent presidential authority to engage in domestic spying in derogation of congressional laws to the contrary.[16] The CRS also rebutted the administration's expansive argument that the AUMF gave it latitude to operate outside the parameters of FISA. After all, the statute already provided an exception to its warrant requirements for the first fifteen days after a congressional declaration of war, and Congress also amended the law after the September 11, 2001, attacks to maximize its effectiveness against terrorism—a clear indication that lawmakers aimed to keep FISA in full force.[17]

Just days after the Congressional Research Service released its report, fourteen constitutional scholars and former government officials, among them prominent conservatives, sent a letter to congressional leaders with striking similar conclusions. The authors also submitted a lengthier rebuttal in response to the administration's White Paper.[18] Those who signed the documents included some of the nation's leading constitutional scholars, many of them former Justice Department attorneys and presidential advisers, as well as a former FBI director and federal judge. Beyond Bush's ideological supporters in and out of Congress who were more concerned about national security and protecting the president from embarrassment, the letters represented the views among many political observers on both sides of the aisle. The authors contended that the administration's arguments for the program collapsed under the weight of constitutional and legal examination.[19] The authors found no basis in the administration's argument that surveillance without court approval was authorized by the AUMF, which empowered the president to use "all necessary and appropriate force against" al Qaeda. According to the Justice Department, spying on the enemy—even if it involved monitoring U.S. phone and e-mail without judicial approval or probable cause—was a "fundamental incident of war" sanctioned by the AUMF. Indeed, this contention was a bold argument. As Congress was drafting the AUMF, the White House sought additional powers authorizing the president to use force "in the United States," as well as overseas—a proposal denied by Congress.[20] By rejecting the administration's proposal, Congress indicated that it never intended for the AUMF to have any force in the United States. As one constitutional scholar wrote in early 2006, "It would be extraordinary if the precisely-crafted FISA framework, which has been explicitly amended by Congress five times since 9/11, could silently be altered in the way that the administration contends, particularly since the AUMF was adopted without there being any reference to NSA, to its mission, to the targeted interception of international communications of United States persons within the United States, or to any aspect of FISA."[21]

Beyond this point, however, the constitutional scholars and former government officials who wrote to the congressional leadership said that Congress had specifically and expressly regulated all electronic surveillance in the United States, declaring that FISA and the criminal code were the "exclusive means by which electronic surveillance ... and the interception of domestic, wire, oral, and electronic communications may be conducted."[22] Moreover, Congress explicitly addressed the question of wiretapping during wartime, limiting warrantless surveillance to the first fifteen days of the conflict. If the president required further warrantless surveillance during wartime, the fifteen days provided enough time for Congress to consider and enact additional authorization—a provision not mentioned in the Justice Department documents. "Rather than follow this course," the authors wrote, "the President acted unilaterally and secretly in contravention of FISA's terms."[23]

It was not the first time that a president made a power grab based on implied congressional authorization. President Harry Truman made similar claims when seizing the steel mills during the Korean War. In response to Truman's overreaching of executive power, Justice Felix Frankfurter declared that it was "one thing to draw an intention of Congress from general language and to say that Congress would have explicitly written what is inferred, where Congress has not addressed itself to a specific situation." But Frankfurter said it was "quite impossible ... when Congress did specifically address itself to a problem, as Congress did to that of seizure, to find secreted in the interstices of legislation the very grant of power which Congress consciously withheld." To discover "authority so explicitly withheld," said the Justice, is "to disrespect the whole legislative process and the constitutional division of authority between the President and Congress."[24] Justice Frankfurter's words seemed amply applicable to the immediate situation in which a president was claiming power to overrun a statute that expressly prohibited such an action.

The administration's reading of *Hamdi* also was highly questionable since the majority Court limited its ruling to individuals who were "part of or supporting forces hostile to the United States or coalition partners in Afghanistan and who engaged in an armed conflict against the United States there."[25] The authors contended the Court's ruling could not be squared with the administration's broad reading of the case as justifying the use of unchecked warrantless domestic spying. "It is one thing ... to say that foreign battlefield capture of enemy combatants is an incident of waging war that Congress intended to authorize. It is another matter entirely to treat unchecked warrantless domestic spying as included in that authorization, especially where an existing statute specifies that other laws are the 'exclusive means' by which electronic surveillance may be conducted."[26]

The legal experts also challenged the administration's claim that under Article II, the president had the inherent constitutional authority to engage in a domestic spying program without judicial oversight. When passing FISA, Congress did not deny that the president had the constitutional power to conduct surveillance for national security purposes. Instead, Congress concluded that "even if the President has the inherent authority in the absence of legislation to authorize warrantless electronic surveillance for foreign intelligence purposes, Congress has the power to regulate the conduct of such surveillance by legislating a reasonable procedure, which then becomes the exclusive means by which such surveillance may be conducted."[27] While the president possessed inherent authority, it could not be construed to be absolute, or that the executive may operate outside the laws passed by Congress under its Article I powers. Congress therefore plainly had the authority to regulate domestic surveillance by government intelligence agencies—a fact recognized by the Justice Department at the time of FISA's passage.[28]

The bipartisan authors, moreover, vigorously asserted that to interpret the AUMF and FISA as allowing unchecked domestic surveillance for the duration of the war on terror did indeed raise serious constitutional questions. The Supreme Court had "never upheld such a sweeping power to invade the privacy of Americans at home without individualized suspicion or judicial oversight." Yet, the NSA surveillance program permitted domestic spying without either of the Fourth Amendment requirements of individual probable cause and a warrant. In fact, the only time the Court considered a case involving national security surveillance, it ruled that the Fourth Amendment prohibited domestic security wiretaps without those protections.[29] Finally, the authors contested the administration's "special needs" argument. The administration referenced a court case—*In re Sealed Case No. 02-001*—to justify venturing beyond the probable cause and warrant requirements of ordinary law enforcement. But the authors pointed out that the *Sealed Case* actually upheld FISA, which "requires warrants issued by Article III federal judges upon an individualized showing of probable cause that the subject is an agent of a foreign power." By contrast, the NSA program neither required individual judicial approval nor did it require a showing that the target of the surveillance was an agent of a foreign power.[30] Above all else, however, critics charged that if the administration wanted additional powers to carry out terrorist surveillance, it should have gone to Congress to amend and operate within the law rather than claim expansive powers beyond the pale of the Constitution.

A Question of History

In early February 2006, Gonzales argued the administration's position before the Senate Judiciary Committee, adding that the president was "the sole organ" for the nation in foreign affairs. This assertion alluded to a 1936 Supreme Court ruling in United States v. Curtis-Wright Export Corporation, which referred to the "exclusive power of the president as the sole organ of the federal government in the field of international relations."[31] But the *Curtis-Wright* decision involved a presidential order imposing an arms embargo—at the behest of Congress—on Bolivia and Paraguay, countries that were then at war with each other. Charged with violating the embargo, the Curtis-Wright company claimed that the arms ban was illegal, an argument rejected by the Court on the grounds that the president had the constitutional authority to conduct foreign affairs. The decision had nothing to do with legitimating executive authority to override a statute passed by Congress under its Article I powers. Gonzales's misuse of *Curtis-Wright* recalled the Iran-Contra hearings in the 1980s, when Colonel Oliver North cited the same opinion in support of his rogue arms-for-hostages operation and the diversion of funds to the Nicaraguan contras. Gonzales's reference to this one line, out of context, from a Supreme Court ruling that could not possibly be construed to support unilateral executive authority was indeed a thin reed on which to hang a constitutional argument to overrun the surveillance law.[32] Gonzales's remark drew a response from *Washington Post* columnist George Will. That "non sequitur," wrote the conservative columnist—a critic of the administration's overreaching—was "refuted by the Constitution's plain language, which empowers Congress to ratify treaties, declare war, fund and regulate military forces, and make laws 'necessary and proper' for the execution of all presidential powers." Those powers "do not include deciding that a law—FISA—is somehow exempted from the presidential duty to 'take care that the laws be faithfully executed,'" he wrote.[33]

Gonzales's testimony before the Senate Judiciary Committee also immediately drew skeptical, if not harsh, responses from committee leaders. The committee's Republican chairman, Senator Arlen Specter, said the federal law barred "any electronic surveillance without a court order." In addition, Senator Patrick Leahy, the panel's ranking Democrat, said that instead of the administration monitoring messages legally, "he's decided to do it illegally."[34] But Gonzales said the president would have been irresponsible not to have authorized the NSA to undertake the surveillance program after the September 11 attacks, and claimed that the executive's long historical practice of undertaking warrantless surveillance of wartime communications amply justified the NSA program. Given the advantages of this historical practice, the administration's surveillance activity was nothing "novel," he said. Like his predecessors, Bush had the inherent constitutional right to conduct warrantless electronic surveillance in a time of armed conflict, which was supplemented by the text and purpose of the AUMF.[35]

Indeed, in the 1970s the Senate Select Committee to Study Governmental Operations with Respect to Intelligence Activities—the so-called Church Committee—found that every president since Franklin D. Roosevelt claimed the authority to carry out warrantless surveillance. But it was perhaps peculiar that Gonzales would both cite but ignore the U.S. government's history in conducting domestic surveillance to justify the administration's expansion of executive power. After all, the Church Committee provided powerful evidence of why the executive should no longer be given exclusive authority to spy on Americans. In investigating the history of domestic spying by the executive branch, the Church Committee found significant past abuses of warrantless electronic surveillance in the name of national security. "While the number of illegal or improper national security taps and bugs conducted during the Nixon administration may have exceeded those in previous administrations, the surveillances were regrettably by no means atypical," the committee said. Unchecked surveillance had enabled the government to "generate vast amounts of information—unrelated to any legitimate government interest—about the personal and political lives of American citizens." The committee noted that unrestrained surveillance not only raised the danger of its use for partisan political purposes and other improper ends, but threatened to chill the exercise of fundamental political freedoms guaranteed under the Bill of Rights. The history of these abuses gave considerable force behind passage of FISA with the aim of curbing the executive's unilateral authority to conduct domestic wiretapping without the benefit of judicial oversight.[36]

The administration's urgent sense to defend the country from a possible second wave of attacks recalled previous eras of national peril. It was not the first time that the balance between national security and civil liberties swung against bedrock constitutional principles of privacy, free expression, and due process. With the threat of an enemy within, real or imagined, the United States confronted these situations before. In 1798, President John Adams signed the Alien and Sedition Acts over concerns that the passions of the French Revolution would be spread to American shores by "Philosophes" and "Jacobins" who infiltrated the country. The year of their enactment witnessed the sinking or commandeering of more than 300 ships by the French. The radical Directory had taken over the revolution, sending hundreds of aristocrats, including the king and queen, to their deaths. Fearing war with France, the Federalists saw Jefferson and his followers' pro-French views as treasonous. The Alien and Sedition Acts resulted in the imprisonment of newspaper editors, protestors, and even a Congressman.[37] Adams's unconstitutional acts, however, paled in comparison to Lincoln's suspension of habeas corpus during the Civil War. By the time of Lincoln's inauguration, seven states had already seceded from the union. After the outbreak of hostilities, Lincoln claimed the internal threat of Confederate saboteurs to suspend the right of due process and to jail "Copperhead" newspaper editors and others who opposed his policies.[38]

Woodrow Wilson's Justice Department responded to the Red Scare of 1919, which began with a series of terrorist bombings around the country, by raiding Communist meetings, arresting more than 5,000 persons, and deporting about 400 suspect aliens with little due process. These activities came after the suppression of civil liberties following America's entry into World War I in 1917 and the Russian Revolution. Wilson urged Congress to pass the Espionage Act, the Trading with the Enemy Act, and the Sedition Act. The Espionage Act's censorship provisions allowed Postmaster General Albert Burleson to suppress journals, letters, and anything else that he viewed as a threat to national security. Even more drastic steps were taken by Franklin D. Roosevelt with the interning of more than 120,000 Japanese Americans following the Japanese attack on Pearl Harbor in December 1941.[39]

This fear of the enemy within again arose in the early 1950s with the Communist witch hunts of Senator Joseph McCarthy. Tenured professors were fired for exercising their Fifth Amendment rights, and writers, actors, and others who worked in Hollywood were blacklisted and held in contempt of Congress for invoking their First Amendment protection and refusing to disclose the names of others who may have had ties to the Communist party. While the constitutional rights of the accused were trampled in show trials before McCarthy's congressional committee, decades later the Soviet archives revealed that the Kremlin did maintain a spy network within the American government. But the times were conducive to considerable fear. The perceived external threat of Communism on the march was translated into an internal threat of Communist infiltration and subversion. After consolidating their grip on Eastern Europe after World War II, the Soviets with their ideology of world revolution tested an atomic bomb in August 1949. Mao instigated a revolution in China, imposing a Communist regime on one-quarter of the world's population. Then, in 1950, Communist North Korea invaded South Korea. At the same time, Alger Hiss and Julius and Ethel Rosenberg were arrested for spying for the Soviets—lending credence to the belief of Communist infiltration. The atmosphere of alarm led to congressional hearings, blacklists, and vastly expanded powers of J. Edgar Hoover's FBI.[40]

In important respects, the September 11, 2001, attacks stand alone in American history. The surprise strike against a civilian population by terrorists trained on foreign soil posed a new and substantial threat to U.S. security. The al Qaeda network operating under the protection of the Islamist Taliban government in Afghanistan and a sworn enemy of the United States was led by

Osama bin Laden, an international terrorist of Saudi descent. After the attacks on the Twin Towers in New York and the Pentagon outside Washington, there was no way of knowing whether other terrorists had infiltrated the country and whether other mass attacks were imminent. Following the attacks the U.S. military and its allies deposed the radical Taliban regime in Afghanistan and began planning for the invasion of Iraq to overthrow Saddam Hussein. At the same time, in nationwide sweeps the government detained more than a 1,000 suspects inside the United States, mostly Muslims, and expanded its war-making authority that included detaining indefinitely U.S. citizens as enemy combatants, denying prisoners access to lawyers or courts, rejecting in some cases the applicability of the Geneva Conventions, expanding its interrogation techniques to include harsher treatment, and establishing secret prisons in foreign countries. The Bush administration also immediately launched its warrantless domestic spying program that ignited vigorous objections about violating Americans' Fourth Amendment assurances that the "right of the people to be secure in their persons, houses, papers, and effects, against unreasonable searches and seizures, shall not be violated, and no warrants shall issue, but upon probable cause."[41] These events occurred mostly at the expense of a compliant Congress, taking a subsidiary role to the president and abrogating its duty to check the executive's expansive assertions of power.

Imperative of New Surveillance Technologies

The decision to allow eavesdropping inside the country without court approval marked a sea change for the NSA, whose mission was to spy on communications overseas. The NSA, based in Fort Meade, Maryland, operated as the nation's largest and most secretive intelligence agency and had always sought to remain out of public view. The agency specialized in cracking codes and operated listening posts around the world to eavesdrop on foreign governments, diplomats, trade negotiators, drug lords, and terrorists. Since the late 1970s, however, the agency began operating under tight restrictions governing spying on Americans. Under the agency's longstanding rules, the NSA may intercept phone calls or e-mail messages on foreign soil, even if those receiving these communications are in the United States. But the agency could only do so by first obtaining a court order on the grounds of probable cause from the Foreign Intelligence Surveillance Court, whose eleven judges meet in closed sessions at the Justice Department. It has typically been the FBI, not the NSA, that has sought FISA warrants to carry out domestic spying. Until Bush issued his presidential order allowing the NSA to carry out warrantless surveillance within the United States, the intelligence agency largely limited its domestic spying to foreign embassies and missions in Washington, New York, and other cities with a court order.[42]

In the panic following the 9/11 attacks, the possibility of using the NSA's full arsenal of new surveillance technologies immediately became part of the urgent imperative to hunt down hidden plotters before they could strike again. Advances in technology involving acoustic engineering and statistical theory combined with the efficient use of computing power offered new capacities to monitor communications from the vast stream of global voice and data traffic. Since the 1990s the shift in market forces away from satellites to fiber optic cable also provided new capabilities to eavesdrop. By the time of the terrorist attacks, nearly all voice and data traffic to and from the United States traveled by fiber optic cable; about one-third of that traffic passed from one foreign country to another through U.S. networks. With a growing fraction of global telecommunications traversing through junctions on U.S. territory, the Bush administration had both the incentive and capability for a new and highly effective kind of espionage.[43]

But the FISA law stood in the way. Until Bush changed the rules, the law prevented the government from tapping into access points on U.S. territory without a warrant to monitor the contents of communications to or from individuals in the United States. Nevertheless, the NSA's operational capabilities in conducting its warrantless spying program ran into a host of legal and political concerns. While the Bush administration refused to say—in public or in closed sessions of Congress—how many Americans had been monitored without court authority, in late May 2006 Seymour Hersh, investigative journalist for the *New Yorker*, reported the number in the tens of thousands.[44] The NSA's powerful computers collected and sifted through thousands of e-mails, faxes, and telephone calls coming in and out of the country before singling out ones for human investigation.

The program's intrusiveness became even more pronounced as artificial intelligence systems filtered and ranked the voice and data traffic in order of probable interest to NSA analysts. Intelligence officers tended to "wash out" the vast majority of leads selected by computers within days or weeks.[45] With the sheer scale of the warrantless program sweeping up tens of thousands of bystanders, considerable doubts arose within the NSA about its legality under the Fourth Amendment. At issue was whether such wide net searches could be judged "reasonable" if they were based on evidence that showed them to be unreliable in the overwhelming number of cases. According to government officials and lawyers with concerns about the legality of the program, the ratio of success to failure carried considerable significance when the subjects of surveillance were American citizens with constitutional protections. Because in most cases the government could not meet the minimum legal definition of probable cause for carrying out surveillance activities, those who devised the plan knew that it would be highly problematic to go through the FISA court for warrants.[46]

Lawyers Revolt

Regardless of the powerful incentive to use the NSA's surveillance capabilities, the ordering of the NSA to spy on American soil without court orders sparked profound concerns within the Bush administration from the start. The spying program stemmed from a high-level intelligence meeting just days after the September 11 attacks. The main architect of the plan was General Michael V. Hayden, then the director of the NSA, who saw opportunity in using the agency's enormous technological prowess in the United States.[47] The idea received support from John Yoo, a Berkeley professor turned deputy chief of the Justice Department's Office of Legal Counsel. Yoo wrote an internal memorandum arguing that the government could use "electronic surveillance techniques and equipment that are more powerful and sophisticated than those available to law enforcement agencies in order to intercept telephonic communications and observe the movement of persons but without obtaining warrants for such uses." Despite the possibility of raising constitutional issues, Yoo wrote, the "government may be justified in taking measures which in less troubled conditions could be seen as infringements of individual liberties."[48]

In the weeks following the attacks, Vice President Dick Cheney and his top legal adviser, David Addington, pushed hard for the NSA to get involved in intercepting purely domestic telephone calls and e-mails without court warrants in the hunt for terrorists.[49] Driving Cheney's forceful approach seemed to be an ideological view that after the September 11 attacks, it was time to right the wrongs that weakened the government's intelligence agencies in the 1970s. Writing in the first volume of his political memoirs, Henry Kissinger had expressed considerable frustration over those who were "eager to dismantle" the government's intelligence apparatus. Intelligence officials, he complained, "deserve[d] better of their country than the merciless assault to which they have been exposed—assaults that threaten to leave us naked in a vital area of our national security."[50] Kissinger's words reflected the strong sentiments of White House and national security officials of the time, but they could have just as well been written by Cheney who long believed in the necessity of reversing what he viewed as power seizures of past Democratic Congresses that usurped the prerogatives that constitutionally belonged to the president. Just as at the height of the Cold War, the United States was now living in an age of ideological confrontation. Radical organizations and groups around the globe were carrying out terrorist outrages, or financing them, transferring weapons and explosives, seeking to cause mass murder of innocents or the overthrow of governments. In Cheney's view, Congress far overreached its authority in the 1970s and 1980s, a trend that had to be reversed in the name of national security.

But the idea of intercepting purely domestic communications ran into flak from some lawyers and officials at the intelligence agency, which was badly scarred by the surveillance scandals in the 1970s and ever since exercised its powerful technology with considerable caution to stay within the parameters of the law. Trained in the agency's rules against domestic spying and resistant to approving any surveillance without court orders, they argued that any wiretapping should be limited to communications into and out of the country—a view that ultimately prevailed. Even with this limitation, the program marked a fundamental expansion of the NSA's domestic spying powers and a decisive break with the provisions of FISA, which required court approval for all eavesdropping on U.S. soil. General Hayden, who aimed to stay within the agreed upon parameters, reportedly accepted the argument that as commander in chief, the president owned the constitutional authority to order surveillance on international communications without court approval—a position vigorously contested by critics across the political spectrum in and out of government. Unlike Cheney and Addington who believed that domestic surveillance without warrants should be done if people were suspected of having links to al Qaeda, Hayden was particularly concerned about ensuring that at least one end of each conversation be outside the United States.[51]

Despite the agreed upon framework for monitoring communications coming in and out of the country, the infighting within the administration over the legality and parameters of the spying program was hardly over. On one side stood a small coterie of hard-liners who led an insurrection against the legal limits on the presidency. These officials included Cheney and his formidable general counsel and legal adviser for many years, David Addington, joined by John Yoo, the theorist behind unhinging the presidency from the limitations placed on it by Congress. Also involved was Timothy E. Flannigan, the deputy White House counsel, and later, then White House counsel, Alberto Gonzales. As Cheney's lead agent in the charge to extend executive powers, Addington— like his boss—long believed that the reforms following Watergate and Vietnam considerably weakened the presidency. To Cheney and Addington, the 9/11 attacks with the threat of other imminent strikes created the urgent imperative to unleash the intelligence agencies. With the support of Secretary of Defense Donald Rumsfeld and CIA Director George Tenet, who only worried about providing legal cover to his agents, Addington and his allies set about drafting a legal argument on behalf of expansive presidential powers during wartime.[52]

With the aim of giving the president maximum powers in the war on terror, Addington found a critical ally early on in John Yoo at the Office of Legal Counsel, a key office in the executive branch that serves as the final arbiter on the legal limits of presidential actions. Yoo, who began authoring legal opinions granting the president expansive wartime powers, later became synonymous with the infamous "torture memo" allowing CIA interrogators to use "coercive methods" short of maiming or killing prisoners. With Yoo's advice, Flannigan wrote the authorization of military force that Congress approved on September 18, 2001. The authorization was drafted in broad terms to cover any unexpected event and the administration immediately claimed it as congressional approval for launching its warrantless surveillance program. At the same time, Yoo was already drafting that legal opinion, completing it on September 25 but keeping it secret for more than three years. It was an extraordinary move, evading Congress, the courts, and key senior administration officials who were likely to object. To minimize dissent, Addington froze out others in the administration. Among those excluded was John B. Bellinger III, the National Security Council's top lawyer who reported to Condoleezza Rice and who Addington and his allies viewed with contempt. With Bellinger kept in the dark regarding a critical issue that was under his purview, Rice's lawyer had no chance to push for vetting the eavesdropping program with the secret court that supervised domestic surveillance—a step the administration was compelled to take several years later.[53]

Representing his political muscle inside the administration, Cheney first briefed the chairman and ranking minority members of the intelligence committees on October 25, 2001, swearing them to secrecy. In previous administrations, they would have met with the president in the Oval Office. But instead the four congressional members were led to the vice president's office in the White House where they learned of the NSA operations from Cheney, Lt. General Michael Hayden of the Air Force, then the agency's director before becoming a full general and principal deputy director of national intelligence, and George J. Tenet, the director of the CIA. Attending the meeting was Senator Bob Graham, who after becoming chairman of the Senate intelligence committee had been told by the president that Cheney had been handed the portfolio for intelligence activities. If nothing else, such news signaled the president's abdication of a vast portion of his executive powers to the vice president, who was an executive branch supremacist and who sought to unhinge the presidency from judicial and congressional oversight.[54]

The eavesdropping program began with virtually no constraints, worrying several agency officials who feared participating in an illegal operation. By mid-2004, concerns spread well beyond national security officials to government lawyers and the federal judge who oversaw the FISA court in the Justice Department. Among those who opposed Cheney, Addington, and their hard-line allies were several Justice Department lawyers, including Deputy Attorney General James Comey, Jack Goldsmith, a former special counsel in the Pentagon, and others. With Comey's backing, these government lawyers challenged efforts to spin what they viewed as implausible justifications for giving the president virtually unlimited wartime powers. They did so at considerable risk to themselves—ostracized and denied promotions, while others later left the administration for jobs in private law firms or academia. Goldsmith and others battled to bring the eavesdropping program within the law. The infighting with Addington and others around Cheney intensified after Goldsmith became head of the Office of Legal Counsel (OLC) in April 2003. Unlike Cheney and Addington, Goldsmith was not an executive power absolutist. After several months in the post, Goldsmith initiated a review of Yoo's March 2003 torture memo, igniting a face-to-face confrontation with Addington, who accused him of altering the rules in midstream and putting American lives at risk. In 2004, with considerable concerns about the legality of the eavesdropping program, Goldsmith also pushed for a reevaluation of the eavesdropping program.[55]

According to the rules worked out, the spying program had to be reviewed by the attorney general every forty-five days. The fierce internal battle over the program's legality came to a head in March 2004 after John Ashcroft was hospitalized with a serious pancreatic condition. In Ashcroft's absence, Comey became acting attorney general. Goldsmith, joined by a former OLC lawyer, Patrick Philbin—who had become Comey's national security aide—raised concerns with the deputy attorney general regarding the legality of the spying program. Comey agreed that there should be no reauthorization of the program. Comey discussed these concerns with Ashcroft the day the attorney general went into the hospital and the two evidently agreed that the program was no longer legal. At a high-level meeting at the White House on March 9, 2004, regarding Justice Department objections, Cheney told his government adversaries that he disagreed with their concerns about the legality of the secret surveillance program. In addition to Cheney, the meeting involved Gonzales, Addington, Andrew Card Jr., Bush's chief of staff, and others. Failing to persuade Comey, Gonzales and Card made a late-night visit on March 10—the eve of the program's expiration—to Ashcroft who lay in a hospital bed battling pancreatitis and recovering from gallbladder surgery. The two aides pressured Ashcroft to reauthorize the NSA's spying program after Comey and other Justice Department officials refused to recertify the legality of the program. But from his hospital bed, in pain and on medication, Ashcroft rebuked them, explaining why he thought the program was illegal. But "that doesn't matter, because I'm not the attorney general," he said pointing to

Comey who had raced to the hospital ahead of Gonzales and Card; "there's the attorney general."[56]

The furious reaction shot beyond Cheney to the Oval Office. With "his penchant for putdown nicknames," reported *Newsweek*, Bush began "referring to Comey as 'Cuomey' or 'Cuomo,' apparently after former New York Governor Mario Cuomo, who was notorious for his Hamlet-like indecision over whether to seek the Democratic presidential nomination in the 1980s."[57] Despite Ashcroft's refusal to abandon his objections, the White House recertified the part of the program in dispute without going through the normal channels of the Justice Department regarding its legality. Bush backed down, however, after Comey, Goldsmith, FBI Director Robert S. Mueller III, Ashcroft's chief of staff, and as many as thirty Justice officials threatened to resign.

The threat of mass resignations signified a resounding vote of no-confidence in Cheney, Addington, and Gonzales by officials who were all Republican political appointees and were known for previously carrying out aggressive antiterrorism initiatives. Comey, who left the administration shortly afterward, later revealed the dramatic details surrounding the Ashcroft showdown in testimony before the Senate Judiciary Committee in May 2007. In that testimony, Comey recounted that Gonzales had tried to "do an end run around the acting attorney general" and "take advantage of a very sick man who did not have the powers of attorney general."[58]

The objections of Judge Colleen Kollar-Kotelly, the federal judge who oversaw the FISA court, helped spur the suspension of the program. The judge, who became the FISA court's presiding judge in May 2002, questioned whether information overheard under the NSA program was being improperly used to obtain wiretap warrants in the court. Like her predecessor, Royce C. Lamberth, who served as head judge at the time of the September 11, 2001, attacks, Kollar-Kotelly had profound reservations about the legality of the warrantless surveillance of phone calls and e-mails. Both judges worried about protecting the court from tainted evidence and demanded that no information obtained by the NSA program be used to obtain warrants from their court. When in mid-2004 Kollar-Kotelly voiced concerns that the NSA program was being used to provide information for FISA warrants, Attorney General Ashcroft temporarily suspended elements of the program. As a result, stricter legal rules were worked out between the NSA and Justice Department, including an expanded and refined checklist to follow in determining whether any probable cause existed to monitor a person's communications. Moreover, Kollar-Kotelly required that high-level Justice officials certify that any information provided to the court be accurate if it involved NSA surveillance evidence, or face possible perjury charges.[59]

Politics

The internal divisions in the administration were mirrored within conservative political circles. The NSA's domestic surveillance program caused widening ideological fissures between neoconservative adherents of national security against small government libertarians and others who viewed it as threatening the core constitutional Fourth Amendment right against unreasonable searches and seizures. "It seems to me that if you're the president, you have to proceed with great caution when you do anything that flies in the face of the Constitution," said Warren Rudman, a former Republican Senator from New Hampshire who also served on several government intelligence advisory boards. Rudman added that he viewed the surveillance program with "grave concern." Despite the administration's arguments on the legality of the program, a number of prominent conservatives disagreed and even accused the White House of extending executive prerogatives to the detriment of the balance of powers. David Keene, chairman of the American Conservative Union, criticized the NSA program as a case of "presidential overreaching" that most Americans would reject. In a *Washington Post* opinion piece, columnist George Will wrote that "conservatives' wholesome wariness of presidential power has been a casualty of conservative presidents winning seven of the past 10 elections." Bob Barr, a Georgia conservative who was one of the Republican Party's most vociferous opponents of government domestic spying before leaving office in 2003, denounced the NSA's warrantless spying program as an "egregious violation of the electronic surveillance laws." He believed the uproar should stand as a test of Republicans' willingness to reign in their president.[60]

The program also faced immediate skepticism among some Republicans in the Senate. Arlen Specter, who chaired the Senate Judiciary Committee, called the program inappropriate and pushed to hold a series of hearings on the matter at the considerable displeasure of the vice president and others in the administration.[61] Specter's sentiments were shared by the likes of centrist Senators Chuck Hagel of Nebraska and John Sununu of New Hampshire, as well as limited government advocates such as Larry Craig of Idaho. Other Republicans supported Bush's right to evade the law to conduct surveillance, arguing that security should come first and that the details could be dealt with later. Leading neoconservatives William Kristol and Gary Schmitt declared that the president possessed the authority to collect foreign intelligence on American soil "as he sees fit" and that Congress could not "legislate for every contingency." Cheney saw the matter entirely through the prism of presidential power. "I believe in a strong, robust executive authority, and I think that the world we live in demands it," he explained to reporters. According to the vice president, the wave of openness and accountability that swept over Washington after the Watergate scandal and Vietnam War proved to be the "nadir of the modern presidency in terms of authority and legitimacy and harmed the president's ability to lead in a dangerous era. But I do think that to some extent now we've been able to restore the legitimate authority of the presidency."[62]

It was the kind of statement that triggered a response even from Republican political observers. "He's living in a time warp," said Bruce Fein, a constitutional lawyer who also served in the Reagan administration. "The great irony is Bush inherited the strongest presidency of anyone since Franklin Roosevelt, and Cheney acts as if he's still under the constraints of 1973 or 1974." Indeed, despite the discarding of the War Powers Act, the legislative veto, the independent counsel statute, and other legacies of the 1970s, the vice president believed that executive power had been severely eroded since the Nixon years. Nonetheless, like so much else, the fault lines seemingly led to Iraq. From the beginning those who supported the Iraq War "found reason to think that all other Bush policies, from torture to domestic surveillance, are justified," said Robert Levy, a conservative legal scholar at the libertarian Cato Institute. "This is just one in a litany of ongoing events that have separated the noninterventionist wing of the Republican Party from the neocon wing."[63]

In the halls of Congress, the debate over the NSA's surveillance program quickly descended into a partisan squabble shortly after it was revealed in December 2005. In February 2006, columnist David Ignatius, writing in the *Washington Post*, pointed out that "rather than seeking a compromise that would anchor the program in law, both the administration and its critics [were] pursuing absolutist agendas—insisting on the primacy of security or liberty, rather than some reasonable balance of the two. This way lies disaster."[64] Rather than seek accommodation, however, the administration asserted far-reaching wartime powers in carrying out the warrantless surveillance program and moved to exploit the issue for political gain. In early 2006, Karl Rove, the president's political adviser, saw opportunity in defining the debate as a new "wedge issue" leading up to the 2006 congressional elections. According to Rove, those in Congress and others were either with the administration or Osama bin Laden, impugning the Democrats for being weak on national security in a world threatened by terrorism. With Bush's poll numbers sinking due to the Iraq War, liberal interest groups were also refusing to compromise, urging Democratic members of Congress to wait until after the 2006 elections when they might have more congressional support. If the elections fell their way, the Democrats would be in a stronger position to force the administration to heed FISA, or perhaps amend it. At the same time, liberal groups wanted more time to pursue court action against the domestic spying program to have it declared unconstitutional.[65]

Between these uncompromising stances, others staked out a middle ground. Republican Senators Lindsey Graham and Arlen Specter urged the White House to seek legal review of the program by the FISA court, while Representative Jane Harman, the ranking Democrat who served on the House Intelligence Committee, argued that it could operate under existing FISA provisions. Others proposed amending FISA to bring the program within the law. But the Bush administration—led by Cheney—refused to seek clear legislative authority and national consensus for the program.[66]

In March 2006, Specter held four days of hearings before the Judiciary Committee, after the Senate Intelligence Committee declined to convene hearings on the NSA program. The hearings were notable as five former judges on the Foreign Intelligence Surveillance Court, including one who resigned in apparent protest over Bush's domestic spying, urged Congress to give the nation's most secretive court formal oversight of the NSA's surveillance program. Several of the judges also challenged the president's constitutional authority to order electronic surveillance on Americans without a warrant. They also warned that the program could endanger criminal prosecutions that stemmed from the surveillance activities. Judge Harold A. Baker, who left the intelligence court to become a sitting judge in Illinois, said the president was bound by the law "like everyone else." If Congress duly enacts a law that is considered constitutional like the Foreign Intelligence Surveillance Act, the "president ignores it at the president's peril."[67]

The testimony of the former judges of the intelligence court indicated the administration's growing isolation over the legality of the eavesdropping program, but the White House continued to maintain that the president had the inherent constitutional authority to order surveillance without warrants in defense of the country. In May 2006, the controversy gained renewed force after *USA Today* reported that the NSA had been secretly amassing the domestic call records of tens of millions of phone company customers since the September 11, 2001, attacks. One major telecommunications carrier reportedly had set up a top secret circuit between its main computer complex and a government-intelligence computer center at Quantico, Virginia.[68] Amid a furor of protests over the covert effort from privacy advocates, members of Congress, and others, the White House moved quickly to shape the debate. Before TV cameras and in a radio address, Bush defended the government intelligence program to prevent another terrorist attack. "The privacy of all Americans is fiercely protected in all our activities," he said. Bush said the government was not trolling through the personal lives or listening to the calls of millions of innocent Americans, but was only analyzing the patterns of contacts they revealed. On Capitol Hill, Democrats expressed outrage while some Republicans voiced concern. "Are you telling me tens of millions of Americans are involved with al-Qaeda?" railed Senator Patrick Leahy, the ranking Democrat on the Senate Judiciary Committee. Senate Finance Chairman Chuck Grassley, an Iowan Republican, asked why the phone companies were not protecting their customers. Senator Specter said he would call executives from any of the companies that provided the NSA their records on cell phone and landline calls made by millions of Americans—"to find out what is going on."[69]

Administration Blocks Investigations

The White House, however, moved adroitly to obstruct any probes into the NSA's surveillance activity. Specter, who had been the leading Republican voice raising questions about the legality of the surveillance program, aimed to issue subpoenas to compel telephone company executives to testify about their cooperation in providing call records to the NSA. But Cheney, maneuvering around Specter, cut a furtive deal with the other Republicans on the Judiciary Committee to block testimony from phone company executives. The incident went public after Specter released to the news media a letter he sent to the vice president. In his letter, Specter accused Cheney of meddling behind his back in the committee's business. Specter wrote that events were unfolding in a "context where the administration is continuing warrantless wiretaps in violation of the Foreign Intelligence Surveillance Act and is preventing the Senate Judiciary Committee from carrying out its constitutional responsibility for congressional oversight."[70]

Moreover, in an unusual and unprecedented intervention, in April 2006 Bush personally sidelined an internal Justice Department probe of the NSA's warrantless eavesdropping program. The president shut down the probe after his attorney general learned that his own conduct would come under scrutiny regarding the administration's domestic surveillance program. It was unclear whether Bush knew at the time of his decision that Gonzales would be a focus of the investigation by the Justice Department's internal ethics watchdog, the Office of Professional Responsibility (OPR). But if the inquiry had been allowed to proceed, it would have examined Gonzales's role in authorizing the surveillance program when he was White House counsel, as well as his oversight of the highly controversial program after he became attorney general. OPR investigators sought to launch their investigation by interviewing Jack Goldsmith, who had been assistant attorney general for the Office of Legal Counsel, and James A. Baker, the counsel for Justice's Office of Intelligence Policy and Review. Both officials had expressed serious reservations about the legality of the NSA program. Moreover, Goldsmith and others in the Office of Legal Counsel had clashed with Gonzales and his White House allies in 2004 over the reauthorization of the program, ultimately forcing a change in its rules.[71]

Nonetheless, Bush personally intervened to terminate the inquiry by denying security clearances to the attorneys who were investigating whether Gonzales and other department lawyers knowingly authorized an unfounded interpretation of the law to give the spying program legal cover. Since its creation more than thirty years previously, the OPR had conducted numerous highly sensitive investigations involving executive branch programs. In a memorandum explaining the reasons for terminating the probe, the OPR's chief lawyer, H. Marshall Jerrett, wrote that since its creation, the office had never before been prevented from obtaining access to information classified at the highest levels. Under sharp questioning from Senate Judiciary Committee Chairman Arlen Specter, Gonzales said that Bush would not grant the access needed for security reasons. "It was highly classified, very important, and many other lawyers had access. Why not OPR?" asked Specter. Gonzales said the "President of the United States makes the decision." It was a highly convenient answer for an attorney general who was to be a focus of an internal investigation—one that critics charged raised serious ethical issues.[72] A conservative critic of the administration's legal rationale for the surveillance program compared Gonzales unfavorably to Elliot Richardson, the Watergate-era attorney general who resigned in 1973 rather than obey Richard Nixon's order to fire special prosecutor Archibald Cox. But a Justice Department official said that the investigation was nothing more than politics, initiated by more than thirty-six Democrats and one House independent.[73]

Congressional Efforts to Pass New Surveillance Legislation

These controversies erupted soon after the Bush administration's nomination of General Michael V. Hayden as the next CIA director triggered a greater uproar than the White House anticipated over his role in the surveillance program and his staunch public defense of it.[74] Facing potentially tough Senate questioning, the White House agreed to brief all twenty-one members of the House Intelligence Committee and all sixteen members of the Senate's judiciary panel.[75] The administration's willingness to conduct the briefings seemed to signal that after months of tough debate, the White House had grown more open to consultation with Congress, including even considering legislation to revise the surveillance law. In July, Specter announced what he termed a "major breakthrough" regarding legislation supported by the White House that would allow the administration to submit the NSA's warrantless surveillance program to the FISA court for review of its legality.[76] In reality, Specter's breakthrough was little more than hyperbole, signifying a major retreat from his earlier insistence that the eavesdropping program must be subject to supervision of the secret intelligence court.[77] Specter negotiated the agreement with Cheney, who got the better of the deal. Republican leaders rallied around the Specter–Cheney deal that would allow—but not require—the secret FISA court to review the legality of the program as a whole and not individual wiretaps, with the aim of portraying their Democratic opponents as soft on terrorism. But by September, a number of Republicans moved to stiffen the terms of the agreement, while others introduced competing bills in the House and Senate with tougher accountability provisions.[78]

Specter's deal garnered a favorable 10:8 vote along party lines on the Senate Judiciary Committee in mid-September. But on the House Judiciary Committee, efforts to water down controls on the surveillance program faced an open rebellion among half a dozen Republican conservatives. "There are enough Republicans with concerns," said Representatives Jeff Flake, an Arizona Republican, who was advocating for a bi-partisan bill that would impose much tougher rules on the warrantless surveillance program. "Once you basically give the president this authority, it's very difficult to pull it back."[79] The widening rift within Republican congressional ranks indicated eroding support for the administration's stance that it had the inherent constitutional authority to bypass the 1978 surveillance law.

In the meantime the White House suffered another reversal when in August 2006, a federal judge in Detroit found the post-9/11 warrantless surveillance program aimed at uncovering terrorist activity to be unconstitutional. The judge ruled that the program violated rights to privacy, free speech, and the separation of powers. The American Civil Liberties Union, which led the lawsuit on behalf of other groups including lawyers, journalists, and scholars, claimed that the plaintiffs had a "well found" belief that their international communications were being intercepted by the government. By "compromising the free speech and privacy rights of the plaintiffs and others," the suit contended, "the program violates the First and Fourth Amendments of the United States Constitution." Filed in early January 2006, the suit also argued that it violated the separation of powers principles, "because it was authorized by President George W. Bush in excess of his Executive authority and contrary to limits imposed by Congress."[80] Within hours of the ruling, the Justice Department filed notice of appeal with the 6th Circuit U.S. Court of Appeals, covering appeals from Kentucky, Michigan, Ohio, and Tennessee. Bush decried the ruling. "I strongly disagree with that decision, strongly disagree," he said, adding that "our appeals will be upheld." The president may have had good reason for believing that the appeal would be upheld as he had appointed six judges to the Cincinnati-based 6th Circuit that gave Republican appointees an 8:6 majority.[81]

Democrats Take Over

With Democratic victories in both houses of Congress in the 2006 November elections and the loss in the courts with other cases pending, the administration faced new legal and political hurdles in its effort to continue the surveillance program. In mid-January 2007, after months of bruising national debate over the reach of the president's wartime powers, the White House abruptly reversed course. Gonzales announced that the surveillance program would be overseen by the FISA court and that the practice of eavesdropping without warrants on Americans suspected of ties to terrorists would come to an end. The Justice Department said that it devised an innovative arrangement with the FISA court that provided for the "necessary speed and agility" to obtain court approval to listen in on international communications of people in the United States while at the same time safeguarding national security. The administration refused to provide critical details on the new procedures, but four congressional members who had been briefed described them as a hybrid effort that involved both individual warrants and the authority to conduct surveillance on more broadly defined groups of people. The reversal came almost a month after President Bush signed a little-noticed statement claiming new powers to open U.S. mail without judicial warrants in emergencies or in foreign intelligence cases, provoking warnings from Democrats and privacy advocates that the administration was trying to circumvent legal restrictions on its authority.[82]

The administration's surprise retreat on its spying activities came after repeatedly rejecting proposals from Congress to revise the electronic surveillance law and stonewalling attempts to investigate the eavesdropping program. The White House, citing national security concerns, declined to discuss publicly or offer evidence of what ailed the 1978 surveillance act. But in May 2007, in a reversal of its January agreement and a sign of the struggle over executive powers between the White House and the Democratic-controlled Congress, senior Bush administration officials declared that they could not assure that the government would continue to seek court approval for the domestic surveillance program. Senior administration officials, including Michael McConnell, the new director of National Intelligence, insisted that the president still had the authority under Article II of the Constitution to conduct surveillance inside the country. Nonetheless, appearing before the Senate Intelligence Committee, McConnell said that all domestic surveillance was now being conducted with court approved warrants. "But I'd just highlight," he said, "Article II is Article

II, so in a different circumstance, I can't speak for the president what he might decide."[83]

The administration's statement about its Article II prerogatives came as the White House was seeking new legislation to update the 1978 law to expand the government's surveillance powers. The White House said that the outmoded law hindered the government's efforts to eavesdrop on telephone calls and e-mails that did not involve Americans or violate the privacy rights of people inside the United States. The proposed legislation was aimed at capturing international telephone calls and e-mail that went from one foreign country to another, but that digitally passed through the U.S. telecommunications system. The measure also proposed giving legal immunity to NSA employees who engaged in warrantless domestic spying and to telecommunications companies that cooperated with the NSA's program before being put under the surveillance act.[84]

The *Washington Post* denounced the administration's bill, saying it would not update the surveillance law, but "gut it" by allowing the government to amass vast amounts of data from American citizens' phone calls and e-mail communications. "This is a dishonest measure, dishonestly presented, and Congress should reject it," the editorial said. "Before making any new laws, Congress has to get to the truth about Bush's spying program."[85] As if taking its cue from the *Washington Post*, in June 2007, seven months after winning slim majorities in the House and Senate, the new Democratic-controlled Congress stepped up pressure to shed light on the legality of the Bush administration's warrantless surveillance policy, which had become one of its most controversial efforts in the battle against terrorism. The Senate Judiciary Committee subpoenaed the White House, Vice President Dick Cheney's office, the Justice Department, and the National Security Council, giving the administration until mid-July to comply with its demand for information.[86] The committee sought documents detailing the administration's authorization and reauthorization of the spying program, the internal deliberations and disputes over its legality, the thwarting of an in-house Justice Department investigation of the policy, and the NSA's agreements with telecommunications companies that cooperated in the surveillance activity.[87] The subpoenas came after eighteen months of the administration ignoring at least nine requests for the documents under both Republican and Democratic leadership. Only three of the nine Republicans on the committee opposed authorizing the subpoenas, which was approved by a 13:3 vote. While Senate Judiciary Committee Chairman Patrick Leahy declared in a letter accompanying the subpoenas that the "administration cannot thwart the Congress's conduct of its constitutional duties with sweeping assertions of secrecy and privilege," White House spokesman Tony Fratto condemned the subpoenas as an act of political partisanship and insisted that the surveillance program was "lawful," "limited," and protected American citizens from terrorist attacks.[88]

But a federal judge who used to preside on the FISA court said that while it was proper for executive branch agencies to conduct such surveillance, "we have found in the history of our country ... that you cannot trust the executive." Speaking at the Washington Convention Center in June 2007, Royce C. Lamberth, who was appointed to the federal bench by President Ronald Reagan and led the FISA court from 1995 to 2002, said that the "executive has to fight and win the war at all costs. But judges understand the war has to be fought, but it can't be at all costs." The country still has to preserve civil liberties, he said. Although the administration claimed that the warrant process was too cumbersome, Lamberth said the special FISA court met the challenge of reacting quickly to the September 11 events. At the time of the attacks, Lamberth was stuck in traffic near the Pentagon when one of the hijacked plans struck the building. With his car engulfed in smoke, Lamberth called on the assistance of federal marshals to get him into the District. By the time they reached him, "I had approved five FISA coverages [warrants] on my cell phone." Lamberth said that because of the national emergency, "We changed a number of FISA procedures, including approving warrants based on oral briefings by the head of the FBI."[89]

Nonetheless, the clash between the executive and legislative branches of government over the subpoenas raised the question whether the Judiciary Committee and the full Senate were poised to cite administration officials for criminal contempt, which could ignite a fierce battle over executive privilege and the constitutional separation of powers. Since 1975, Congress had cited ten senior executive branch officials for contempt for failing to produce subpoenaed documents.[90] But in each case, the executive branch had cut a deal with Congress before any criminal proceedings were pursued. In the immediate case, Congress seemingly had grounds for citing executive officials with criminal contempt if they failed to comply with its demands for information. The 1978 surveillance law made it a felony to conduct surveillance without a warrant, even though the president's legal team claimed that his wartime powers permitted him to bypass such laws at his discretion. Moreover, if Bush refused to negotiate and claimed privilege to avoid complying with the subpoenas, he could conceivably be charged with ordering a crime under the FISA statute. According to constitutional scholar Jonathan Turley, both Democrats and Republicans had not wanted to "recognize that this president may have ordered criminal offenses. But they may be on the road to do that, because the way Congress can get around the executive privilege in court is to say, 'we're investigating a potential crime.'"[91]

The showdown over the surveillance program intensified in July 2007, after a small group of Senate Democrats demanded the appointment of a special counsel to investigate whether Attorney General Gonzales committed perjury in his testimony about the domestic spying dispute that erupted in March 2004. In his sworn testimony before the panel in 2006 and 2007, Gonzales denied that the dispute involved the surveillance program, saying it centered on other intelligence activities. The testimony seemed to conflict with that of former Deputy Attorney General James Comey who revealed dramatic details of a threatened mass resignation of Justice Department officials over the legality of the surveillance program and a late-night confrontation at the bedside of ailing Attorney General John Ashcroft. In a separate development, Gonzales's testimony received another hit when FBI Director Robert Mueller III told the House Judiciary Committee that the March 2004 dispute involved the NSA's counterterrorist eavesdropping program, again seemingly contradicting the attorney general's statements that there were never any disagreements inside the Bush administration about the program.[92]

Congress Caves in to President's Surveillance Bill

As Congress and the White House squared off over the subpoenas—even working behind the scenes to resolve the dispute—in July 2007, the U.S. Circuit voted 2:1 to vacate Judge Taylor's decision. Representing the politics on the court, the two judges who made up the majority, both Republican appointees, did not rule on the spying program's legality. Instead, they declared that the plaintiffs had no standing to sue because they failed to demonstrate that they had been the targets of clandestine surveillance. The "plaintiffs do not—and because of the State Secrets Doctrine cannot—produce any evidence that any of their own communications have ever been intercepted by the NSA," the majority said. Despite the dissenting opinion of Judge Ronald Lee Gilman, the lone Democratic appointee, the ruling seemed indicative of the usual practice of the courts to resort to doctrines like standing in order to avoid intense political controversies.[93]

On July 17, 2007, the day before the deadline for responding to the subpoenas, Senate Judiciary Chairman Patrick Leahy granted an extension of time at the request of the White House counsel and the counsel to the vice president.[94] Soon after, the White House intensified efforts to update the surveillance law before the congressional recess in August. The push for change stemmed from a classified ruling earlier in the year by the special intelligence court, concluding that warrants were required for intercepting communications between two overseas locations that passed through routing stations in the United States.

Generally, the surveillance law placed no restrictions on foreign-to-foreign communications. But because much of that traffic passed through U.S. territory, the court charged with enforcing the 1978 surveillance law said that the government could not monitor these communications without a warrant.[95]

Under pressure from Bush, the House and Senate, racing to complete a final rush of legislation before its month-long break, approved changes to FISA, despite serious reservations from many Democrats about the scope of the executive branch's new surveillance powers. For months, Democrats refused to extend the administration new wiretapping powers until it turned over documents about the surveillance program. The White House refused to yield, however, even after Congress issued subpoenas for the information. While the administration and its Republican allies pushed for action to safeguard the country as intelligence officials spoke of "chatter" among al Qaeda suspects, Democrats who opposed the legislation accused the White House of fear mongering and political capitulation by fellow Democrats. Senator Russ Feingold, who served on the Intelligence Committee, gave the administration a backhanded compliment. The White House, he said, "has identified the one major remaining weakness in the Democratic Party, and that's its unwillingness to stand up to the administration when it's making a power grab regarding terrorism and national security." Representative Jane Harman, Democrat of California, said the administration "very skillfully played the fear card," adding that with the "chatter up in August, the issue of FISA reform got traction. Then they ran out the clock."[96]

The administration claimed that its spying program became seriously impaired after the FISA court required warrants to intercept foreign-to-foreign communications passing through telecommunication switches on American soil. When in April 2007 the administration proposed sweeping measures to modernize the surveillance law, it was treated as dead on arrival by the Democratic opposition, especially since it gave Attorney General Alberto Gonzales—discredited in the eyes of congressional Democrats—broadened oversight of the program. By mid-July, the administration's intelligence briefings by Mike McConnell, director of National Intelligence, on the intelligence gap together with the release of a National Intelligence estimate on terrorism prompted a series of talks between White House officials and Democratic congressional leaders. Congressional Democrats responded by trying to craft a narrow bill that would preserve court oversight—not so narrow as to demand that the security agency seek individual court warrants that would overly burden the spying program, but enough that would allow the court to review and approve agency procedures soon after the surveillance began. The administration, however, insisted on broad authority for the attorney general and the National

Intelligence director to approve surveillance, with the court relegated to merely certifying that no abuses occurred long after the eavesdropping occurred. As the talks intensified in the days before the congressional recess, what appeared to be a deal in the making collapsed after the two sides failed to reach agreement. With time running out, both the Senate and House approved the Republican bill without stronger court oversight.[97]

The new law went far beyond solving what the administration depicted as small technical issues relating mostly to monitoring foreign-to-foreign communications that were routed through the United States—a technological problem that did not exist when Congress passed the surveillance law in 1978. Instead of fixing that anomaly, the White House and its allies on Capitol Hill pressured Congress in the name of fighting terrorism into voting for changes that considerably expanded the legal limits of the government's ability to monitor millions of phone calls and e-mail messages going into and out of the country. The law allowed the NSA for the first time to conduct much of its surveillance without warrants. Previously, if the government was conducting surveillance inside the country, the government needed warrants approved by the FISA court to monitor telephone conversations, e-mail messages, and other electronic communications between individuals in the United States and overseas. The new law addressed the growing fraction of international communications passing through fiber optic cables and switching stations on American soil. By altering the legal definition of what constituted "electronic surveillance," the measure gave exclusive authority to the director of Intelligence and attorney general—executive branch officials—to approve eavesdropping without warrant, court supervision, or accountability as long as one of the people communicating was "reasonably believed" to be outside the country. These terms all but emasculated the FISA court, relegating it to merely reviewing the government's procedures in intercepting communications well after the fact. The law therefore went far beyond resolving the issue of intercepting foreign-to-foreign communications to potentially allowing the government to eavesdrop on millions of Americans calling or e-mailing internationally. Nonetheless, in a nod to the Fourth Amendment, the law still required warrants for intercepting purely domestic conversations between two Americans.[98]

The new surveillance law, which would remain in force for six months, also gave the director of Intelligence and the attorney general greater coercive powers to force telecommunications companies to cooperate with its surveillance operations. This provision met resistance from the telecommunications carriers, which were facing major lawsuits for having secretly cooperated with the NSA and which favored greater legal protections through court-approved warrants ordering them to comply. With the lawsuits pending, the administration lobbied to give legal immunity to the telecommunications companies.[99] Congress agreed to give immunity to the telecoms but refused to make it retroactive, keeping the lawsuits alive.

Despite the administration's political victory in winning approval for its surveillance bill, senior House Democrats pledged to create a more acceptable, permanent change in the FISA law that would provide for greater judicial oversight and protections for civil liberties. Typifying the sentiment among much of the House Democratic leadership, Speaker Nancy Pelosi said the measure did "violence to the Constitution of the United States."[100] Nevertheless, such words rang hollow as House and Senate Democrats, who proposed and quickly abandoned their own bills aimed at fixing the internet-age problem, could not escape accusations of caving in to another expansion of presidential power at the expense of one of the nation's key accountability laws that checked unrestrained executive discretion to spy on Americans. While the Republicans followed the president's lead, many of the sixteen Democrats in the Senate and forty-one in the House who voted for the bill said that they acted in the name of national security. But the spectacle left the *New York Times* "wondering what the Democrats—especially their feckless Senate leaders—plan to do with their majority in Congress if they are too scared of Republican campaign ads to use it to protect the Constitution and restrain an out-of-control president."[101] Moreover, despite Democratic promises to fix the law by restoring judicial oversight before it came up for renewal after six months, their wholesale retreat on the matter raised questions of whether they could ever face down accusations by the White House of being soft on terrorism. This question had significance since the new law gave the government vastly expanded powers to intercept, without judicial oversight, every communication going into and out of the country.

If nothing else, the measure with its six-month sunset provision promised a continuing clash between Congress and the White House regarding the parameters of the new surveillance law. The larger issue, however, involved the potential long-term consequences of unchecked domestic surveillance on civil liberties. In the 1970s, the Church Committee documented the long history of domestic spying abuses that culminated during the Nixon years. Congress enacted FISA to rein in the presidency after its enormous abuses of the nation's intelligence agencies. The 1978 surveillance law established a clear and explicit process of judicial oversight for domestic eavesdropping—a process that the Bush administration swept aside with claims that it infringed on the president's constitutional powers as commander in chief, that this inherent authority was supplemented by the enactment of the AUMF, and that national security demanded unchecked surveillance powers. Few, if any, questioned the necessity of tracking terrorist activity inside and outside the country, only that it be done within the law under judicial supervision to ensure fundamental constitutional protections. Benjamin Franklin gave prescient warning two centuries ago—"they that can give up essential liberty to obtain a little temporary safety deserve neither liberty nor safety."[102] Similarly, the majority Court in the *Hamdi* decision cautioned that it was in the most difficult times that the country's critical freedoms and liberties were most sorely tested, and "it is in those times that we must preserve our commitment at home to the principles for which we fight abroad."[103]

Epilogue

In early August 2006, the Senate passed sweeping bi-partisan legislation aimed at streamlining and increasing government transparency under the FOIA. Introduced by Senate Judiciary Committee Chairman Patrick Leahy and John Cornyn, a Republican member of the panel, the measure passed unanimously. The bill represented the first major strengthening of the FOIA in more than a decade and was expected to help reverse the troubling trends of excessive delays and evasion of compliance by government agencies. In drafting the measure, which was expected to pass the House, Leahy and Cornyn hoped to bolster the nation's key sunshine law by restoring meaningful deadlines for agency compliance under the FOIA, imposing real consequences on federal agencies for missing the law's twenty-day statutory deadline, and clarifying that the FOIA applies to government records held by outside private contractors. The bill also would establish a FOIA hotline service for all federal agencies and create a FOIA ombudsman to provide FOIA requestors and federal agencies with a meaningful alternative to costly litigation.[1]

While Leahy expected the president to sign the FOIA measure, the administration's obsession with secrecy took another turn. In late August, the administration claimed that the White House Office of Administration was not covered by the freedom of information law, even though the office had its own FOIA officer and responded to sixty-five requests in the previous year. The claim also contradicted the White House's own website—as of August 23, 2007—insisting that the office was covered by the FOIA. The administration's assertion came on the heels of Vice President Cheney's claim that he stood immune from the inspection and classification reporting requirements mandated by a presidential executive order. The fight to immunize the Office of

Administration from the FOIA pointed to the larger battle over access to an estimated 5 million e-mail messages that inexplicably vanished from White House computers. According to congressional investigators, the messages from the Office of Administration contained important evidence on the controversial firing of nine U.S. attorneys who apparently refused to use their positions to help Republicans win elections. "What exactly does the administration want to hide?" asked the *New York Times*. "It is hard to believe the administration's constant refrain that there is nothing to the prosecutor scandal when it is working so hard to avoid letting the facts about it get out."[2]

Soon after the administration made its arguments about the status of the Office of Administration to a federal judge, J. William Leonard, the federal government's chief classification authority, abruptly announced his resignation. The announcement aroused immediate suspicions that he was being ousted as director of the Information Security Oversight Office for challenging the vice president. Since becoming director of the ISOO in 2002, Leonard had developed a reputation for integrity as an official spokesman for a credible classification policy and an outspoken critic of classification practices. In 2006, he noted that few, if any, would deny that too much government information was being classified. "The integrity of the security classification program is essential to our nation's continued well-being," he said. These sentiments led him into a highly publicized clash with the vice president's office, which decided in 2003 to stop complying with ISOO's inspection and reporting requirements. The vice president's office claimed that it was exempt from classification oversight procedures under a presidential order on grounds that it was not an "entity within the executive branch." In 2006, Leonard twice urged Cheney's aide David Addington to reconsider the vice president's noncompliance, but was ignored. In January 2007, Leonard appealed to Attorney General Alberto Gonzales requesting his interpretation as to whether the vice president's office was subject to reporting on its classification activities. While the attorney general ignored his appeal, the episode turned the vice president and his extreme secrecy claims into an object of public ridicule. In retribution, the vice president tried to abolish the ISOO and to amend the presidential order to include a provision exempting the vice president's office from oversight; both recommendations, however, were rejected by an inter-agency group. Leonard's unexpected resignation invited speculation that the imbroglio with Cheney's office and the vice president's public humiliation played a role in his departure.[3]

On August 27, 2007, Attorney General Alberto Gonzales, whose tenure had been scarred by controversy and accusations of perjury before Congress, announced his resignation. Gonzales arrived in Washington as a loyal lawyer from Texas with an inspiring life story as the son of Mexican migrants, but no experience in the nation's capital. He derived his power almost exclusively from his relationship with the president who affectionately called him "Fredo." He departed bloodied after prolonged and withering criticism for his frequent misstatements and memory lapses in testimony before Congress. His testimony relating to the prosecutors' firings were often contradicted by his top aides and by documents. Moreover, his statements to Congress about the administration's warrantless domestic surveillance program also were undermined by numerous credible sources, including the testimony of Robert Mueller, the director of the FBI. While Vice President Dick Cheney and his top legal adviser, David Addington, comprised the intellectual force behind the administration's executive overreaching, Gonzales nevertheless shaped and articulated the public arguments for extending presidential powers in a time of war. His dogged defense of the president's wartime powers that often bypassed the laws of the land earned the growing enmity of those in and out of Congress on both sides of the aisle. In matters involving warrantless domestic spying, detention of suspects indefinitely as "enemy combatants," extreme interrogation methods, and defying congressional subpoenas, Gonzales came to be seen more as the president's legal retainer than an independent legal thinker upholding the Constitution. Gonzales's ouster was a "reflection that the Democrats are on the offensive and have more power than they used to," said Bush's former press secretary Ari Fleischer. "The president doesn't have a lot of armor left, and the fact that they were able to force him out is a chink in whatever armor he has left."[4]

Indeed, the Democrats' oversight offensive also extended to approving a bill to override Bush's executive order granting former presidents and vice presidents and their heirs the power to block indefinitely the release of their White House records under the Presidential Records Act. The measure overwhelmingly passed the House in March by a veto-proof 333:93 margin and cleared the Senate Homeland Security and Governmental Affairs Committee in June. In September 2007, however, White House secrecy took a new twist when Senator Jim Bunning, a Kentucky Republican, objected to floor consideration of the bill, temporarily putting a hold on a vote on the measure. The maneuver raised speculation that the administration had found a congressional agent to help torpedo the legislation. Senator Dianne Feinstein sought to push the legislation through under the Senate's unanimous consent rule that allows noncontroversial bills to be considered on an expedited basis. But her effort was blocked by Bunning, who did not state the reasons for his opposition to the bill on the floor. "This bill was offered in the spirit of the First Amendment and the principle of freedom of information upon which our nation was founded," stated Senator Joseph Lieberman. "I call on my colleagues to refrain from procedural roadblocks and allow the public access to the important historical records of their elected leaders." Nonetheless, the White House threatened to veto the bill if it passed Congress, claiming that it infringed on the president's rights of executive privilege. The veto threat posed a challenge to the newly elected Democratic Congress regarding whether it could marshal the votes to overturn the veto and uphold one of the nation's cornerstone open government statutes passed in the 1970s.[5]

As this procedural maneuvering played out on the Senate floor, a federal district court struck down part of Bush's executive decree on the presidential records law. The lawsuit against Bush's executive order was brought by Public Citizen on behalf of itself and several other academic and public interest groups. The executive order rewriting the presidential records law that allowed former presidents and vice presidents as well as their designated representatives, surviving family members, and even heirs to block the release of their presidential materials comprised a key element in the Bush-Cheney administration's broad secrecy initiatives. Since the president issued his executive order in November 2001, historians and other researchers had faced lengthy delays in obtaining the records of former Presidents Reagan and Bush, as well as their respective vice presidents because of the unlimited time the order permitted for "privilege reviews" by the office holders and their representatives. Judge Kollar-Kotelly, however, concluded that these significant delays violated the PRA's public access mandate and were not, as the government argued, required by the Constitution. The judge, however, did not rule on the other aspects of Bush's executive order, finding them "unripe" as no former president or vice president had yet exerted a unilateral veto power granted under the decree. The court victory, according to Public Citizen, indicated a "rejection of the government's unfounded constitutional theories of executive privilege" and sounded a "warning shot suggesting that the other provisions of the order are unlawful as well."[6]

The embattled White House also came under more aggressive investigation by the Committee on Oversight and Government Reform under the Chairman Representative Henry A. Waxman. The committee pressed its investigation on whether White House officials violated the presidential records law by using e-mail accounts maintained by the Republican National Committee and the Bush-Cheney 2004 campaign for official White House communications. The Presidential Records Act required the president to preserve and maintain records related to the activities, deliberations, decisions, and policies of his administration. But in what critics charged was an effort to skirt the law and the judgment of history itself, as well as more immediate congressional and media investigations, White House officials used their RNC e-mail accounts to avoid scrutiny and even had many of the e-mail records destroyed. Waxman's investigation found that the number of White House officials who were given RNC e-mail accounts was higher than previously disclosed. In March 2007, White House spokesperson Dana Perino said that only a "handful of officials" had RNC e-mail accounts. She later revised her estimate to fifty "over the course of the administration." The committee, however, learned from the RNC that at least eight White House officials were making extensive use of the RNC accounts, including Karl Rove, the president's senior adviser, Andrew Card, the former White House chief of staff, and many other officials in the Office of Political Affairs, the Office of Communications, and the Office of the Vice President. Moreover, the RNC preserved no e-mails for fifty-one of the eighty-eight officials who frequently used the alternative accounts. The RNC saved only 130 e-mails sent to Karl Rove during Bush's first administration and no e-mails sent by Rove prior to November 2003. "For many other White House officials," the committee found, "the RNC has no e-mails from before the fall of 2006."[7]

On August 24, 2007, the Bush-Cheney administration confirmed for the first time that American telecommunications companies played a central role in the NSA's domestic spying program after claiming for more than a year that any participation by them was a "state secret." The disclosure that the government had eavesdropped without warrants on thousands of telephone calls in which one party was outside the United States came in an unusual interview that National Intelligence Director Mike McConnell gave to the *El Paso Times*. Although the administration had long claimed that discussing publicly such intelligence issues would harm national security, McConnell made his remarks in an apparent effort to strengthen support for the recently broadened surveillance authority Congress had hastily approved before its August recess—even as Democrats threatened to revise the legislation for giving too much power to the executive branch. "Under the president's program, the terrorist surveillance program, the private sector had assisted us, because if you're going to get access, you've got to have a partner," McConnell said. He revealed this activity while praising Congress for giving the telecoms immunity from lawsuits or criminal sanctions if they continued to assist the NSA in its domestic spying program. It was also vital, he said, that Congress absolve the companies retroactively. AT&T and other major telecommunications firms were being sued over their role in allowing eavesdropping without warrants on overseas communications of Americans suspected of terrorist associations. "That would be a nice twofer," protested the *New York Times*, "protect a deep-pockets industry that may have broken the law, and cut off judicial scrutiny of Mr. Bush's decision to ignore FISA in the first place."[8]

After Congress reconvened following its summer recess, Bush said that the temporary surveillance law hurriedly passed in August must be made permanent and expanded. The measure, which Congress set to expire in six months, allowed the government to monitor, without court approved warrants, international communications between Americans and overseas contacts, as long as foreigners were the target of the eavesdropping. The legislation also gutted the judicial oversight of the federal intelligence surveillance court regarding the government's surveillance activities, leaving enormous discretion in the hands of the executive branch. If the law was not made permanent and expanded, Bush declared on a visit to the super-secret National Security Agency's headquarters in Fort Meade, Maryland, "Our national security professionals will lose critical tools they need to protect our country." Congress passed the temporary measure at the urgent request of the Bush-Cheney administration, which said that the modernization of communications technology had made FISA outdated and created a critical gap in the nation's terrorist surveillance capabilities. But civil liberties groups, Democrats, and others argued that the temporary changes granting the government the right to spy on American soil without court oversight went too far. In light of the administration's effort to expand presidential authority and eviscerate the original 1978 surveillance law that was passed to rein in unfettered executive power, Democrats aimed to change the law to provide additional oversight whenever the government eavesdropped on U.S. residents with overseas parties.[9]

The day before Bush pressed his case at the NSA's headquarters to expand the government's authority to eavesdrop without warrants, McConnell testified before Congress that the NSA had not conducted wiretapping without court orders on the telephones of any American since at least February 2007. The national intelligence director told the House Judiciary Committee that since he took office that month, the government had only conducted electronic surveillance with court approved warrants. In January, the administration had announced an agreement to permit the secret intelligence court to oversee the NSA's spying program and that it would adhere to the thirty-year-old surveillance law that regulated the government's domestic spying activities. Although McConnell's testimony was the first time that he publicly stated that the warrantless surveillance program had ended, he nevertheless argued for permanently expanding the surveillance powers granted under the temporary measure.[10]

The government's termination of the warrantless program and its more cautious approach stemmed from the thin Democratic victories in the November 2006 congressional elections. McConnell's testimony came as the Democratic-controlled Congress was gearing up for another legislative battle to revise the nation's key surveillance law to provide for more judicial oversight and to protect civil liberties. Congressional Democrats came to accept the concept of warrantless surveillance of international communications, but they argued for a stronger oversight role for the special intelligence court in reviewing the eavesdropping after it had been carried out to ensure the adequate protection of Americans' privacy rights.[11]

But in October 2007, two months after promising that they would roll back the expansive surveillance powers granted to the administration under the temporary measure, congressional Democrats appeared to be ready to compromise. Nervous at being tagged soft on terrorism if they insisted on strict curbs on gathering intelligence, they proposed a bill in the House that would keep some of the expansive eavesdropping authority that the administration won in August for six months. The bill, proposed by Democratic leader of the House Intelligence and Judiciary Committees, would impose quarterly audits by the Justice Department inspector general, empower the foreign intelligence court to grant one-year "umbrella" warrants in advance for intercepting overseas communications, and require the administration to disclose details of the program. It would not, however, give retroactive legal immunity to the telecommunications companies that participated in the surveillance program—a top priority of the administration.[12]

Glossary

AUMF (Authorization to Use Military Force): Congress passed the AUMF as an emergency measure seven days after the September 11, 2001, attacks on the United States by the al Qaeda terrorist group. The emergency measure authorized the president to "use all necessary and appropriate force against those nations, organizations, or persons he determines planned, authorized, committed, or aided the terrorist attacks of September 11, 2001 ... in order to prevent any future acts of international terrorism against the United States."

Executive Order 12667: This order was issued by President Ronald Reagan shortly before leaving office, the executive order set the procedures for asserting executive privilege by former and incumbent presidents against disclosure of presidential materials under the Presidential Records Act. It created a notification process that required the U.S. archivist to give former and incumbent presidents thirty days' notice before releasing an ex-president's records. The order also required the archivist to inform the former and sitting presidents of any records that raised a substantial question of executive privilege. After thirty days, the archivist could release the records unless the incumbent or former president claimed privilege, or unless the incumbent instructed the archivist to extend the review period. In addition, the order allowed a former president to go to the courts if the archivist denied his privilege claim.

Executive Order 12958: This order was issued in 1995 by President Bill Clinton to address over-classification problems, the executive order called for the declassification of documents after twenty-five years unless disclosure would harm national security, assist in the development of weapons of mass destruction, or identify confidential informants.

Executive Order 13233: This order was issued by President George W. Bush on November 1, 2001, the controversial executive order erected new barriers to obtaining access to former presidents' White House materials under the 1978 Presidential Records Act. The order authorized former presidents and vice presidents, their designated representatives or surviving family members and heirs to withhold materials in seeming perpetuity by asserting executive privilege. The order required that a "specific need" for information be demonstrated; placed the burden on the person requesting materials to bring a lawsuit in order to challenge a denial of access; expanded the types of records exempt from disclosure; and relieved the U.S. archivist of affirmative responsibilities under the presidential records law to carry out the systematic release of presidential records to the public. The order provided a double veto over disclosure. Only when both the former president and incumbent president authorized access could the U.S. archivist release an ex-president's materials to the public.

FACA (Federal Advisory Committee Act): This act was passed in 1972 to curb the domination of government advisory groups by special interests and their unaccountable influence over public policy. Under the statute, presidential and other federal advisory committees that include nongovernmental participants must publicly announce their meetings, hold their meetings in public, take minutes of meetings, and allow for differing views to be represented. The law also allows for public access to minutes and other records, reports, and transcripts, but exempts open access to information that is classified or deals with national security.

FISA (Federal Intelligence Surveillance Act): Congress passed FISA as a result of the intelligence-gathering abuses of the administration of Richard M. Nixon when the National Security Agency and the Federal Bureau of Investigation spied on civil rights and anti–Vietnam War activists. Following extensive hearings on these abuses, in 1978 Congress passed FISA, which required the NSA and FBI to obtain a warrant any time they sought to monitor communications inside the country. Before doing so, the law required that the intelligence agencies establish probable cause that the target of electronic surveillance was a foreign power or agent of a foreign power. The law also established the FISA court, a secret panel that could grant government authority to wiretap Americans after a showing of probable cause. In passing the statute, Congress aimed to limit any claim of inherent presidential authority and provided that FISA serve as the "exclusive means" by which surveillance could be carried out on American soil.

FOIA (Freedom of Information Act): This act was signed into law by President Lyndon B. Johnson in 1966 to make government information publicly available. The nation's cornerstone sunshine law granted citizens the right to access all federal government information limited only by nine exemptions governing national security, private commercial or trade secrets, law enforcement, personal privacy, and other matters. In 1974, Congress overrode a veto by President Gerald Ford to strengthen the law, adding important provisions speeding up responses, providing for judicial review, reducing fees, and allowing the courts to review in camera classified information to determine whether it was being properly withheld under the law's nine exemptions.

GAO (General Accountability Office): Initially created in 1921, Congress expanded the GAO's responsibilities from traditional finance and accounting activities to assessments of the effectiveness of executive agencies. Through a series of legislative measures from the 1940 to the 1980s, the agency was empowered to launch investigations or evaluations on its own initiative or at the request of a congressional committee, subcommittee, or member of Congress. In 1980, Congress granted the agency the authority to sue the executive branch to compel the disclosure of documents in cases in which it refused to comply with requests for information. The law also allowed the comptroller general—the head of the GAO—to pursue court actions against the president and his principal advisers and assistants, and against those units within the Executive Office of the President whose sole function was to advise and assist the president, for information that would not be available under the Freedom of Information Act.

Homeland Security Act of 2002: Signed into law on November 25, 2002, by President George W. Bush, the act folded 170,000 employees from twenty-two agencies into a new cabinet-level super-agency charged with defending the nation against terrorism. The massive government reorganization to defend the country stemmed from the terrorist attacks on New York and Washington on September 11, 2001.

ISOO (Information Security Oversight Office): Established by President Jimmy Carter in 1978 under Executive Order 12065, "National Security Information," the ISOO operates within the National Archives and Records Administration and is responsible to the president for policy and oversight of the government-wide security classification program. It now derives its authority from Executive Orders 12958, "Classified National Security Information," and 12829, "National Industrial Security Program," as amended.

PRA (Presidential Records Act): Passed in 1978 following the constitutional struggle surrounding access to President Richard M. Nixon's tapes and records for the Watergate investigations and trials, this law overturned the long-running tradition of private ownership of presidential records that dated to the beginning of the Republic by declaring that after

January 20, 1981, the records of all presidents and vice presidents would be the property of the American people. The law allowed citizens to review all materials, including confidential communications with advisers, twelve years after a president leaves office. The act also assured that the most sensitive records relating to national security, foreign relations, financial and trade secrets, and personal privacy were exempt from disclosure.

Notes

Introduction

1. Letter from James Madison to W. T. Barry, August 4, 1822, in *Complete James Madison* (Harper and Brothers, 1953).

2. David Banisar, "Government Secrecy: Decisions without Democracy" (July 2007), OpenTheGovernment.org.

3. Arthur Schlesinger, Jr., quoted in Ibid.

4. Ibid.

5. John Adams, "A Dissertation on the Canon and Feudal Law" (1765), available at http://teachingamericanhistory.org/library/index.asp?document=43.

6. Patrick Henry, "The Debates in the Convention of the Commonwealth of Virginia, on the Adoption of the Federal Constitution" (June 9, 1788).

Chapter 1

1. Patrick Leahy and John Cornyn, "Democrat, Republican Senators Work Together to Reform FOIA," *Quill* 94, no. 7 (September 2006): 4.

2. See FOIA, 5 U.S.C. Section 552 (b). The statute's nine exemptions include (1) classified information; (2) internal agency personnel rules and practices; (3) information specifically exempted from disclosure by statute; (4) private commercial and trade secret information; (5) interagency or intra-agency privilege communications; (6) personnel, medical, or similar files, the disclosure of which would constitute a clearly unwarranted invasion of personal privacy; (7) information compiled for law enforcement purposes; (8) information relating to reports for or by an agency involved in regulating financial institutions; and (9) geological information concerning oil wells.

3. William Safire, "Free Speech v. Scalia," *New York Times*, April 29, 1985.

4. Office of the White House Press Secretary, *Statement by the President Upon Signing S. 1160*, July 4, 1966.

5. See "Bill Moyers on the Freedom of Information Act," *NOW* (April 5, 2002), at http://www.pbs.org/now/commentary/moyers4.html.

6. See Cong. Rec., House, "Freedom of Information Act—Veto Message from the President of the United States" (H. Doc. No. 93-383), 93rd Cong., 2d sess., November 18, 1974, 36243.

7. See Warren Weaver, "U.S. Information Act: Difficulties Despite Successes," *New York Times*, August 8, 1977; "Public Access to FBI Files Called Informer Deterrent," *New York Times*, November 10, 1977; "CIA Aide Deplores Data-Release Law," *New York Times*, April 6, 1979; Allen Weinstein, "Open Season on Open Government," *New York Times*, June 10, 1979; and Editorial, "Too Much Freedom of Information?" *New York Times*, June 29, 1979.

8. See "A Memorandum for the Executive Departments and Agencies Concerning the Law Enforcement Amendments to the Freedom of Information Act, 5 U.S.C. Sec.552, Enacted as the Freedom of Information Reform Act of 1986, Sections 1801–1804 of the Anti-Drug Abuse Act of 1986, 100 stat. 3207-48" (October 27, 1986), at http://www.usdoj.gov/04foia/86agmemo.htm. Also see Howell Raines, "Reagan Order Tightens the Rules on Disclosing Secret Information," *New York Times*, April 3, 1982.

9. See Senator Daniel Patrick Moynihan, "Report of the Commission on Protecting and Reducing Government Secrecy" (Moynihan Commission), 1997.

10. Quoted in David Westphal, "Bush Proclaims Belief in Open Government," *Sacramento Bee*, April 15, 2005.

11. See Kenneth Jost, "Government Secrecy," CQ Online (December 2, 2005), at http://library.cqpress.com/cqresearcher/php?id=cqresrre20; and "Report of the Commission on Protecting and Reducing Government Secrecy," Senate Document 105-2, Pub. L. 236, 103rd Cong., Washington, DC: U.S. Government Printing Office, 1997, xxi.

12. Allison Mitchell, "Cheney Rejects Access to Terror Brief," *New York Times*, May 20, 2002.

13. Ibid.

14. Editorial, "Mr. Cheney's Imperial Presidency," *New York Times*, December 23, 2005; and James Tranto, "The Weekend Interview with Dick Cheney: A Strong Executive," *Wall Street Journal*, January 28, 2006.

15. Charlie Savage, "Hail to the Chief—Dick Cheney's Mission to Expand or Restore the Powers of the Presidency," *Boston Globe*, November 26, 2006; and James Crawley, "Lordy, Lordy, Look Who's 40," *Richmond Times-Dispatch*, July 2, 2006.

16. See Cong. Rec., House, Proceedings and Debates of the 93rd Cong., 2d sess., November 19, 1974, 36593; Cong. Rec., House, Proceedings of the 93rd Cong., 2d sess., November 20, 1974, 36624; and Cong. Rec., Senate, Proceedings and Debates of the 93rd Cong., 2d sess., November 21, 1974, 36865. The biggest complaints about the 1974 amendments came from the national defense, law

enforcement, and intelligence communities, as well as private corporations, which criticized the law for fostering industrial espionage. See Weaver, "U.S. Information Act"; Allen Weinstein, "Open Season on Open Government"; Deirdre Carmody, "Measures to Shield U.S. Data Criticized," *New York Times*, May 4, 1980; and Richard Hallor, "Pentagon Aide Sees Information Act Abuses," *New York Times*, July 19, 1981.

17. Savage, "Hail to the Chief—Dick Cheney's Mission to Expand or Restore the Powers of the Presidency"; and Crawley, "Lordy, Lordy, Look Who's 40."

18. Adam Clymer, "Government Openness at Issue as Bush Holds on to Records," *New York Times*, January 3, 2003; and Alison Leigh Cowan, "Battling over Records of Bush's Governorship," *New York Times*, February 11, 2002.

19. See Bruce P. Montgomery, "Congressional Oversight: Vice President Richard B. Cheney's Executive Branch Triumph," *Political Science Quarterly* 120, no. 4 (Winter 2005–2006): 581–618.

20. See Pub. L. No. 95-591, 92 Stat. 2523 (1978) (codified as amended at 44 U.S.C. 2201 et seq). Bush Executive Order No. 13233 may be seen at the Public Citizen Litigation Group website at http://www.citizen.org/litigation/briefs/FOIAGOVSEC/articles.cfm?=ID=7116.

21. Finlay Lewis, "White House Secrecy Stance Stirs Debate," *San Diego Union-Tribune*, December 5, 2002; and The Judicial Watch 2002, "'State of the Union' Report: A Failure of Leadership," February 1, 2002, available at http://www.judicialwatch.org/archive/ois/specials/bushenforce.htm.

22. Ellen Nakashima, "Bush View of Secrecy Is Stirring Frustration," *Washington Post,* March 3, 2002; and Clymer, "Government Openness at Issue."

23. See Memorandum from John Ashcroft, Attorney General, to Heads of all Federal Departments and Agencies, October 12, 2001, available at http://www.usdoj.gov/oip/foiapost/2001foiapost19.htm.

24. Letter to the Editor, "What Our Government Is Hiding," *Washington Post*, December 6, 2002.

25. Memorandum from Janet Reno, Attorney General, for Heads of Departments and Agencies, The Freedom of Information Act, October 4, 1993. Reno's memorandum stated that "it shall be the policy of the Department of Justice to defend the assertion of a FOIA exemption only in those cases where the agency reasonably foresees that disclosure would be harmful to an interest protected by that exemption. Where an item of information might technically or arguably fall within an exemption, it ought not to be withheld from a FOIA requester unless it need be. It is my belief that this change in policy serves the public interest by achieving the Act's primary objective—maximum responsible disclosure of government information—while preserving essential confidentiality. Accordingly, I strongly encourage your FOIA officers to make 'discretionary disclosures' whenever possible under the Act."

26. See Philip Taubman, "Supporters of Disclosure Act See Threat in U.S. Shift on Lawsuits," *New York Times*, May 5, 1981. The procedural change made by

Smith reversed the policy of Attorney General Griffin B. Bell in 1977 that agencies seeking to withhold requested information must show that disclosure would be "demonstrably harmful" to the government. Bell's directive aimed to encourage disclosure and reduce the number of lawsuits that were being filed when agencies denied information requests.

27. Editorial, "Critics Say the New Rule Limits Access to Records," *New York Times*, February 27, 2002; and Editorial, "The Day Ashcroft Censored Freedom of Information," *San Francisco Chronicle*, January 6, 2002.

28. Memorandum from Andrew Card, Assistant to the President and Chief of Staff, to Heads of Executive Departments and Agencies re: Action to Safeguard Information Regarding Weapons of Mass Destruction and Other Sensitive Documents Related to Homeland Security (March 19, 2002), available at http://www.usdoj.gov/oip/foiapost/2002foiapost10.htm.

29. Memorandum from Laura L. S. Kimberly, Acting Director, Information Security Oversight Office, to Departments and Agencies re: Safeguarding Information Regarding Weapons of Mass Destruction and Other Sensitive Records Related to Homeland Security, March 19, 2002, available at http://www.usdoj.gov/oip/foiapost/2002foiapost10.htm.

30. Keith Anderson, "Is There Still a Sound Legal Basis?: The Freedom of Information Act in the Post-9/11 World," *Ohio State Law Journal*, 64 (2003): 1627–28.

31. See *A Citizen's Guide on Using the Freedom of Information Act and the Privacy Act of 1974 to Request Government Records*, H. Rep., 107-371, 107th Cong., 2d sess., 2002; and Reporters Committee for Freedom of the Press, *Homefront Confidential: Freedom of Information,* 2005, available at http://www.rcfp.org/homefrotconfidential/foi.html.

32. Reporters Committee for Freedom of the Press, *Homefront Confidential: Freedom of Information,* 2005, available at http://www.rcfp.org/homefrotconfidential/foi.html.

33. See U.S. General Accounting Office, Report to the Ranking Minority Member, Committee on the Judiciary, U.S. Senate, "Freedom of Information Act: Agency Views on Changes Resulting from New Administration Policy," September 2003.

34. National Security Archive, "The Ashcroft Memo: Drastic Change Or More Thunder Than Lightning," Freedom of Information Act Audit, March 14, 2003, available at http://www.gwu.cdu/~nsarchiv/NSAEBB/NSAEBB84/execsum.htm; and OMB Watch, "GAO Report Indicates Less FOIA Information Under Ashcroft," September 22, 2003, available at http://www.ombwatch.org/article/1821/-1/233.

35. Clymer, "Government Openness at Issue."

36. James V. Grimaldi and Guy Gugliotta, "Chemical Plants Are Feared as Targets," *Washington Post*, December 16, 2001; Pew Internet & American Life Project, "One Year Later: September 11 and the Internet" (2002), available at http://www.pewinternet.org/reports/pdfs/PIP_9-11_Report.pdf; and Reporters Committee for Freedom of the Press, "Homefront Confidential" (2005), available at http://www.rcfp.org/homefrontconfidential/foi.html.

37. See The Electronic FOIA Amendments of 1996 (E-FOIA), Pub. L. No. 104-231, 110 Stat. 3048.

38. White House, Office of the Press Secretary, Statement by the President upon Signing the EFOIA, October 2, 1996.

39. See Homeland Security Efforts: Hearing Before the House Comm. on Science, 107th Cong., 32 (2002) (statement of James K. Kallstrom, Special Adviser to Governor Pataki on Counter-Terrorism; Grimaldi and Gugliotta, "Chemical Plants Are Feared as Targets"; and Neil King Jr. and Alan Cullison, "Al Qaeda Papers Show Efforts to Acquire Weapons," *Wall Street Journal*, November 19, 2001.

40. Anthony Loyd, "Al-Qaeda Tested Terror Weapons: Preliminary Experiments Were Done on Animals," *Ottawa Citizen*, December 29, 2001.

41. See Richard Clarke, Keynote Address: "Threats to U.S. National Security: Proposed Partnership Initiatives Toward Preventing Cyber Terrorist Attacks," *DePaul Business Law Journal,* 33, 35 (1999); Kristen Elizabeth Uhl, "The Freedom of Information Act Post-9/11: Balancing the Public's Right to Know, Critical Infrastructure Protection, and Homeland Security," *American Law Review* 53 (2003–2004): 283–84, notes 126, 132; Jay Lyman, "Worries Mount over Terrorist Cyber Assault," *NewsFactor Network*, June 27, 2002.

42. William J. Boyd, "U.S. Is Tightening Rules on Keeping Scientific Secrets," *New York Times*, February 17, 2002.

43. White House, Office of the Press Secretary, Address to a Joint Session of Congress and the American People, September 20, 2001, available at http://www.whitehouse.gov/news/releases/2001/09/200110920-8.

44. Press Release, White House, Executive Order Establishing Office of Homeland Security (October 8, 2001) (establishing the Office of Homeland Security and the Homeland Security Council), available at http://www.whitehouse.gov/news/releases/2001/10/20011008-1.html.

45. The Critical Infrastructure Information Security Act of 2001, S. 1456; and Reporters Committee for Freedom of the Press, "Homefront Confidential" (2005), available at http://rcfp.org/homefrontconfidential/foi.html.

46. Press release, Senate Committee on Governmental Affairs, "Lieberman, Specter Offer Homeland Defense Legislation" (October 11, 2001), available at http://www.senate.gov/~gov_affairs/ 101101homedefpress.htm.

47. See National Commission on Terrorist Attacks upon the United States, *The 9/11 Commission Report: Final Report of the National Commission on Terrorist Attacks upon the United States* (July 22, 2004); and Kenneth Jost, "Re-examining 9/11," *CQ Researcher* (June 4, 2004): 493–516.

48. See Office of Homeland Security, "National Strategy for Homeland Security" (July 2002), available at http://www.whitehouse.gov/homeland/book/nat_strat_hls.pdf.

49. See A Legislative Proposal to Create a New Cabinet Department of Homeland Security, H. Doc. 107-227 (June 18, 2002). Also see OMB Watch, "Bush Seeks FOIA Exemption in Homeland Security Bill" (June 19, 2002), available at http://www.ombwatch.org/articleview/844/1/233; and Michael Isikoff and Daniel

Klaidman, "Executive: Why the White House Said Yes to a 9-11 Inquiry," *Newsweek* (September 30, 2002): 6.

50. Alison Mitchell, "Limits Sought on Access to Company Data," *New York Times*, November 28, 2001.

51. A Legislative Proposal to Create a New Cabinet Department of Homeland Security, H. Doc. 107-227 (June 18, 2002); and Mitchell, "Limits Sought on Access to Company Data."

52. See Securing Our Infrastructure: Private/Public Information Sharing: Hearing before the Senate Committee on Government Affairs, Senate, 107th Cong., 2002, 97-103; USA Patriot Act of 2001, Pub. L. No. 107-56, Stat. 272, 2001; and Homeland Security Act of 2002, H.R. 5005, 107th Cong. 2(4), 2002.

53. H.R. Rep. No. 107-609, 2002, 220; and Uhl, "The Freedom of Information Act Post-9/11," 294, note 190.

54. Homeland Security Act of 2002, H.R. 5005, 107th Cong. 214(a)(1) (2002).

55. Paul McMasters, "We Have Enough Secrecy," *Cincinnati Post*, September 17, 2002.

56. See 5 U.S.C. 552 (b) (1)-(9) (2002); and Reporters Committee for Freedom of the Press, "Homefront Confidential," 2005.

57. See Amendment to Scale Back FOIA Exemption for Homeland Security Department (July 25, 2002), available at http://www.fas.org/sgp/news/2002/07/leahy-foia.html.

58. See Statement of Senator Patrick Leahy on Introduction of The Restoration of the Freedom of Information Act (March 12, 2003), available at http://www/leahy.senate.gov/press/200303/031203e.html. Leahy's statement said that "Senator Bennett stated in the [Senate Governmental Affairs] Committee's July 25, 2002 mark up that the Administration had endorsed the compromise. He also said that industry groups had reported to him that the compromise language would make it possible for them to share information with the government without fear of the information being released to competitors or to other agencies that might accidentally reveal it."

59. Tamara Lytle, "Secrecy Provisions in Homeland Security Department Draws Scrutiny," Knight-Ridder Tribune News Service, November 14, 2002.

60. Darren Samuelsohn, "Senate in Home Stretch on Cabinet-level Bill with FOIA Exemption," *Environment & Energy Daily* (November 18, 2002), available at Westlaw, 11/13/02 EEP-EED art.2.

61. Mark Tapscott, "Too Many Secrets," *Washington Post*, November 20, 2002.

62. James Kuhnhenn and Drew Brown, "Legislation Would Make It Easier for Agencies to Snoop, While Permitting Greater Government Secrecy," Knight-Ridder Tribune Service, November 21, 2002.

63. Editorial, "Secrecy, Bureaucracy May Be a Poor Mix in New Superagency," *Yakima Herald-Republic* (Yakima, Washington), November 21, 2002. The FOIA

exemptions and criminal penalties for disclosing information were contained in a subsection of the Homeland Security Act, entitled the "Critical Infrastructure Act of 2002" (CIIA). See Homeland Security Act of 2002, H.R. 5005, 107th Cong. 214 (a)(1) (2002).

64. See Homeland Security Act of 2002, H.R. 5005, 107th Cong. 214 (a)(1) (2002); also see Statement by U.S. Senator Patrick Leahy, "On Introduction of the Restoration of Freedom of Information Act" ("Restore FOIA") (March 12, 2003), available at http://leahy.senate.gov/press/200303/021203e.html; and John W. Dean, FindLaw Forum: "Tom Ridge's Appearance Before Congress Is Another Nixon-Style Move by the Bush Administration" (April 12, 2002), available at http://www.cnn.com/2002/LAW/04/columns/fl.dean.ridge.04.12.

65. Christina E. Wells, "National Security Information and the Freedom of Information Act," *Administrative Law Review* (2004): 1195, 1214.

66. White House, Office of the Press Secretary, Homeland Security Act of 2002 Signing Statement, November 25, 2002; Douglas Turner, "Bush Draws Veil of Secrecy Around Government's Files," *Buffalo News*, December 2, 2002.

67. See Charlie Savage, "Cheney Aide Is Screening Legislation: Advisor Seeks to Protect Bush Power," *Boston Globe*, May 28, 2006. According to Savage, the leading architect of the signing statements was David Addington, Cheney's legal adviser and chief of staff. "The statements assert the president's right to ignore the laws because they conflict with his interpretation of the Constitution."

68. S. 609, 108th Cong. (2003).

69. Statement of Senator Patrick Leahy on Introduction of the Restoration of Freedom of Information Act (March 12, 2003), available at http://leahy.senate.gov/press/200303/031203e.html.

70. Kenneth Jost, "Government Secrecy," *CQ Researcher* (December 2, 2005), available at http://library.cqpress.com/cqresearcher/document.php?id=cqresrre20.

71. See letter from Henry A. Waxman, Ranking Minority Member of House Committee on Government Reform, to Christopher Shays, chairman of the Subcommittee on National Security, Emerging Threats, and International Relations of the Committee on Government Reform (March 1, 2005); and OpenTheGovernment.org, "Secrecy Report Card 2006," available at http://www.openthegovernment.org.

72. Society of Environmental Journalists, "SEJ urges Homeland Security Dept. to Limit NEPA Secrecy Proposal," July 14, 2004, available at http://www.sej.org/foia/fallout.htm#111802; Society of Environmental Journalists, "SEJ Opposes EPA's Proposal to Limit TRI Toxic Collection" (January 13, 2006), available at http://www.sej.org.foia/fallout.htm#111802; Society of Environmental Journalists, "SEJ Opposes Wastewater Security Bill's Secrecy Provisions" (May 22, 2006), available at http://www.sej.org/foia.htm#111802; and OMB Watch, "Defense Department Seeks New FOIA Exemption" (May 22, 2005), available at http://www.ombwatch.org/article/2822/1/233?TopicID=1. Also see Christopher H. Schmitt and Edward T. Pound, "Keeping Secrets" (December 13, 2003), available at http://wwwusnews.com.

73. Society of Environmental Journalists, "SEJ Opposes Rider with New FOIA Exemption for Satellite Data and Studies on Earth Sciences" (September 10, 2004), available at http://www.sej.org/foia/fallout.htm#111802; and Waxman Report, "Secrecy in the Bush Administration," 12.

74. OMB Watch, "Defense Department Seeks New FOIA Exemption" (May 2, 2005), available at http://www.ombwatch.org/article/2822/1/233?TopicID=1; and National Security Archive, "DIA Versus the Facts, What DIA Told the U.S. Congress to Get a Freedom of Act Exemption for DIA Operational Files," available at http://www.gwu.edu~nsarchiv/nsaebb/nsaebb34/facts.html.

75. OMB Watch, "Terrorism Information Sharing Faces Several Hurdles" (December 5, 2006), available at http://ombwatch.org/article/3658/1/1?TopicID=1.

76. Eric Lichtblau and Adam Litak, "On Terror, Spying and Guns, Ashcroft Expands Reach," *New York Times*, March 15, 2003.

77. Society of Environmental Journalists, "SEJ Letter Re: Withdrawal of Web Access to Congressional Research Service Reports" (November 12, 2003), available at http://www.sej.org/foia/fallout.htm#111802.

78. SEJ, "SEJ Joins News Media in Challenging Homeland Security Maritime Secrecy" (July 16, 2004), available at http://www.sej.org.foia/fallout.htm#111802.

79. SEJ, "SEJ Urges OMB to Withdraw Peer Review Proposal" (May 14, 2004), available at http://www.sej.org.foia/fallout.htm#111802.

80. Clymer, "Government Openness at Issue."

81. U.S. House of Rep., Committee on Government Reform—Minority Staff Special Investigation Division, "Secrecy in the Bush Administration," Prepared for Rep. Henry A. Waxman (hereafter Waxman Report), September 14, 2004, 11–12.

82. Society of Environmental Journalists, "SEJ Speaks on Freedom of Information" (November 15, 2006), available at http://www.sej.org/foia/fallout.htm#111802; and Waxman Report, "Secrecy in the Bush Administration," 14–15.

83. See S. 3678, "A Bill to Amend the Public Health Service Act with Respect to Health Security and All-Hazards Preparedness and Response, and for Other Purposes," Public Law No. 109-417; Mark Tapscott, "New Anti-Disease Agency Would be Exempt from FOIA," Knight Ridder/Tribune Service, November 10, 2005, available at http://www.mctdirect.com/public/FOI-nov-1—2005.htm; OMB Watch, "A New Ultra-Secret Government Agency" (November 29, 2005), available at http://www.ombwatch.org/article/3195/-1%7Bcategory_; and OMB Watch, "Secretive Biodefense Legislation Moves Forward" (September 26, 2006), available at http://www.ombwatch.org/article/3598/1/1?TopicID=1; and Associated Press, "FOI Advocates Troubled by Bill Cloaking Federal Agency," December 4, 2005, available at http://www.firstamendmentcenter.org/news.aspx?id=16135.

84. See Christopher Lee, "Cold War Data Made Secret Again," *Washington Post*, August 21, 2006; and Editorial, "A Fixation with Secrecy," *New York Times*, August 26, 2006.

85. Associated Press, "Defense Dept. to Fund University Study on Altering the FOIA," July 8, 2006, available at http://www.firstamendmentcenter.org/news.aspx?id=17125; and Associated Press, "Terrorism Study Still Worries Open-Records

Advocates," September 9, 2006, available at http://www.firstamendmentcenter.org/news.aspx?id=17433.

86. Waxman Report, "Secrecy in the Bush Administration," 12–14.

87. Sidney Blumenthal, "Comment & Debate: Cheney's Vice-like Grip: Bush Has Granted His Deputy the Greatest Expansion of Powers in American History," *The Guardian,* February 24, 2006; see also OMB Watch, "Vice President Refuses to Disclose Classification Data" (June 13, 2006), available at http://www.ombwatch.org/article/3468/1/233?TopicID=1.

88. See White House, Office of the Press Secretary, Executive Order No. 13292, "Further Amendment to the Executive Order 12958, As Amended, Classified National Security Information" (March 25, 2003), available at http://www.fas.org/sgp/bush/eoamend.html; and Jane E. Kirtley, "Transparency and Accountability in a Time of Terror: The Bush Administration's Assault on Freedom of Information," *Communications Law and Policy,* 11 (2006): 502–3.

89. See Mark Silva, "Cheney Keeps Classification Activity Secret," *Chicago Tribune* (May 27, 2006), available at http://www.chicagotribune.com/news/nationworld/chi-0605270039may27,1,1588921.story; and Letter from Steven Aftergood, Director, Project on Government Secrecy, Federation of American Scientists to William Leonard, Director, Information Security Oversight Office (May 30, 2006), available at http://www.fas.org.

90. Mark Silva, "Cheney Keeps Classification Activity Secret"; and Letter from Steven Aftergood to William Leonard.

91. See Letter from William J. Leonard, Director of Information Security Oversight Office, to David S. Addington, Assistant to the President and Chief of Staff to the Vice President, June 8, 2006; Letter from William J. Leonard, Director of Information Security Oversight Office, to David S. Addington, Assistant to the President and Chief of Staff to the Vice President, August 23, 2006; Letter from William J. Leonard, Director of Information Security Oversight Office, to Alberto Gonzales, Attorney General, January 9, 2007; and *Secrecy News,* "ISOO Asks Attorney General to Rule on Cheney's Role," 2007, no. 14 (February 6, 2007), available at http://www.fas.org/blog/secrecy.

92. Peter Baker, "Cheney's Defiance in Archives Dispute Reveals Wider Battle," *Washington Post,* June 22, 2007; Scott Shane, "Agency Is Target in Cheney Fight on Secrecy Data," June 22, 2007; Barton Gellman and Jo Becker, "A Different Understanding with the President," *Washington Post,* June 24, 2007; and Jim Rutenberg, "White House Drops Vice President's Dual-Role Argument as Moot," *New York Times,* June 27, 2007.

93. Vanessa Blum, "Administration Won One FOIA Fight, but Battle Is Far from Over," *The Recorder,* December 16, 2002.

94. *Center for National Security Studies v. U.S. Department of Justice,* 215 F.Supp.2d 94 (D.C.C. 2002).

95. See Reporters Committee for Freedom of the Press, "Homefront Confidential," 2005; and *Center for National Security Studies v. U.S. Department of Justice,* 215 Supp.2d 94 (D.C.C. 2002).

96. *Center for National Security Studies v. United States Department of Justice*, 215 F.Supp.2d (D.C.C. 2002), 102; and Reporters Committee for Freedom of the Press, "Homefront Confidential," 2005.

97. *Center for National Security Studies v. United States Department of Justice*, 331 F.3d (D.C.C. 2003), 926–28.

98. Ibid., 940.

99. Keith Anderson, "Is There a Sound Legal Basis?: The Freedom of Information Act in the Post-9/11 World," *Ohio State Law Journal*, 64 (2003): 1639; and OMB Watch, "Secrecy Wins In Court" (June 20, 2003), available at http://www.ombwatch.org/article/1608/-1/233.

100. See Steve Fairnaru, "Court Says Detainees' ID Can Be Kept Secret," *Washington Post*, June 18, 2003.

101. See *ACLU v. Hudson County*; and Reporters Committee for Freedom of the Press, "Homefront Confidential," 2005.

102. Julia Preston, "Judge Orders U.S. to Release Files on Abu Ghraib," *New York Times*, September 16, 2004.

103. Julia Preston, "ACLU Gains in Its Quest for CIA Documents on Detainees," *New York Times*, February 3, 2005; Editorial, "The Costly Right to Know," *New York Times*, February 2, 2005.

104. Kate Zernike, "Government Defies an Order to Release Iraq Abuse Photos," *New York Times*, July 23, 2005.

105. Ibid.

106. Julia Preston, "Judge Says U.S. Must Release Prison Photos," *New York Times*, May 27, 2005.

107. Julie Preston, "Officials See Risk in the Release of Photos and Videotapes of Iraqi Prisoner Abuse," *New York Times,* August 12, 2005.

108. See *American Civil Liberties Union v. U.S. Department of Defense*, 389 F.Supp.2d (S.D.N.Y.2005), 575–78; and Julia Preston, "Judge Orders Release of More Prison Abuse Photos," *New York Times*, September 30, 2005.

109. Jane E. Kirtley, "Transparency and Accountability in a Time of Terror: The Bush Administration's Assault on Freedom of Information," *Communication Law & Policy*, 11 (2006): 502; Also see Press Release, ACLU, "ACLU Releases First Government Authentication of Abu Ghraib Abuse Images Along with One New Photo," April 11, 2006, available at http://www.aclu.org/safefree/torture/2497 prs20060411.html.

110. National Security Archive, "Return of the Fallen: Pentagon Releases Hundreds More Casualty Homecoming Images," April 28, 2005, available at http://www.gwu.edu~nsarchiv/nsaebb/nsaebb152/index/htm.

111. Dana Milbank, "Curtain Ordered for Media Coverage of Returning Coffins," *Washington Post*, October 21, 2003.

112. National Security Archive, "Return of the Fallen: Pentagon Releases Hundreds More War Casualty Homecoming Images."

113. See *Associated Press v. U.S. Department of Defense*, 395 F.Supp.2d 15 (S.D.N.Y.2005); Reporters Committee for Freedom of the Press, "Judge Orders the Release of Detainee Information," September 21, 2006, available at https://rcfp.org/news/2006/0921-foi-judgeo.html; and Elaine Hargrove, "Transcripts of Guantanamo Tribunals Released," *SILHA Bulletin* (Winter 2006).

114. See Hargrove, "Transcripts of Guantanamo Tribunals Released"; and Reporters Committee for Freedom of the Press, "Judge Orders Release of Detainee Information."

115. Paul K. McMasters, "What We Can't Know Hurts Us," First Amendment Center (February 6, 2005), available at http://www.firstamendmentcenter.org/commentary.aspx?id=14787&pr.

116. Testimony of Walter Mears Before the Subcommittee on Terrorism, Technology and Homeland Security of the Senate Judiciary Committee, Openness in Government and Freedom of Information: Examining the OPEN Government Act of 2005 (March 15, 2005), available at http://judiciary.senate.gov/print_testimony.cfm?id=1417&wit_id=4078.

117. Associated Press, "Study: Journalists Face Long FOIA Delays," September 9, 2005.

118. Associated Press, "Agencies Missing FOIA Deadlines, AP Finds," March 13, 2006.

119. Alan Johnson, "Feds Less Eager to Share Records; Study Finds a Slower Response to Requests," *Columbus Dispatch*, July 1, 2006.

120. Associated Press, "Government Slower Under Open-Records Law," July 27, 2006; and OMB Watch, "Attorney General Gives Thumbs Up to Agencies on FOIA Plans," available at http://www.ombwatch.org/article/3625/1/233?TopicID=1.

121. Patrick Leahy and John Cornyn, "Democrat, Republican Senators Work Together to Reform FOIA," *Quill* 94, no. 7 (September 2006): 4.

122. See OpenTheGovernment.org, "FOIA's 40th Anniversary; Agencies Respond to the President's Call for Improved Disclosure," July 4, 2006.

123. Executive Order No. 13392, 70 Fed. Reg.75,373 (December 14, 2005).

124. Associated Press, "Agencies Missing FOIA Deadlines."

125. See OMB Watch, "Attorney General Gives Thumbs Up to Agencies on FOIA Plans."

126. See Opening Statement of John Cornyn, U.S. Senate Committee on the Judiciary, Openness in Government and Freedom of Information: Examining the OPEN Government Act of 2005 (March 15, 2005), available at http://judiciary.senate.gov.member_statement.cfm?id=1417&wi.

127. OMB Watch, "FOIA Continues to Get Congressional Attention" (June 13, 2005), available at http://www.ombwatch.org/article/2871/-1/233.

128. Jane Kirtley, "Transparency and Accountability in a Time of Terror"; also see Liz Sidoti, "Bills Would Shield DIA Documents from FOIA," *San Francisco Gate* (December 12, 2005), available at http://sgate.com.cgi-bin/article.cgi?file=/n/a/2005/12/12/national/w162812S57.DTL.

129. See Associated Press, "FOIA Bill Advances But Unlikely to Pass This Year," September 28, 2006; and OMB Watch, "Open Government Act Clears Senate Committee Hurdle" (September 26, 2006), available at http://www.ombwatch.org/article/35891/1/229?TopicID=1.

130. OMB Watch, "Government Receives Poor Grades on Secrecy" (September 12, 2006), available at http://www.ombwatch.org/article/35891/1/229?TopicID=1.

131. Scott Shane, "Secrets to be Declassified Under New Rule at 25," *New York Times*, December 21, 2006; and Jon Wiener, "You're Mistaken If You Think Declassifying Government Documents Means Making Them Available," *Los Angeles Times*, January 4, 2007.

132. Karen DeYoung and Walter Pincus, "CIA to Air Decades of Its Dirty Laundry," *Washington Post*, June 22, 2007.

133. See Jim Abrams, "Democrats Cite Administration Secrecy in Pushing Open Government Agenda," Associated Press, March 14, 2007; OMB Watch, "FOIA Reform Kicks Off in the House" (February 2, 2007), available at http://www.omb watch.org/article/3731/1/1/478.

134. Richard Nixon, Statement Establishing a New System for Classification and Declassification of Government Documents Relating to National Security (March 8, 1972), available at http://www.americanpresidency.org.

Chapter 2

1. Presidential Records Act of 1978.

2. See Executive Order 13233 of November 1, 2001: Further Implementation of the Presidential Records Act.

3. See Statement of Professor Jonathan Turley, Hearings Regarding Executive Order 13233 and the Presidential Records Act, Subcommittee on Government Efficiency, Financial Management and Intergovernmental Relations and the Committee on Government Reform, House of Rep., 107th Cong., 1st and 2d sess., April 24, 2002, 404–33; and Marcy Lynn Karin, "Out of Sight, but not Out of Mind: How Executive Order 13,233 Expands Executive Privilege While Simultaneously Preventing Access to Presidential Records," *Stanford Law Review* 2, no. 55 (November 2002): 529–42.

4. *Nixon v. Administrator of General Services*, 433 U.S. 425 (1977).

5. Statement of Jonathan Turley, Hearings Regarding Executive Order 13233 and the Presidential Records Act; Hearings before the Subcommittee on Government Efficiency, Financial Management and Intergovernmental Relations and the Committee on Government Reform House of Representatives, 107th Cong., 1st and 2d sess., November 6, 2001; April 11 and 24, 2002, 404–5.

6. See Office of the Attorney General, State of Texas, John Cornyn, May 3, 2002, Opinion No. JC-0498 Re: Interpretation of Texas Govern Code Section 441.201 concerning the official records of a former governor, available at

www.oag.state.tx.us/opinopen/opinions/op49cornyn/jc-0498.htm. Also see Lucius Lomax, "W's Paper Chase: Bush Attempts to Have His State Papers Declared Federal Property," *Austin Chronicle*, September 28, 2001; and Alison Leigh Cowan, "Battling over Records of Bush's Governorship," *New York Times*, February 11, 2002.

7. Carl M. Cannon, "Nixon's Revenge," *National Journal* 34, no. 2, January 12, 2002.

8. See John D. McKinnon, "Legal Worries over Missing Emails Grow; White House May Face Questions over Past Probes," *Wall Street Journal* (April 16, 2007).

9. Letter from George Washington to James Madison, May 5, 1789, in John C. Fitzpatrick, ed. *The Writings of George Washington, 1732–1799* (Washington, DC: U.S. Government Printing Office, 1931–1944), 311.

10. See Appendix 10, Presidential Records Act of 1978, Hearings before a Subcommittee of the Committee on Government Operations, House of Rep., 95th Cong., 2d sess., on H.R. 10998 and Related Bills, February 23, 28; March 2 and 7, 1978, vi. See also Carl McGowan, "Presidents and Their Papers," *Minnesota Law Review* 68 (1983): 409; and John C. Fitzpatrick, ed., *The Writings of George Washington from the Original Manuscript Sources, 1745–1799*, I (Washington, DC: U.S. Government Printing Office, 1976), xl.

11. See Appendix 10: "Handling of Presidential Records: Historical and Current Practice, Presidential Records Act of 1978," Hearings before a Subcommittee of the Committee on Government Operations, House of Rep., 95th Cong., 2d sess. on H.R. 10998 and Related Bills, February 23, 28; March 2 and 7, 1978, 467–87; McGowan, "Presidents and Their Papers," 409, 412; Frank L. Schick, Renee Schick, and Mark Caroll, *Records of the Presidency: Presidential Papers and Libraries from Washington to Reagan* (Phoenix: Oryx Press, 1989), 39, 45, 56, 68, 77, 79, 82, 85, 93, 101, 105, 109, 133; and Kenneth W. Duckett and Francis Russell, "The Harding Papers: How Some Were Burned ... And Others Were Saved," *American Heritage* 16 (February 1965): 24–31, 102–10; John McDonough, R. Gordon Hoxie, and Richard Jacobs, "Who Owns Presidential Papers?" *Manuscripts* 27, no. 1 (Winter 1975): 2–11; and Larry Berman, "The Evolution and Value of Presidential Libraries," in *The Presidency and Information Policy,* Center for the Study of the Presidency, Proceedings, vol. 4, no. 1, 1981.

12. See H. G. Jones, *The Records of a Nation: Their Management, Preservation, and Use* (New York: Atheneum, 1969), 157.

13. Text of letter of agreement between Richard Nixon and Arthur F. Sampson reprinted in Cong. Rec., 93rd Cong., 2d sess., 1974, 120 Pt. 25: 33965.

14. Editorial, "Presidential Records and the Public Interest," *Washington Post*, September 15, 1974.

15. Presidential Recordings and Materials Preservation Act, U.S. Code, vol. 44 (1974). Also see Cong. Rec., 93rd Cong., 2d sess., 1974, 120, pt. 25, 33848, 33850–51, 33855, 33857, 33860.

16. *Nixon v. Administrator of General Services*, 433 U.S. 425 (1977), 441.

17. *Nixon v. Administrator*, 433 U.S. 425 (1977), 441, 443, 444.

18. *Nixon v. Administrator*, 433 U.S. 425 (1977), 451.

19. *Nixon v. Administrator*, 433 U.S. 425 (1977), 452–53.

20. *United States v. Nixon*, 418 U.S. (1974), 705

21. *Nixon v. Administrator*, 433 U.S. 425 (1977), 484.

22. *Nixon v. Administrator*, 433 U.S. 425 (1977), 493, 503.

23. *Nixon v. Administrator*, 433 U.S. 425 (1977), 504, 520.

24. *Nixon v. Administrator*, 433 U.S. 425 (1977), 545.

25. Presidential Records Act of 1978, Pub. L. No. 95-591 (codified at 44 U.S.C.).

26. Presidential Records Act of 1978, sec. 2202.

27. See Presidential Records Act of 1978, 44 U.S.C. secs. 2201–7 for terms and conditions of the law.

28. Presidential Records Act of 1978, sec. 2206 (3).

29. See Marcy Lynn Karin, "Out of Sight, But Not Out of Mind: How Executive Order 13,233 Expands Executive Privilege While Simultaneously Preventing Access to Presidential Records," *Stanford Law Review*, 55 (November 2002).

30. 124th Cong. Rec. (1978), 36844; and House Report 107-790, Presidential Records Act Amendments of 2002.

31. See Alexandra K. Wigdor and David Wigdor, "The Future of Presidential Papers," in *The Presidency and Information Policy*, Center for the Study of the Presidency, Proceedings, vol. 4, no. 1, 1981.

32. Statement of Deputy Assistant Attorney General Larry A. Hammond, Hearing before the Senate Committee on Governmental Affairs on S. 3494, 95th Cong., 2d sess. (1978), 14.

33. See *New York Times*, "Carter Imposes Restrictions on His Staff's Use of Presidential Papers," December 18, 1980.

34. Memorandum from John G. Roberts to Fred F. Fielding, Threat to Deliberative Privilege Posed by the Presidential Records Act, September 9, 1985.

35. Ibid.

36. See U.S. House Subcommittee on Government Information, Justice, and Agriculture of the Committee on Government Operations, Statement on Behalf of the Office of General Counsel to the Clerk of the House of Representatives, 99th Cong., 2d sess. (April 29, 1986), 3; and Seymour Hersh, "A Reporter at Large: Nixon's Last Cover-up," *New Yorker*, December 14, 1992, 86.

37. Stanley I. Kutler, "Presidential Materials: Nixon's Ghost at Justice," *Wall Street Journal*, April 1, 1986.

38. See *Public Citizen v. Burke*, 843 F.2d 1473 (D.C.C. 1988).

39. See Executive Order 12667, 54 C.F.R. 3403 (1989) [hereafter Reagan Order].

40. Statement of Jonathan Turley, Hearings on Executive Order 13233.

41. Neil A. Lewis, "White House Delays Release of Reagan Papers," *New York Times*, June 9, 2001.

42. Elizabeth Bumiller, "Bush Keeps a Grip on Presidential Papers," *New York Times*, November 2, 2001; Editorial, "Cheating History," *New York Times*, November 15, 2001.

43. Executive Order 13233, sec. 3 (d) (1) (2) and sec.4.

44. *American Historical Association, et al. v. National Archives and Records Administration, et al.*, Memorandum of Points and Authorities in Support of Plaintiff's Motion for Summary Judgment, February 8, 2002.

45. See *Public Citizen v. Burke*, 843 F.2d (D.C.Cir. 1988); and *Nixon v. Freeman*, 670 F.2d 346 (D.C.Cir. 1982).

46. *Nixon v. Freeman*, 670 F.2d (D.C.Cir. 1982), 356–59.

47. See *Public Citizen v. Burke*, 843 F.2d (D.C.Cir. 1988), 1479.

48. *American Historical Association v. National Archives and Records Administration*, 10.

49. Statement of Jonathan Turley, Hearings on Executive Order 13233.

50. Executive Order 13233, sec. 3 (d) and sec.11.

51. Executive Order 13233, sec. 11.

52. Executive Order 13233, sec.10.

53. See Final Report of the National Study Commission on Records and Documents of Federal Officials, 1977, note 27, 13; and Statement of Jonathan Turley, Hearings on Executive Order 13233.

54. Marcy Lynn Karin, "Out of Sight, But Not Out of Mind."

55. *United States v. Reynolds*, 345 U.S. (1953), 1, 7.

56. Letter from George Washington Parke Curtis to John Pickett, April 17, 1857, quoted in McGowan, 412.

57. See Ken Ringle, "Shaken Foundation: Nixon Family, Political Heirs Split over Institute Honoring Drug Tycoon," *Washington Post*, April 9, 1997; James Sterngold, "Library and Legacy Adrift as the Nixon Sisters Feud," *New York Times*, March 25, 2002; and John-Thor Dahlburg and Stuart Pfeifer, "For Feuding Nixon Sisters, Finally a Peace with Honor," *Los Angeles Times*, August 9, 2002.

58. See Joseph Sax, "Playing Darts with a Rembrandt," 82 (1999); and Executive Order 13233, sec. 10.

59. Executive Order 13233, sec. 4.

60. Richard Reeves, "Writing History to Executive Order," *New York Times,* November 16, 2001.

61. Ben Gose and Dan Curry, "Historians Attack Bush Executive Order," *Chronicle of Higher Education*, November 16, 2001.

62. Linda Kulman, "Who Owns History? Historians the Bush Administration Wrangle over Access to Presidential Records," *U.S. News & World Report*, April 29, 2002.

63. Adam Clymer, "Government Openness at Issue as Bush Holds on to Records," *New York Times*, January 3, 2003; and Gose and Curry, "Historians Attack Bush Executive Order on Presidential Records."

64. Clymer, "Government Openness at Issue."

65. Public Citizen, "Public Citizen Sues to Block Implementation of Executive Order on Presidential Records," Press Release, November 28, 2001.

66. Emily Eakin, "Presidential Papers as Smoking Guns," *New York Times*, April 13, 2001.

67. Adam Clymer, "House Panel Seeks Release of Presidential Papers," *New York Times*, October 10, 2002.

68. Clymer, "Government Openness at Issue."

69. Editorial, "Follow-Up/Unseal the Presidential Papers," *San Francisco Chronicle*, August 18, 2003.

70. Cong. Rec., Senate, July 31, 2003, 10621–87.

71. See *American Historical Association v. National Archives & Records Administration*, No. 01-2447; and Testimony of Scott L. Nelson, Attorney, Public Citizen Litigation Group, Hearings on the Presidential Records Act and Executive Order 13233 Before the Subcommittee on Information Policy, Census and National Archives of the House Committee on Oversight and Government Reform, March 1, 2007.

72. Testimony of Scott L. Nelson, Hearings on the Presidential Records Act and Executive Order 13233.

73. Ibid.

74. See H.R. 1255: The Presidential Records Act Amendments of 2007, 110th Cong., 1st sess.; Editorial, "Sunshine on History," *New York Times*, March 12, 2007; "National Briefing in Washington: House Passes Open-Records Measures," *New York Times,* March 15, 2007; and bill.

75. Dan Froomkin, "Countless White E-Mails Deleted," *Washington Post*, April 12, 2007; and Sheryl Gay Stolberg, "Missing E-Mail May be Related to Prosecutors," April 13, 2007. The controversy over the firing of the nine U.S. attorneys involved whether they were pressured to act in the interests of the Republican Party and lost their jobs for failing to do so. According to the *New York Times*, the firing offenses of the prosecutors who were purged during the 2006 congressional election year were that they would not "indict Democrats they investigated, they investigated important Republicans, or they would not try to suppress the votes of Democratic-leaning groups with baseless election fraud cases." Moreover, a "disproportionate number of the prosecutors pushed out, or considered for dismissal, were in swing states. The main reason for the purge ... appears to have been an attempt to tip states like Missouri and Washington to Republican candidates for House, Senate, governor and president." See Editorial, "Why This Scandal Matters," *New York Times,* May 19, 2007.

76. John D. McKinnon, "Legal Worries over Missing Emails Grow; White House May Face Questions over Past Probes," *Wall Street Journal*, April 16, 2007; Sidney Blumenthal, "Follow the E-Mails," Salon.com (March 29, 2007), available at http://www.salon.com; and Dan Froomkin, "Countless White House E-Mails Deleted," *Washington Post*, April 12, 2007.

77. Daniel Schulman, "The Emails the White House Doesn't Want You to See" (March 30, 2007), available at http://www.motherjones.com.

78. Kenneth Jost, "Can E-Mail Unlock White House Secrets?" *Legal Times*, January 22, 1996.

79. Steven V. Roberts, "When the Moving Trucks Pull Up to the White House Door," *New York Times*, November 17, 1988.

80. Editorial, "What's in Those Files?" *Washington Post*, January 19, 1993; Stephen Lebaton, "Judge Sees Plan by White House to Defy Orders and Purge Data," *New York Times*, January 15, 1993; Michael York, "Court Bars Destruction of Records," *Washington Post*, January 7, 1993.

81. Editorial, "A Special Place in History for Mr. Bush," *New York Times*, March 1, 1995.

82. Schulman, "The Emails the White House Doesn't Want You to See."

83. Weekly Compilation of Presidential Documents, 10 (September 16, 19/4), 1117–18.

84. Quoted in David Greenberg, *Nixon's Shadow: History of an Image*, New York: W. W. Norton, 2003, 212–13.

85. Dan Froomkin, "The Next Bush Scandal," *Washington Post*, April 10, 2007.

86. Quoted in Daniel Schulman, "The Emails the White House Doesn't Want You to See."

87. Carl M. Cannon, "Nixon's Revenge," *National Journal* 34, no. 2 (January 12, 2002): 96.

88. Statement of Jonathan Turley, Hearings on Executive Order 13233.

Chapter 3

1. See Report of the National Energy Policy Development Group (May 2001), available at http://www.bookstore.gpo.gov, accessed 23 June 2003. Also see Stephen J. Hedges and William Neikerk, "Bush Faces Power Struggle in Devising U.S. Energy Plan," *Chicago Tribune*, February 5, 2001.

2. Patrick Crow, "U.S. Oil and Gas Industry Has High Expectations from Bush Administration on Energy Issues," *Oil and Gas Journal* 99, no. 7 (February 12, 2001): 66–72.

3. Report of the National Energy Policy Development Group; and Howard Fineman and Michael Isikoff, "At the Table," *Newsweek*, May 14, 2001.

4. Mike Allen and Dana Milbank, "Cheney Role Offers Strengths and Liabilities," *Washington Post*, May 17, 2001.

5. See National Energy Policy, Report of the National Energy Policy Development Group, May 2001.

6. The task force also included the director of the Federal Emergency Management Agency; the assistant to the president and deputy chief of staff for policy; the assistant to the president for economic policy; and the assistant to the president for intergovernmental affairs.

7. Waxman and Dingell requested that the GAO's investigation specifically seek the following: (1) a complete list of all NEPDG members and staff, and an

identification of any members or staff who were not full-time employees of the federal government; (2) a complete list of all NEPDG meetings, including the date, location, and attendees of each meeting; (3) the criteria used to determine which nonfederal entities would be invited to the meetings and an identification of the person or persons responsible for extending invitations under those criteria; (4) an accounting of the legal authorities pursuant to which the NEPDG was organized and was conducting its business; and (5) an accounting of all direct and indirect costs associated with the task force. See *Walker v. Cheney*, Complaint for Declaratory and Injunctive Relief, U.S. District Court for the District of Columbia, Civil Action 1, 02cv00340, 8.

8. Although the White House refused to divulge who the energy task force met with, aides said the representatives at the meetings included 118 energy industry or corporate groups, forty renewable energy providers, twenty-two unions, thirteen environmental groups, five academics, sixty-three government groups, six energy efficiency proponents, and a consumer group. See Allen and Milbank, "Cheney Role Offers Strengths and Liabilities."

9. Allen and Milbank, "Cheney Role Offers Strengths and Liabilities."

10. *Walker v. Cheney*, Complaint for Declaratory and Injunctive Relief, 11.

11. Mike Allen, "Cheney Spurns GAO Request," *Washington Post*, June 19, 2001.

12. Ibid.

13. Mark Hosenball, T. Trent Gegax, and Rich Thomas, "Lobbyists at the White House Table," *Newsweek*, May 14, 2001, 19–22; and Martha Brant and Tamara Lipper, "A New Capitol Clash," *Newsweek*, February 11, 2002, 28–29.

14. Letter from David M. Walker, Comptroller General of the General Accounting Office, to the Vice President of the United States, August 17, 2001.

15. Ellen Nakashima, "Can GAO Make Cheney Blink?" *Washington Post*, August 3, 2001, A17.

16. Ibid.

17. In 1980 Congress vested the GAO's comptroller general with the authority to enforce the agency's investigative powers by bringing civil action in the U.S. District Court for the District of Columbia. The law, however, precludes the comptroller general from filing suit under three situations: (1) where records at issue relate to the activities that have been designated by the president as foreign intelligence or counterintelligence activities; (2) where a specific statute exempts the records from disclosure; and (3) where, within twenty days of filing of the comptroller general's report, the president or the director of the Office of Management and Budget certifies to the comptroller general and Congress that disclosure could be reasonably expected to impair substantially the operations of the government.

18. Ellen Nakashima, "Cheney Defies GAO's Disclosure Demand," *Washington Post*, September 7, 2001.

19. Ellen Nakashima, "Environmental Group Sues for Records of Energy Task Force," *Washington Post*, December 12, 2001.

20. Editorial, "The Enron Post-Mortem," *New York Times*, January 4, 2002.

21. Robert Bryce, "Enron: The Inside Story: Friends in High Places," *The Guardian*, November 6, 2002.

22. Bryce, "Enron: The Inside Story." Also see Dana Milbank and Dan Morgan, "GAO Vows to Sue for Cheney Files: Hill Probes Enron Influence on Task Force," *Washington Post*, January 26, 2002; and Public Citizen, "Memo Shows Enron Division Headed by Army Secretary Thomas White Manipulated California Electricity Market" (May 8, 2002), available on Public Citizen website at http://www.publiccitizen.org/pressroom/release.cfm?ID=1106, accessed March 9, 2006.

23. Mike Allen, "Cheney, Aides Met With Enron 6 Times in 2001," *Washington Post*, January 9, 2002.

24. Ibid.

25. Martha Brant and Tamara Lipper, "A New Capitol Clash," *Newsweek*, February 11, 2002, 29.

26. Elizabeth Bumiller, "Congress Rebuffed on Energy Documents," *New York Times*, January 18, 2002.

27. Senator Carl Levin of the Senate Committee on Armed Services and the Permanent Subcommittee on Investigations of the Senate Committee on Government Affairs; Senator Joseph I. Lieberman, Chairman of the Senate Committee on Governmental Affairs; Senator Ernest F. Hollings, Chairman of the Senate Committee on Commerce; and Senator Byron L. Dorgan, Chairman of the Subcommittee on Treasury and General Government of the Senate Committee on Appropriations, and the Subcommittee on Consumer Affairs, Foreign Commerce, and Tourism of the Senate Committee on Commerce, Science, and Transportation, joined the previous congressional request that the GAO investigate the composition and practices of the NEPDG. See letter from Hon. Carl M. Levin, Hon. Joseph I. Lieberman, Hon. Ernest F. Hollings, and Hon. Byron L. Dorgan to Hon. David M. Walker, January 22, 2002.

28. Milbank and Morgan, "GAO Vows to Sue for Cheney Files."

29. Ibid.

30. Ibid.

31. Dana Milbank, "Cheney Refuses Records Release: Energy Showdown with GAO Looms," *Washington Post*, January 28, 2002.

32. Ibid.

33. Ibid.

34. Ibid.

35. Ibid.

36. Liz Mariantes, "Lawsuit Will Test Right to Privacy in the White House" (January 31, 2002), http://www.csmonitor.com.

37. Ibid.

38. The facts of Cheney's refusal to disclose information about the energy task force were strikingly similar to the controversy surrounding First Lady Hillary Rodham Clinton's Health Care Task Force, which was created in 1993 to develop a

proposal for reforming health care in the United States. As was the case with the vice president's energy task force, many individuals and private groups had concerns about the operation of the Health Care Task Force, including the identities of the individuals participating in the meetings of the task force, how often the meetings occurred, and how decisions were being made. One of these groups, the Association of American Physicians and Surgeons, filed a lawsuit for access to information about the Health Care Task Force's operations. See *Association of American Physicians and Surgeons, Inc. v. Hillary Rodham Clinton*, 813 F. Supp. 82, 95 (D.D.C. 1993).

39. Mariantes, "Lawsuit Will Test Right to Privacy."

40. Dana Milbank, "White House Girds for Protracted Legal Fight," *Washington Post*, February 22, 2002, A4.

41. On January 30, 2002, Comptroller General David Walker notified the President Pro Tempore of the U.S. Senate and the speaker of the House of Representatives that the GAO was preparing to file suit for the records in dispute. The comptroller general filed suit seeking declaratory and injunctive relief on February 22, 2002, specifically relying upon his statutory authority to investigate and evaluate his right to obtain access to documents.

42. Dana Milbank, "GAO Takes White House to Court," *Washington Post*, February 22, 2002.

43. Milbank, "White House Girds for Protracted Fight."

44. See *Walker v. Cheney*, Complaint for Declaratory and Injunctive Relief, U.S. District Court for the District of Columbia, Civil Action No. 1:02cv00340.

45. See Milbank, "GAO Takes White House to Court"; and Don Van Natta Jr., "Agency Files Suit for Cheney Papers on Energy Policy," *New York Times*, February 23, 2002.

46. Van Natta Jr., "Agency Files Suit for Cheney Papers on Energy Policy."

47. Dana Milbank and Ellen Nakashima, "Energy Department Ordered to Release Documents," *Washington Post*, February 28, 2001, A1; and Don Van Natta Jr., "Judge Orders Release of Energy Panel Files," *New York Times*, February 28, 2002.

48. Ibid.

49. Associated Press, "Bush Not Worried about Energy Papers," March 1, 2002.

50. Susan Cornwell, "Analysis: White House Digs In on Task Force Records," Reuters, March 3, 2003.

51. Ibid.

52. Ibid.

53. Editorial, "Cheney's Intransigence," JSOnline, *Milwaukee Journal/Sentinel*, March 4, 2002.

54. See *Judicial Watch v. U.S. Department of Energy, et al.*, U.S. District Court for the District of Columbia, Civil Action No. 01-0981 (PLF).

55. Judicial Watch Press Release, "Judge Orders Release of Agency Energy Task Force Documents."

56. Dana Milbank and Mike Allen, "Energy Contacts Disclosed," *Washington Post,* March 26, 2002, A1; and Associated Press, "Documents Reveal Energy Head Met No Environmentalists," March 26, 2002.

57. Milbank and Allen, "Energy Contacts Disclosed."

58. Associated Press, "Documents Reveal Energy Head Met No Environmentalists."

59. Milbank and Allen, "Energy Contacts Disclosed."

60. Richard A. Oppel Jr., "White House Acknowledges More Contacts with Enron," *New York Times*, May 23, 2002.

61. Richard A. Oppel Jr., "White House Acknowledges More Contacts with Enron;" and James Toedtman, "Looking for Answers/Senate Panel Hits Bush, Cheney with Enron Subpoena," *Newsday*, May 23, 2002.

62. Editorial, "A Familiar Name; More on Enron's Ties to the White House," *Columbus Dispatch*, June 1, 2002.

63. Editorial, "More and More Slime," *Charlotte Gazette*, May 22, 2002.

64. Ibid.

65. *Judicial Watch v. National Energy Policy Development Group*, Civil Action 01-1530 (EGS); and *Sierra Club v. Vice President Richard Cheney, et al.*, Civil Action 02-631 (EGS), U.S. District Court for the District of Columbia, July 12, 2002.

66. See *Judicial Watch v. National Energy Policy Development Group*, Civil Action 01-1530 (EGS); and *Sierra Club v. Vice President Richard Cheney, et al.*, Civil Action 02-631 (EGS), U.S. District Court for the District of Columbia. Also see *Nixon v. Administrator of General Services*, 433 U.S. 425 (1977).

67. See *Nixon v. Administrator of General Services*, 433 U.S. 425 (1977); and *Judicial Watch v. National Energy Policy Development Group,* Civil Action No. 01-1530 (EGS); and *Sierra Club v. Vice President Richard Cheney, et al.*, Civil Action No. 02-631 (EGS), U.S. District Court for the District of Columbia.

68. Neely Tucker, "White House Told to Turn over More Data on Energy Panel," *Washington Post*, August 3, 2002.

69. Don Van Natta Jr., "Cheney Argues Against Giving Congress Records," *New York Times*, September 28, 2002; and Neely Tucker, "Cheney-GAO Showdown Goes to Court," *Washington Post,* September 28, 2002, A5.

70. Ibid.

71. Michael C. Dorf, "A Brief History of Executive Privilege from George Washington Through Dick Cheney" (February 6, 2002), http://www.findlaw.com/dorf/20020206.html. Also see Dana Milbank, "Is Judge's Past Prologue in Cheney Case?" *Washington Post*, November 26, 2002. In the Clinton case, the Supreme Court refused to reconsider the U.S. Court of Appeals for the 8th Circuit's ruling in favor of Kenneth Starr, the independent prosecutor. The appellate court accepted many of the arguments made by Bates. The court rejected the White House claim that Starr failed to demonstrate a "demonstrated, specific need" for the documents. In addition, the court agreed with Bates's legal team that presidential advisers would not be moved to temper the candor of their remarks and dismissed other White House arguments as mere political concerns. In *Walker v. Cheney*, the Bush

administration made many of the same arguments as the Clinton White House did, especially concerning the intrusive nature of the GAO's request on presidential and vice presidential autonomy.

72. *Walker v. Cheney*, U.S. District Court for the District of Columbia, Civil Action No. 02-0340 (JDB), December 9, 2002.

73. Ibid., 25–26, 29–30.

74. Neely Tucker, "Suit Versus Cheney Is Dismissed," *Washington Post*, December 10, 2002.

75. Ibid.

76. Ibid.

77. Dana Milbank, "GAO Ends Fight with Cheney over Files," *Washington Post*, February 8, 2003.

78. Ibid.

79. Ibid.

80. Ibid.

81. John W. Dean, "The Ongoing Fight between the Supreme Court and Congress as Illustrated by the GAO/Cheney Suit" (June 8, 2004), http://writ.news.findlaw.com/dean/20020201.html.

82. Erwin Chemerinksy, "The Constitutional Jurisprudence of the Rehnquist Court," in Martin H. Belsky, ed., *The Rehnquist Court: A Retrospective*, New York: Oxford University Press, 2002, 197–98.

83. Peter Brand and Alexander Bolton, "GOP Threats Halted GAO Cheney Suit," *The Hill*, February 19, 2003; and T. J. Halstead, "The Law: *Walker v. Cheney*: Legal Insulation of the Vice President from GAO Investigations," *Presidential Studies Quarterly* 33, no. 3 (September 2003): 646.

84. Letter from GAO Comptroller General David M. Walker to Representative Henry Waxman, February 7, 2003; and Halstead, "The Law: *Walker v. Cheney*," 642–43.

85. Remarks by Henry Waxman, "Cheney Task Force Records and GAO Authority," U.S. House of Representatives, Committee on Government Reform, Minority Office (February 12, 2003), http://www.house.gov/reform/min.

86. John W. Dean, "The General Accounting Office Drops its Suit Against Vice President Cheney" (June 22, 2004), http://writ.news.findlaw.com/dean/20030214.html.

87. U.S. Congress, Senate, 96th Cong., Senate Report No. 96-570 (1980), 5.

88. Ibid., 8.

89. Ibid., 2.

90. Bernard Rosen, *Holding Government Bureaucracies Accountable,* New York: Praeger, 1989, 75.

91. Mathew D. McCubbins and Terry Sullivan, eds., *Congress: Structure and Policy,* Cambridge: Cambridge University Press, 1987. Also see Anthony King, ed., *Both Ends of the Avenue: The Presidency, the Executive Branch, and Congress in the 1980s,* Washington, DC: American Enterprise Institute, 1983; and Joel Aberbach,

Keeping a Watchful Eye: The Politics of Congressional Oversight, Washington, DC: Brookings Institution, 1990.

92. Susan Page, "Bush Unscathed by Investigations," *USA Today,* August 13, 2003.

93. Mike Allen, "GAO Cites Corporate Shaping of Energy Plan," *Washington Post,* August 26, 2003.

Chapter 4

1. *Judicial Watch v. National Energy Policy Development Group*; *Sierra Club v. Vice President Richard Cheney, et al.*, Memorandum Opinion, U.S. District Court for the District of Columbia; *Judicial Watch v. United States Department of Energy, et al.,* Civil Action No. 01-0981 (PLF); and *Natural Resources Defense Council v. U.S. Department of Energy,* Civil Action No. 01-2545 (PLF). Judicial Watch sent FOIA requests to the Departments of Agriculture, Commerce, Energy, Interior, Treasury, and to the Environmental Protection Agency, and Office of Management and Budget.

2. *Sierra Club v. Vice President Richard Cheney, et al.*, Memorandum Opinion, U.S. District Court for the District of Columbia.

3. Dan Van Natta Jr. and Neela Banerjee, "Review Shows Energy Industry's Recommendations to Bush Ended Up Being National Policy," *New York Times*, March 28, 2002.

4. Dan Van Natta Jr., "Bush Energy Paper Followed Industry Push," *New York Times*, March 27, 2002.

5. See Van Natta Jr. and Banerjee, "Review Shows Energy Industry's Recommendations to Bush Ended Up Being National Policy"; and Franz Neil, "NDRC Details Company Contacts with Energy Plan Committee," *Chemical Week* 164, no. 22, May 29, 2002, 13.

6. U.S. Supreme Court, *In Re: Richard B. Cheney, et al. Petition for Writ of Certiorari* (September 2003), appendix B, 98a, 109a; Judicial Watch press release, "JW Victory: Court Rules Against Cheney, Energy Task Force" (July 12, 2002), http://www.judicialwatch.org; Sierra Club press release, "Judge Issues Opinion Against Cheney Energy Task Force" (July 12, 2002), http://www.sierraclub.org; Dana Milbank, "Suit on Cheney Energy Files to Proceed," *Washington Post*, July 13, 2002; and Warren Richey, "In Cheney Case, Court Reviews Executive Power" (April 27, 2004), http://www.csmonitor.com.

7. Richey, "In Cheney Case, Court Reviews Executive Power."

8. David Stout, "Supreme Court Refuses to Order Cheney to Release Energy Papers," *New York Times*, July 24, 2004.

9. Henri E. Cauvin, "Cheney Loses Ruling on Energy Panel Records," *Washington Post*, July 9, 2003; and Neil A. Lewis, "Court Blocks Effort to Protect Secret Cheney Files," *New York Times*, July 9, 2003.

10. Ibid.; and Associated Press, "Court Won't Stop Suit on Energy Task Force," July 9, 2003. Also see U.S. Supreme Court, *In Re: Richard B. Cheney, Petition for a Writ of Certiorari, No. 03-475,* September 2003, 8.

11. U.S. Supreme Court, *In re: Richard B. Cheney, Vice President of the United States, et al., Petition for Writ of Certiorari, No. 03-475* (September 2003), 7.

12. Charles Lane, "High Court Will Review Ruling on Cheney Task Force Records," *Washington Post,* December 16, 2003; Linda Greenhouse, "Justices Will Hear Appeal on Cheney's Energy Panel," *New York Times,* December 16, 2003; Kirk Semple, "Cheney Energy Group Case to Get High Court Hearing," *New York Times,* December 15, 2003; Robert S. Greenberger, "The Economy: Court to Rule on Energy Task Force: Cheney Claims Privilege in Not Disclosing Contacts will be Decided by Justices," *Wall Street Journal,* December 16, 2003; and David G. Savage, "Supreme Court to Hear Cheney Case: Justices Will Determine Whether the Vice President Most Reveal Documents that Show Who Attended Energy Task Force Meetings," *Los Angeles Times,* December 16, 2003.

13. See *U.S. v. Nixon,* 418 U.S. 704–5 (1974); and Savage, "Supreme Court to Hear Cheney Case."

14. Greenhouse, "Justices Will Hear Appeal."

15. Anne Gearan, "Supreme Court: Presidential Power Is Central to Energy Task Force Lawsuit," *Charleston Gazette,* December 16, 2003.

16. Warren Richey, "Court to Enter Fray over Energy Policy Task Force," *Christian Science Monitor,* December 16, 2003.

17. Editorial, "The Bush Administration: Bright Light Must Shine on Energy Policymaking," *Los Angeles Times,* December 21, 2003; Editorial, "A Question of Access," *St. Petersburg Times,* December 18, 2003; Editorial, "Energy Task Force Shouldn't be an Issue," *Austin American Statesman,* December 18, 2003; Editorial, "High Court to Weigh White House Secrecy," *Albuquerque Journal,* December 18, 2003; Editorial, "Cheney: Three-Time Loser?" *Palm Beach Post,* December 20, 2003; Dana Milbank, "Under Bush, Expanding Secrecy," *Washington Post,* December 23, 2003; and Editorial, "Supreme Folly," *Arizona Daily Star,* December 16, 2003.

18. Michael Janofsky, "Scalia's Trip with Cheney Raises Questions of Impartiality," *New York Times,* February 6, 2004.

19. Ibid.

20. Quotations cited in Supreme Court case *Cheney v. U.S. District Court for the District of Columbia,* On Writ of Certiorari to the United States Court of Appeals for the District of Columbia, Motion to Recuse, No. 03-475, 4–7.

21. Janofsky, "Scalia's Trip with Cheney Raises Questions of Impartiality"; and Associated Press, "Scalia Defends Hunting Trip with Cheney," February 12, 2004.

22. *Cheney v. U.S. District Court for the District of Columbia,* On Writ of Certiorari to the United States Court of Appeal for the D.C. Circuit, Motion to Recuse, No. 03-475, 3–4.

23. Charles Lane, "Court Leaves Up to Scalia a Recusal from Energy Case," *Washington Post,* March 2, 2004.

24. Memorandum of Justice Scalia, *Richard B. Cheney v. U.S. District Court for the District of Columbia*, No. 03-475, March 18, 2004.

25. Jeffrey Rosen, "The Justice Who Came to Dinner," *New York Times*, February 1, 2004.

26. Joan Biskupic, "Scalia Scoffs at Notion that He's Biased Toward Cheney," *USA Today*, April 26, 2004, 2A.

27. *Cheney v. U.S. District Court for the District of Columbia*, No. 03-475, Reply Brief for the Petitioners, April 2004, 1.

28. Society of American Archivists Press Release, "The U.S. Supreme Court Asked to Reject the Government's Claim That It May Conduct the Public's Interest in Secret" (March 18, 2004), http://www.archivists.org.

29. Joan Biskupic, "Justices Weigh Release of Energy Documents," *USA Today*, April 26, 2004; and Associated Press, "Supreme Court Hears Arguments on Cheney's Secret Energy Panel," April 27, 2004.

30. *Cheney v. U.S. District Court for the District of Columbia*, No. 03-475, Brief Amici Curiae of the Reporters Committee for Freedom of the Press, American Society of Newspaper Editors, and Society of Professional Journalists in Support of Respondents, 1–4.

31. *United States v. Nixon*, 418 U.S. 683 (1974), 688, 703–6.

32. *Nixon v. Administrator of General Services*, 433 U.S. 425 (1977), 707.

33. "Advising the President," *Wall Street Journal*, June 24, 2004, 12.

34. Editorial, *New York Times*, April 27, 2003.

35. Stout, "Supreme Court Refuses to Order Cheney to Release Energy Papers"; William Branigan, "Cheney Energy Documents Remain Sealed," *Washington Post*, June 24, 2004; and Warren Richey, "Cheney Wins a Round on Paper Trail" (June 25, 2004), http://www.csmonitor.com.

36. Richey, "Cheney Wins a Round on Paper Trail."

37. Tom Curry, "Cheney's Win: More Than Legal" (June 24, 2004), http://www.msnbc.com.

38. John A. Lukey, "At the Court, Inflating the White House's Power," *Washington Post*, July 4, 2004.

39. Bruce Fein, "Pyrrhic Secrecy Victory," *Washington Times*, July 29, 2004.

40. *Cheney v. U.S. District Court for the District of Columbia*, 124 S. Ct. 2489 (2004).

41. Louis Klarevas, "Can You Sue the White House? Opening the Door for Separation of Powers Immunity in Cheney v. District Court?" *Presidential Studies Quarterly* 34, no. 4 (December 2004): 865.

42. Richey, "Cheney Wins a Round on Paper Trail."

43. Ibid.

44. Curry, "Cheney's Win: More than Legal."

45. Branigan, "Cheney Energy Documents Remain Sealed."

46. Curry, "Cheney's Win: More than Legal"; and Stout, "Supreme Court Refuses to Order Cheney to Release Energy Papers."

47. Joan A. Lukey, "At the Court, Inflating the White House's Power," *Washington Post*, July 4, 2004, B2.

48. See *In Re: Richard B. Cheney*, No. 02-5354 (D.C.Cir. 2005).

49. See *In Re: Richard B. Cheney*, No. 02-5354 (D.C.Cir. 2005), 7–8.

50. See *In Re: Richard B. Cheney*, No. 02-5354 (D.C.Cir. 2005), 12–13.

51. Carol D. Leonnig and Jim VandeHei, "Cheney Wins Court Ruling on Energy Panel Records," *Washington Post*, May 11, 2005. Also see David Stout, "Appeals Court Backs Cheney in Secrecy Case," *New York Times*, May 11, 2005; and David G. Savage, "Court Lets Cheney Keep Talks Secret" (May 11, 2005), http://www.latimes.com.

52. *In Re: Richard B. Cheney*, No. 02-5354 (D.C.Cir. 2005), 7–8.

53. *Hearings Before Subcommittee on Intergovernmental Relations of the Committee on Government Operations*, U.S. Senate, 92nd Cong., 1st sess. On S. 1637, S. 1964, and S. 2064, Part I, June 10 and 11, 1971.

54. *Senate Report No. 92-1098*, The Federal Advisory Committee Act, U.S. Senate, 92nd Cong, September 7, 1972, 5.

55. *Senate Hearings Before Subcommittee on Intergovernmental Relations of the Committee on Government Operations on S. 3067*, 91st Cong., 2d sess., 1970, 32.

56. See *Federal Advisory Committee Act Amendments of 1989*, Hearings on S. 444, 101st Cong., 1st sess., 1989, 6.

57. *Hearings Before Subcommittee on Government Operations*, House of Representatives, 92nd Cong., 1st sess. On H.R. 4383, November 4, 1971, 1.

58. Ibid., 54.

59. Ibid., 13–14. Also see *Senate Report No. 92-1098*, 1972, 6.

60. *Federal Advisory Committee Act, 5 U.S.C. App. As Amended*, Sec. 3(2) (b), Sec. 5(c), Sec. 10(a)(1) and (3).

61. U.S. House, *Federal Advisory Committee Standards Act, Report No. 92-1017*, 92nd Cong., 2d sess., 1972, 7–8.

62. See *Hearings Before Subcommittee on Government Operations*, House of Rep., 92nd Cong., 1st sess on H.R. 4383, November 4, 1971, 17.

63. Adam Clymer, "Government Openness at Issue as Bush Holds on to Records," *New York Times*, January 3, 2003; Mark Tapscott, "Too Many Secrets," *Washington Post*, November 20, 2002; Jim Rutenberg, "White House Keeps a Grip on Its News," *New York Times*, October 14, 2002; Laura Parker, Devin Johnson, and Tony Locy, "Secure Often Means Secret Post-9/11," *USA Today*, May 16, 2002, 1A; Linda Greenhouse, "A Penchant for Secrecy," *New York Times*, May 5, 2002; and John Giuffo, "The FOIA Fight," *Columbia Journalism Review Online Report* (March/April 2002), http://www.cjr.org.

64. Dana Milbank and Justin Blum, "Document Says Oil Chiefs Met with Cheney Task Force," *Washington Post*, November 16, 2005; and Justin Blum, "Big Oil Participation at Issue," *Washington Post*, November 23, 2005.

65. Milbank and Blum, "Document Says Oil Chiefs Met with Cheney Task Force"; and Blum, "Big Oil Participation at Issue."

Chapter 5

1. See Pub. L. 95-511, Title I, 92 Stat. 1796 (October 25, 1978), codified as amended at 50 U.S.C. sec. 1805 (a) (3) (2003 & Supp. 2005).

2. 50 U.S.C. sec. 1809 (a) (1); and Congressional Research Service, Memorandum, "Presidential Authority to Gather Foreign Intelligence Information," January 5, 2006, 27.

3. 50 U.S.C. 1809; 18 U.S.C. 2511 (2) (f); and David Cole and Martin S. Lederman, "The National Security Agency's Domestic Spying Program: Framing the Debate," *Indiana Law Journal* 81, no. 1355 (Fall 2005).

4. James Risen and Eric Lichtblau, "Bush Lets U.S. Spy on Callers Without Courts," *New York Times*, December 16, 2005.

5. Barton Gellman, Dafna Linzer, and Carol D. Leonnig, "Surveillance Net Yields Few Suspects," *Washington Post*, February 5, 2006.

6. See David Johnson, "Federal Agents Expand Probe into Wiretap Leak; Law Enforcement, Intelligence Services Come Under Scrutiny," *New York Times*, February 12, 2006; Walter Pincus, "Prosecution of Journalists Is Possible in NSA Leaks," *Washington Post*, May 22, 2006; Walter Pincus, "Silence Angers Judiciary Panel," *Washington Post*, June 7, 2006; and Dan Eggen, "Grand Jury Probes Leak at NSA," *Washington Post*, July 29, 2006.

7. Eric Lichtblau, "Senate Panel Rebuffed on Documents on U.S. Spying," *New York Times*, February 2, 2006.

8. Letter from Assistant Attorney General William E. Moschella to Chairman Roberts and Vice Chairman Rockefeller of the Senate Select Committee on Intelligence and Chairman Hoekstra and Ranking Minority Member Harman of the House Permanent Select Committee on Intelligence, December 22, 2005; and U.S. Department of Justice, "Legal Authorities Supporting the Activities of the National Security Agency Described by the President," January 19, 2006.

9. Authorization for Use of Military Force, Pub. L. 107-40, 115 Stat. 223 (2001). Also see CRS Report RS22357, *Authorization for Use of Military Force in Response to the 9/11 Attacks, Pub. L. 107-40): Legislative History.*

10. *Hamdi v. Rumsfeld*, 542 U.S. 507 (2004); and U.S. Department of Justice, "Legal Authorities Supporting the Activities of the National Security Agency Described by the President," January 19, 2006, 12.

11. Ibid., 11–12.

12. Ibid., 13.

13. Ibid., 29.

14. See John Cary Sims, "What NSA Is Doing … and Why It's Illegal," *Hastings Constitutional Law Quarterly*, 33 (Winter/Spring 2006).

15. "Legal Authorities Supporting Activities of the National Security Agency," 37–38.

16. Congressional Research Service, Memorandum, "Presidential Authority to Gather Foreign Intelligence Information," 29–32.

17. Ibid., 36–37.

18. See "February 2, 2006 Letter from Scholars and Former Government Officials to Congressional Leadership in Response to Justice Department White Paper of January 19, 2006," in David Cole and Martin S. Lederman, ed., "The National Security Agency's Domestic Spying Program: Framing the Debate," *Indiana Law Journal*, 81 (May 2006): 1414–24.

19. See "January 9, 2006 letter from Scholars and Former Government Officials to Congressional Leadership in Response to Justice Department Letter of December 22, 2005," in David Cole and Martin S. Lederman, ed., "The National Security Agency's Domestic Spying Program; Framing the Debate," *Indiana Law Journal*, 81 (May 2006). The journal reprinted four documents that, taken together, set forth the basic arguments concerning the lawfulness of the secret NSA surveillance program. Two of the documents derived from the Justice Department in support of the program. The other two documents constituted rebuttals to the administration on statutory and constitutional grounds.

20. Tom Daschel, "Power We Didn't Grant," *Washington Post,* December 23, 2005.

21. See John Cary Sims, "What NSA Is Doing … and Why It's Illegal," *Hastings Constitutional Law Quarterly*, 33 (Winter/Spring 2006), available through LexisNexis.

22. 50 U.S.C., sec 1809 (9a) (1).

23. January 9, 2006, Letter from Scholars and Former Government Officials to Congressional Leadership, 1365.

24. See *Youngstown Sheet & Tube Co. v. Sawyer*, 343 U.S. (1952), 579, 609.

25. *Hamdi v. Rumsfeld*, 542 U.S. 507 (2004), 518–19.

26. January 9, 2006, Letter from Scholars and Former Government Officials to Congressional Leadership, 1366.

27. H.R. Rep. No. 95-1283, pt. 1 (1978), 24; and January 9, 2006, Letter from Scholars and Former Government Officials to Congressional Leadership, 1368.

28. January 9, 2006, Letter from Scholars and Former Government Officials to Congressional Leadership, 1368.

29. January 9, 2006, Letter from Scholars and Former Government Officials to Congressional Leadership, 1369; and *United States v. United States District Court*, 407 U.S. 297 (1972).

30. January 9, 2006, Letter from Scholars and Former Government Officials to Congressional Leadership, 1370.

31. U.S. Supreme Court, *United States v. Curtis-Wright Export Corporation*, 299 U.S. 304 (1936).

32. Sean Wilentz, "Mr. Cheney's Minority Report," *New York Times*, July 9, 2007.

33. George Will, "No Checks, Many Imbalances," *Washington Post*, February 16, 2006.

34. David Stout, "Defense of Eavesdropping Is Met with Skepticism in Senate," *New York Times,* February 6, 2006.

35. See Statement of Attorney General Alberto R. Gonzales to the U.S. Senate Judiciary Committee (February 6, 2006), available at http://news.findlaw.com/hdocs/docs/nsa.gonz20606stmnt.html. Gonzales's statement derived from the Justice Department's January 19, 2006 memo to Congress. See U.S. Department of Justice, "Legal Authorities Supporting the Activities of the National Security Agency Described by the President," 16–17.

36. See Supplementary Detailed Staff Reports on Intelligence Activities and the Rights of Americans, Book III, Final Report of the Select Committee to Study Governmental Operations with Respect to Intelligence Activities, U.S. Senate, April 23, 1976; and S. Rep. No. 95-604(I), 9-15, 1978 U.S.C.C.A.N, 3911–16. Also see Congressional Research Service, Memorandum, "Presidential Authority to Conduct Warrantless Electronic Surveillance to Gather Foreign Intelligence Information, 12–13. The Senate Judiciary Committee's report "Background" section includes a detailed history of executive branch surveillance activities dating to the 1930s.

37. See Craig R. Smith, "The Patriot Act in Historic Context," Center for the First Amendment Studies, available at http://www.csulb.edu/~crSmith/whitepaper/patriots.htm.

38. Ibid.

39. Ibid.; and Fareed Zakaria, "Freedom v. Security: Delicate Balance: The Case for Smart Profiling as a Weapon in the War on Terror," *Newsweek* (July 8, 2002), 26.

40. Craig R. Smith, "The Patriot Act in Historic Context"; and Fareed Zakaria, "Freedom v. Security."

41. U.S. Constitution, Amendment IV.

42. Risen and Lichtblau, "Bush Lets U.S. Spy on Callers."

43. Boston Gellman, Dafna Linzer, and Carol D. Leonnig, "Surveillance Net Yields Few Suspects," *Washington Post*, February 5, 2006; Jeffrey Richelson, "Desperately Seeking Signals: The National Security Agency's Echelon Program," *Bulletin of Atomic Scientists* 56, no. 2 (March/April 2000); Eric Lichtblau and James Risen, "Spy Agency Mined Vast Data Trove, Officials Report," *New York Times*, December 24, 2005; James Bamford, "Big Brother Is Listening," *Atlantic Monthly* (April 2006); and John Cary Sims, "What NSA Is Doing . . . and Why It's Illegal," *Hastings Constitutional Law Quarterly*, 33 (Winter/Spring 2006).

44. Seymour M. Hersh, "National Security Department: Listening In," *New Yorker* (May 29, 2006): 25.

45. Baron Gellman, Dafna Linzer, and Carol D. Leonnig, "Surveillance Net Yields Few Suspects"; Risen and Lichtblau, "Bush Lets U.S. Spy on Callers"; Jeffrey Richelson, "Desperately Seeking Signals: The National Security Agency's Echelon Program," *Bulletin of Atomic Scientists* 56, no. 2 (March/April 2000); Lichtblau and Risen, "Spy Agency Mined Vast Data Trove"; James Bamford, "Big Brother Is Listening," *Atlantic Monthly* (April 2006); and John Cary Sims, "What NSA Is Doing . . . and Why It's Illegal," *Hastings Constitutional Law Quarterly*, 33 (Winter/Spring 2006).

46. Baron Gellman, Dafna Linzer, and Carol D. Leonnig, "Surveillance Net Yields Few Suspects"; and Risen and Lichtblau, "Bush Lets U.S. Spy on Callers."

47. Scott Shane and Eric Lichtblau, "Cheney Pushed U.S. to Widen Eavesdropping," *New York Times*, May 14, 2006.

48. Risen and Lichtblau, "Bush Lets U.S. Spy on Callers"; and Barton Gellman and Jo Becker, "A Different Understanding with the President," *Washington Post*, June 24, 2007.

49. Shane and Lichtblau, "Cheney Pushed U.S. to Widen Eavesdropping."

50. Henry Kissinger, *White House Years*, Boston: Little, Brown, 1979, 658.

51. Shane and Lichtblau, "Cheney Pushed U.S. to Widen Eavesdropping."

52. Gellman and Becker, "A Different Understanding with the President"; and Danile Klaidman, Stuart Taylor Jr., and Evan Thomas, "Palace Revolt," *Newsweek*, February 6, 2006, 35–40; and Chitra Ragavan, "Cheney's Guy," *U.S. News & World Report*, May 29, 2006.

53. Gellman and Becker, "A Different Understanding with the President"; and Klaidman, Taylor, and Thomas, "Palace Revolt."

54. Gellman and Becker, "A Different Understanding with the President."

55. Klaidman, Taylor, and Thomas, "Palace Revolt"; Ragavan, "Cheney's Guy."

56. Dan Eggen, "Official: Cheney Urged Wiretaps," *Washington Post*, June 7, 2007; Klaidman, Taylor, and Thomas, "Palace Revolt"; and David Cole, "The Grand Inquisitors," *New York Review of Books* 54, no. 12 (July 19, 2007): 53–54.

57. Klaidman, Taylor, and Thomas, "Palace Revolt."

58. Dan Eggen, "Official: Cheney Urged Wiretaps," *Washington Post*, June 7, 2007; Klaidman, Taylor, and Thomas, "Palace Revolt"; and David Cole, "The Grand Inquisitors."

59. Carol D. Leonnig, "Secret Court Judges Were Warned About NSA Spy Data," *Washington Post*, February 9, 2006; Risen and Lichtblau, "Bush Lets U.S. Spy on Callers"; Dan Eggen, "Official: Cheney Urged Wiretaps," *Washington Post*, June 7, 2007; Klaidman, Taylor, and Thomas, "Palace Revolt"; and Michael A. Fletcher, "Senators Subpoena the White House," *Washington Post*, June 28, 2007.

60. Neil King Jr., "Wiretap Furor Widens Republican Divide: While Security Camp Claims Justification, Civil Libertarians See an Intrusion on Rights," *Wall Street Journal*, December 22, 2005; and Will, "No Checks, Many Imbalances."

61. Carl Hulse and Jim Rutenberg, "Specter's Uneasy Relationship with the White House Is Revealed in Letter to Cheney," *New York Times*, June 8, 2006.

62. Neil King Jr., "Wiretap Furor Widens Republican Divide"; and Peter Baker and Jim VandeHei, "Clash in Latest Chapter in Bush Effort to Widen Executive Power," *Washington Post*, December 21, 2005.

63. Neil King Jr., "Wiretap Furor Widens Republican Divide"; and Peter Baker and Jim VandeHei, "Clash in Latest Chapter in Bush Effort to Widen Executive Power."

64. David Ignatius, "The Wrong Wiretap Debate," *Washington Post*, February 8, 2006.

65. Ibid.; and Will, "No Checks, Many Imbalances."

66. David Ignatius, "The Wrong Wiretap Debate"; Hulse and Rutenberg, "Specter's Uneasy Relationship"; Walter Pincus, "Specter Offers Compromise on NSA Surveillance," *Washington Post*, June 9, 2006; and Jonathan Weisman, "Republican Rift over Wiretapping Widens," *Washington Post*, September 6, 2006; and Jonathan Weisman, "GOP Leaders Back Bush on Wiretapping," *Washington Post*, September 14, 2006.

67. See U.S. Senate, *Hearings before the Senate Judiciary Committee on NSA III: Wartime Executive Powers and the FISA Court*, March 28, 2006; and Eric Lichtblau, "Judges on Secret Panel Speak Out on Spy Program," *New York Times*, March 29, 2006.

68. Hersh, "National Security Department: Listening In."

69. Susan Page, "NSA Secret Database Report Triggers Fierce Debate in Washington," *USA Today*, May 11, 2006; Bill Nichols and John Diamond, "Controversy Shadows Hayden Confirmation," *USA Today*, May 11, 2006; Dan Eggen, "Negroponte Had Denied Domestic Call Monitoring," *Washington Post*, May 15, 2006; Elizabeth Drew, "Power Grab," *New York Review of Books* 53, no. 11 (June 22, 2006), available at http://www.nybooks.com/articles/19092.

70. Hulse and Rutenberg, "Specter's Uneasy Relationship."

71. See Murray Waas, "Internal Affairs," *National Journal* 39, no. 11 (February 17, 2007): 34–37.

72. Ibid.

73. March Sherman, "Gonzales: Bush Blocked Eavesdropping Probe," Associated Press, July 18, 2006; and Dan Eggen, "Bush Thwarted Probe into NSA Wiretapping," *Washington Post*, July 19, 2006.

74. Drew, "Power Grab."

75. Charles Babington and Dafna Linzer, "More Lawmakers to be Privy to Classified Briefings," *Washington Post*, May 17, 2006.

76. Weisman, "Republican Rift over Wiretapping Widens."

77. Walter Pincus, "Specter Offers Compromise on NSA Surveillance," *Washington Post*, June 9, 2006.

78. Weisman, "GOP Leaders Back Bush"; and Weisman, "Republican Rift over Wiretapping Widens."

79. Ibid.

80. See *American Civil Liberties Union; American Civil Liberties Union Foundation; American Civil Liberties Union of Michigan; Council on American-Islamic Relations; Council on American-Islamic Relations Michigan; Greenpeace, Inc.; National Association of Criminal Defense Lawyers; James Bamford; Larry Diamond; Christopher Hitchens; Tara Mcelvey; and Barnett R. Rubin v. National Security Agency/Central Security Service*, Complaint for Declaratory and Injunctive Relief, U.S. District Court, Eastern District of Michigan, Southern Division, Case No. 06-CV-10204, January 17, 2006.

81. Adam Liptak, "Experts Fault Reasoning in Surveillance Decision," *New York Times*, August 19, 2006; and Dan Sewell, "Hard to Predict 6th Circuit's NSA Ruling," *Seattle Post-Intelligencer*, April 19, 2006.

82. Eric Lichtblau and David Johnston, "Court to Oversee U.S. Wiretapping in Terror Cases," *New York Times*, January 18, 2007; David Johnston and Scott Shane, "Senators Demand Details on New Eavesdropping Rules," *New York Times*, January 19, 2007; and Dan Eggen, "Spy Court Orders Stir Debate on Hill," *Washington Post*, January 19, 2007. Also see Dan Eggen, "Bush Warned About Mail-Opening Authority," *Washington Post*, January 5, 2007.

83. James Risen, "Administration Pulls Back on Surveillance Agreement," *New York Times*, May 2, 2007.

84. Ibid.

85. Editorial, "Spying on Americans," *Washington Post*, May 2, 2007.

86. Keith Perine, "Senate Panel Issues Subpoenas for Information on NSA Surveillance Program," *CQ Today* (June 27, 2007), available at http://public.cq.com/docs/cqt/news110-000002541798.html.

87. Charlie Savage, "Panel Pushes for Files on Spy Program," *Boston Globe* (June 28, 2007), available at http://www.boston.com/news/nation/articles/2007/06/28/panel_pushes_for_files_on_spy_program.

88. Josh Meyer, *Los Angeles Times*, "Wiretap Subpoenas Prod Administration," June 28, 2007; and Tom A. Peter, "Subpoenas Target Administration's Wiretapping Program," *Christian Science Monitor* (June 29, 2007), available at http://www.csmonitor.com/2007/0628/p99s01-duts.html.

89. Michael J. Sniffen, "Ex-Surveillance Judge Criticizes Warrantless Taps," Associated Press, June 24, 2007.

90. Charlie Savage, "Panel Pushes for Files on Spy Program."

91. David Edwards and Muriel Kane, "Legal Expert: White House Stonewalling May Force Congress to Charge President with Criminal Offenses" (June 27, 2007), available at http://rawstory.com/php?story=6648.

92. Associated Press, "Democrats Demand Perjury Inquiry for Gonzales," July 26, 2007; and David Johnston and Scott Shane, "FBI Chief Gives Account at Odds with Gonzales's," *New York Times*, July 27, 2007.

93. See U.S. Court of Appeals for the Sixth Circuit, *American Civil Liberties Union, et al. v. National Security Agency, et al.*, Nos. 06-2095/2140 (decided July 6, 2007). Also see Associated Press, "Federal Court Dismisses Domestic Spying Lawsuit," July 6, 2007; Amy Goldstein, "Lawsuit Against Wiretaps Rejected," *Washington Post*, July 7, 2007; and Adam Liptak, "Panel Dismisses Suit Challenging Secret Wiretaps," *New York Times*, July 7, 2007. The decision by the 6th Circuit court left a group of cases pending before a U.S. District Court Judge and the U.S. Court of Appeals for the 9th Circuit in California as the major remaining legal challenges to the NSA warrantless domestic spying program.

94. U.S. Senator Patrick Leahy, "Leahy Grants Administration Request for Extension, Urges White House to Use Time to Gather Information to Turn Over," available at http://leahy.senate.gov/press/200707/071707a.html.

95. Carl Hulse and Edmund L. Andrews, "House Approves Changes in Eavesdropping," *New York Times*, August 5, 2007; Carol D. Leonnig and Ellen

Nakashima, "Ruling Limited Spying Effort," *Washington Post*, August 3, 2007; and Michael Abramowitz and Jonathan Weisman, "Hill, White House Draw Battle Lines," *Washington Post*, August 3, 2007.

96. Eric Lichtblau, James Risen, and Mark Mazzetti, "Reported Drop in Surveillance Spurred a Law," *New York Times*, August 11, 2007. Also see Hulse and Andrews, "House Approves Changes in Eavesdropping"; Leonnig and Nakashima, "Ruling Limited Spying Effort"; and Abramowitz and Weisman, "Hill, White House Draw Battle Lines."

97. Lichtblau, Risen, and Mazzetti, "Reported Drop in Surveillance Spurred a Law."

98. Katherine Shrader, "Spy Chief Gets Voice in Eavesdropping Program," Associated Press, August 7, 2007; Charles Babington, "House Approves Foreign Wiretap Bill," Associated Press, August 5, 2007; and Michael Abramowitz and Jonathan Weisman, "Hill, White House Draw Battle Lines," *Washington Post*, August 3, 2007; and James Risen, "Bush Signs Law to Widen Reach for Wiretapping," *New York Times*, August 6, 2007.

99. Risen, "Bush Signs Law to Widen Reach for Wiretapping"; and Shrader, "Spy Chief Gets Voice in Eavesdropping Program."

100. Hulse and Andrews, "House Approves Changes in Eavesdropping."

101. Editorial, "The Fear of Fear Itself," *New York Times*, August 7, 2007.

102. See Benjamin Franklin, *Historical Review of Pennsylvania, from Its Origin: Embracing, Among Other Subjects, the Various Points of Controversy Which Have Arisen, from Time to Time, Between the Several Governors and the Assemblies Founded on Authentic Documents* (Philadelphia: E. Olmstead and W. Power, 1812); and John Bartlett, *Familiar Quotations*, 16th ed., 311.

103. *Hamdi v. Rumsfeld*, 542 U.S. 507, 532 (2004).

Epilogue

1. See Statement of Patrick Leahy, Chairman, Senate Judiciary Committee, on Passage of the Open Government Act, Senate Proceedings (August 3, 2007), available at http://www.leahy.gov.

2. Editorial, "White House Shell Game," *New York Times*, August 24, 2007.

3. See Secrecy News, "ISOO Director Leonard to Step Down" (September 28, 2007), available at http://www.fas.org/blog/secrecy; National Coalition for History, "Information Security Oversight Chief Leonard Retires" (September 28, 2007), available at http://www.historycoalition.org/2007/09/28/information-security-oversight-chief-leonard-retires.

4. Michael A. Fletcher and R. Jeffery Smith, "Gonzales-Bush Loyalty a Two-Way Street," *Washington Post*, August 27, 2007; Sheryl Gay Stolberg, "Departures Offer Chance for a Fresh Start as Term Ebbs," *New York Times*, August 28, 2007; Eric Lichtblau and Scott Shane, "Gonzales Loyal to Bush, Held Firm on War Policies," *New York Times*, August 28, 2007; Editorial, "The House Lawyer Departs," *New York Times*, August 28, 2007.

5. *Kansas City Star*, "Records Bill Clears Hurdle in the Senate" (June 13, 2007), available at http://www.kansascity.com; Todd J. Gillman, "Anonymous Senator Puts Hold on Bill Unsealing Presidential Papers," *Dallas Morning News*, September 19, 2007; National Coalition for History, "Anonymous Hold Placed on Senate Presidential Records Bill" (September 8, 2007), available at http://history coalition.org/2007/09/06/anonymous-hold-placed-on-senate-presidential-records-bill; National Coalition for History, "Senator Lieberman Tells Congress to Stop Blocking Presidential Records Bill," available at http://historycoalition.org/2007/10/03/Senator-lieberman-tells-colleagues-to-stop-blocking-presidential-records-bill; and Cong. Rec., Senate, September 24, 2007, S11996.

6. See *American Historical Association v. National Archives and Records Administration*, No. 01-2447; and Public Citizen, "Federal Court Strikes Down Bush Executive Order on Presidential Records" (October 1, 2007), available at http://www.citizen.org/pressroom/release.cfm?ID=2524.

7. See U.S. House of Rep., Committee on Oversight and Government Reform, Majority Staff, Interim Report: Investigation of Possible Presidential Records Act Violations, prepared for Chairman Henry A. Waxman (June 2007), available at http://oversight.house.gov/story.asp?ID=1362.

8. Eric Lichtblau, "Role of Telecom Firms in Wiretap Is Confirmed," *New York Times*, August 24, 2007; and Editorial, "The Spy Chief Speaks*," New York Times*, August 26, 2007.

9. Associated Press, "Bush: Strengthen Eavesdropping Law," September 19, 2007.

10. Associated Press, "Bush: Strengthen Eavesdropping Law"; and James Risen, "Warrantless Wiretaps Not Used, Officials Says," *New York Times*, September 19, 2007.

11. Risen, "Warrantless Wiretaps Not Used."

12. See Eric Lichtblau and Carl Hulse, "Democrats Seem Ready to Extend Wiretap Powers," *New York Times*, October 9, 2007; and Ellen Nakashima, "Democrats to Offer New Surveillance Rules," *New York Times*, October 8, 2007.

Bibliography

Books

Aberbach, Joel D. *Keeping a Watchful Eye: The Politics of Congressional Oversight.* Washington, DC: Brookings Institution, 1990.

Belsky, Martin H., ed. *The Rehnquist Court: A Retrospective.* New York: Oxford University Press, 2002.

Collins, Herbert R., and David B. Weaver, eds. *Wills of U.S. Presidents.* New York: Communications Channels, 1976.

Franklin, Benjamin. *Historical Review of Pennsylvania, from Its Origin: Embracing, Among Other Subjects, the Various Points of Controversy Which Have Arisen, from Time to Time, Between the Several Governors and the Assemblies Founded on Authentic Documents.* Philadelphia: E. Olmstead and W. Power, 1812.

Friedman, Leon, and William F. Levantrosser, eds. *Watergate and Afterward: The Legacy of Richard M. Nixon.* Westport, CT: Greenwood Press, 1992.

Greenberg, David. *Nixon's Shadow: History of an Image.* New York: W. W. Norton, 2003.

Jones, H. G. *The Records of a Nation: Their Management, Preservation, and Use.* New York: Atheneum, 1969.

Kirkland, Philip B. *Watergate and the Constitution.* Chicago: University of Chicago Press, 1978.

Kissinger, Henry A. *White House Years.* Boston: Little, Brown, 1979.

———. *Years of Upheaval.* New York: Simon & Schuster, 1982.

———. *Years of Renewal.* New York: Simon & Schuster, 1999.

Kulter, Stanely I. *The Wars of Watergate: The Last Crisis of Richard Nixon.* New York: Alfred A. Knopf, 1990.

McClure, Charles R., Peter Hermon, and Harold C. Relyea, eds. *United States Government Information Policies: Views and Perspectives.* Norwood, NJ: Ablex, 1993.

McCubbins, Mathew D., and Terry Sullivan, eds. *Congress: Structure and Policy.* Cambridge: Cambridge University Press, 1987.

Nelson, Anna K., ed. *The Records of Federal Officials: A Selection of Materials from the National Study Commission on Records and Documents of Federal Officials.* New York: Garland Publishing, 1978.

Rosen, Bernard. *Holding Government Bureaucracies Accountable.* New York: Praeger, 1989.

Schick, Frank L., Renee S. Schick, and Mark Carroll. *Records of the Presidency: Presidential Papers and Libraries from Washington to Reagan.* Phoenix: Oryx Press, 1989.

Articles

Anderson, Keith. "Is There Still a Sound Legal Basis? The Freedom of Information Act in the Post-9/11 World." *Ohio State Law Journal* 64 (2003): 1627–75.

Bretscher, Carl. "Presidential Records Act: The President and Judicial Review Under the Records Acts." *George Washington Law Review* 60, no. 5 (June 1992): 1477–1508.

Canon, Carl M. "Nixon's Revenge." *National Journal* 34, no. 2 (January 2002).

Castano, Sylvia E. "Disclosure of Federal Officials' Documents Under the Freedom of Information Act: A Limited Application." *Houston Law Review* 18, no. 13 (March 1981): 641–54.

Clarke, Richard. "Threats to U.S. National Security: Proposed Partnership Initiatives Toward Preventing Cyber Terrorist Attacks." *DePaul Business Law Journal* 12 (1999): 25–40.

Cole, David. "The Grand Inquisitors." *New York Review of Books* 54, no. 12 (July 2007): 50–54.

Cole, David, and Martin S. Lederman, eds. "The National Security Agency's Domestic Spying Program: Framing the Debate." *Indiana Law Journal* 81 (May 2006).

Duckett, Kenneth W., and Francis Russell. "The Harding Papers: How Some Were Burned ... and Others Were Saved." *American Heritage* 16 (February 1965): 18–31.

Halstead, T. J. "The Law: *Walker v. Cheney*: Legal Insulation of the Vice President from GAO Investigations." *Presidential Studies Quarterly* 33, no. 3 (September 2003): 635–48.

Hersh, Seymour M. "National Security Department: Listening In." *New Yorker* (May 29, 2006): 25–26.

Karin, Marcy Lynn. "Out of Sight, But Not Out of Mind: How Executive Order 13,233 Expands Executive Privilege While Simultaneously Preventing Access to Presidential Records." *Stanford Law Review* 55 (November 2002).

Kirtley, Jane E. "Transparency and Accountability in a Time of Terror: The Bush Administration's Assault on Freedom of Information." *Communications Law and Policy* 11 (2006).

McDonough, John, R. Gordon Hoxie, and Richard Jacobs. "Who Owns Presidential Papers?" *Manuscripts* 27, no. 1 (Winter 1975): 2–15.

Relyea, Harold C. "The Rise and Pause of the U.S. Freedom of Information Act." *Government Publications Review* 10, no. 1 (1983): 18–29.

Sims, John Cary. "What NSA Is Doing . . . and Why it's Illegal." *Hastings Constitutional Law Quarterly* 33 (Winter/Spring 2006).

Spencer, Patricia L. "Nixon v. Administrator of General Services." *Akron Law Review* 11 (Fall 1977): 368–82.

Uhl, Kristen Elizabeth. "The Freedom of Information Act Post-9/11: Balancing the Public's Right to Know, Critical Infrastructure Protection, and Homeland Security." *American Law Review* 53 (2003–2004).

Wells, Christina E. "National Security Information and the Freedom of Information Act." *Administrative Law Review* 56 (2004).

Newspapers and Wire Services

Associated Press, June 7, 1999–August 7, 2007

Austin Chronicle, September 28, 2001

Boston Globe, November 10, 2003–June 28, 2007

Buffalo News, December 2, 2002

Charlotte Gazette, May 22, 2002–December 16, 2003

Chicago Tribune, February 5, 2001

Christian Science Monitor, December 16, 2003–August 20, 2007

Chronicle of Higher Education, November 16, 2001

Cincinnati Post, September 17, 2002

Columbus Dispatch, June 1, 2002–July 1, 2006

CQ Researcher, June 4, 2004–December 2, 2005

Environment & Energy Daily, November 18, 2002

Guardian, November 6, 2002

The Hill, February 19, 2003

Knight-Ridder Tribune News Service, November 14, 2002–November 10, 2005

Los Angeles Times, August 9, 2002–June 28, 2007

Newsday, May 23, 2002

NewsFactor Network, June 27, 2002

New York Times, August 8, 1977–August 7, 2007

Ottawa Citizen, December 29, 2001

Recorder, December 16, 2002

Reuters, March 3, 2003

San Diego Union-Tribune, December 5, 2002

San Francisco Chronicle, January 6, 2002–August 18, 2003

San Francisco Gate, December 12, 2005

Seattle Post-Intelligencer, April 19, 2006

USA Today, August 13, 2003–April 26, 2004

U.S. News & World Report, May 29, 2006
Wall Street Journal, December 16, 2003–April 16, 2007
Washington Post, September 15, 1974–August 3, 2007
Yakima Herald-Republic, November 21, 2002

Government Documents

U.S. Congress, Congressional Record, 1974–2007
U.S. Congress, House Hearings, 1972–2007
U.S. Congress, House Reports, 1971–2006
U.S. Congress, Senate Hearings, 1972–2007
U.S. Congress, Senate Reports, 1972–2007

Court Records

American Civil Liberties Union, et al., v. National Security Agency, et al., U.S. District Court for the Sixth Circuit, Nos. 06-2095/2140 (July 6, 2007).

American Civil Liberties Union v. National Security Agency/Central Security Service, Complaint for Declaratory and Injunctive Relief, U.S. District Court, Eastern District of Michigan, Southern Division, Case No. 06-CV-10204 (January 17, 2006).

American Historical Association, et al., v. National Archives and Records Administration, et al., Memorandum of Points and Authorities in Support of Plaintiff's Motion for Summary Judgment, No. 01-2447 (February 8, 2002).

American Historical Association v. Peterson, 876 F.Supp.1300, 1320 (D.D.C. 1995).

Armstrong v. Bush, 924 F.2d 282, 288 (U.S.App.D.C. 1991).

Association of American Physicians and Surgeons, Inc., v. Hillary Rodham Clinton, 813F.Supp.82, 95 (D.C.C. 1993).

Cheney v. U.S. District Court for the District of Columbia, Civil Action No. 03-475 (2004).

Cheney v. U.S. District Court for the District of Columbia, On Petition for a Writ of Certiorari to the U.S. Court of Appeals for the District of Columbia Circuit, Brief in Opposition of Respondent Sierra Club, Civil Action No. 03-475 (2004).

Cheney v. U.S. District Court for the District of Columbia, Writ of Certiorari to the U.S. Court of Appeals for the District of Columbia Circuit, Brief for the Petitioners, Civil Action No. 03-475 (2004).

David M. Walker v. Richard B. Cheney, U.S. District Court for the District of Columbia, Civil Action No. 02-0340 (JDB) (2002).

Hamdi v. Rumsfeld, 542 U.S. 507 (2004).

In Re: Richard B. Cheney, et al., Petition for Writ of Certiorari, U.S. Supreme Court, No. 03-475, U.S. (September 2003).

In Re: Richard B. Cheney, No. 02-5354 (D.C.Cir. 2005).

In Re: Richard B. Cheney, Vice President of the United States, et al., U.S. Court of Appeals for the District of Columbia Circuit, No. 02-5354 (May 10, 2005).

Judicial Watch v. National Energy Policy Development Group, Civil Action No. 01-1530 (EGS) and *Sierra Club v. Vice President Richard Cheney, et al.*, Civil Action No. 02-631, U.S. District for the District of Columbia (EGS) (July 12, 2002).

Judicial Watch v. U.S. Department of Energy, et al., U.S. District Court for the District of Columbia, Civil Action No. 01-0981 (PLF).

Nixon v. Administrator of General Services, 433 U.S. 425 (1977).

Nixon v. Burke, 843 F.2d 1473 (D.C.Cir. 1988).

Nixon v. Freeman, 670 F.2d 346 (1982).

United States v. Curtis-Wright Export Corporation, 299 U.S. 304 (1936).

United States v. Nixon, 418 U.S. 683 (1974).

Walker v. Cheney, Complaint for Declaratory and Injunctive Relief, U.S. District Court for the District of Columbia, Civil Action No. 1:02cv00340.

Walker v. Cheney, U.S. District Court for the District of Columbia, Civil Action No. 02-0340 (JDB) (December 9, 2002).

Internet Sources

http://chronicle.com

http://judiciary.senate.gov

http://library.cqpress.com/cqresearcher/php?id=cqresrre20

http://sgate.com

http://www.aclu.org

http://www.americanpresidency.org

http://www.bostonglobe.com

http://www.chicagotribune.com

http://www.citizen.org

http://www.csmonitor.com

http://www.fas.org

http://www.findlaw.com

http://www.firstamendmentcenter.org

http://www.foi.missouri.edu/bushinfopolicies/index.html

http://www.gao.gov.com

http://www.gwu.edu/~nsarchiv.com

http://www.house.gov/reform/min/invest_energy/energy.htm

http://www.latimes.com

http://www.msnbc.com

http://www.newsweek.com

http://www.nybooks.com

http://www.nytimes.com

http://www.oag.state.tx/opinopen/opinions/op49cornyn/jc-0498.htm
http://www.ombwatch.org
http://www.openthegovernment.org
http://www.publiccitizen.org
http://www.rcfp.org/homefrontconfidential/foi.html
http://www.salon.com
http://www.sej.org
http://www.senate.gov
http://www.usdoj.gov/oip/foiapost/2002foiapost10.htm
http://www.washingtonpost.com
http://www.whitehouse.gov

Index

Executive Order 13233, ix–x, 6, 35–37,
45, 57; court ruling against, 158;
litigation and legislation to reverse,
51–53, 157–58; provisions of,
47–50

Executive Order 13292, 20–21

Executive Order 13392, 29

executive powers, 4, 5, 6, 15, 24, 32;
abuse of, 123; FACA lawsuit
against vice president and energy
task force, 81–83, 88, 103, 108,
110, 119–20; GAO lawsuit against
vice president and energy task
force, 71, 73, 77; restoration of,
viii; surveillance, 125, 129–31,
133; war on terror, 136–37, 141

executive privilege: FACA lawsuit
against vice president, 102, 109–
12, 119–20; GAO lawsuit against
vice president, 84; Nixon litigation, 45, 48–49, 53; presidential
records, 35–39, 45, 47–50, 53

FACA. *See* Federal Advisory Committee
Act

FBI. *See* Federal Bureau of Investigation

Federal Advisory Committee Act
(FACA), x, xi, 12, 14, 60; enactment of, 116–18; lawsuit against
vice president and energy task
force, 73–74, 76, 81–82; provisions of, 97–98; rulings by appeals
court and Supreme Court, 102,
104–11, 114–16, 119–20; Sullivan
decision, 100–101

Federal Aviation Administration, 17–18

Federal Bureau of Investigation (FBI),
xi, 3, 6, 11, 16, 23, 25; domestic
spying, 123; surveillance warrants,
133, 148

Federal Regulatory Commission, 19

Fein, Bruce, 71, 141

Feinstein, Diane, 13

FISA. *See* Foreign Intelligence Surveillance Act

FOIA. *See* Freedom of Information Act

Ford, Gerald R., 2, 32, 56; administration of, 4–5

Foreign Intelligence Surveillance Act
(FISA), vii, xi, xii; enactment and
provisions of, 123–24; revisions of,
146, 148, 149–52, 159–61; violation of, 125–30, 134–36, 139,
141–43

Foreign Intelligence Surveillance Court,
123, 133, 134, 137, 139, 144–46;
judges on, 142, 148; revised role
of, 150–51

Fourth Amendment, xii, 129, 133, 134,
140, 145, 151

Frankfurter, Felix, 128

Franklin, Benjamin, 153

Freedom of Information Act (FOIA),
vii, ix, 1–3, 5, 7, 109; Ashcroft
memorandum, 6–8, 27, 29–30,
32; creation of secret information
categories, 3, 16–17; delays and
denials, 27–29; elimination of
website data, 9–10; homeland
security bill, 11–15; legal battles,
23–26, 67, 74, 76–78; legislation
to strengthen, 29–30, 32, 155;
national security exemption, 3–4;
proposed exemptions, 15–20, 155

Friedman, Paul, 77–78

GAO. *See* General Accountability
Office

General Accountability Office (GAO),
vii, x, 6, 8, 9, 15; energy task force
investigation, 60–61, 63–67, 69–
70; FOIA, 28; lawsuit against vice
president and energy task force,
59–60, 71–77, 80, 82–94, 98,
109, 113, 119; report on energy
task force, 94–95

Geneva Conventions, 27, 133
Ginsberg, Ruth Bader, 113
Goldsmith, Jack, 138, 143
Gonzales, Alberto R., 4, 22, 29;
    congressional investigation of,
    149, 157; energy task force
    litigation, 75; Executive Order
    13233, 46; firing of U.S. attorneys,
    53, 155; surveillance program,
    129–31, 136, 139, 143–44, 146,
    150
Graham, Lindsey, 142
Guantanamo Bay, 25, 27

Hagel, Chuck, 140
Hamdi v. Rumsfeld, 125–26, 128, 153
Harris, Benjamin, 48
Hastert, Dennis, 72
Hatch, Orrin, 72
Hayden, Gen. Michael V., 135–36,
    137, 144
Health and Human Services Depart-
    ment, 19
Hellerstein, Alvin K., 25–26
Henry, Patrick, xii
Hersh, Seymour, 134
Hiss, Alger, 132
Homeland Security: Department of,
    11–15, 30; Office of, 7, 9
Homeland Security Act, 11–15
Hoover, J. Edgar, 132
Horn, Steven, 50–51

Ignatius, David, 141
Immigration and Naturalization Service,
    23, 25
Independent counsel statute, viii
Information Security Oversight Office,
    16, 22, 155
Iran, 33
Iran-Contra, vii, 54–55, 56, 112, 125,
    130
Iraq, 25, 26, 27, 33, 94

Jefferson, Thomas, 131
Johnson, Lyndon B., 2
Judicial Watch, x, 6, 60–61, 67,
    70; FACA lawsuit against vice
    president and energy task force,
    81–82, 97–100, 103, 115; FOIA
    lawsuit against vice president
    and energy task force, 73–74,
    76–78, 98–99; rulings by appeals
    court and Supreme Court, 109,
    112–15
Justice Department: domestic surveil-
    lance, 127–28; FACA lawsuit
    against vice president and energy
    task force, 103; firing of U.S.
    attorneys, 53, 155; FOIA, 22–23,
    25, 27–28; FOIA policy, drafting
    of, ix, 6–8; GAO lawsuit against
    vice president and energy task
    force, 73, 93; lawyers' revolt over
    surveillance program, 135–39;
    Office of Legal Counsel, 43, 135,
    137, 138, 143; Office of Profes-
    sional Responsibility investigation,
    143–44, 147; presidential records,
    44–46; revision of FISA rules,
    146–47

Keene, David, 140
Kennedy, Anthony, 111–12
Kerry, John, 113
Kessler, Gladys, 23–24, 76, 78
Kissinger, Henry, 32, 135
Knutson, Karen, 115, 121
Kollar-Kotelly, Colleen, 52, 139, 158
Kristol, William, 140

Laden, Osama bin, 133, 141
Lamberth, Royce C., 148
Lautenberg, Frank, 120–21
Lay, Kenneth, 68–69, 71, 80, 99, 103
Leahy, Patrick, 8, 11, 15, 29–30, 155;
    Cheney-Scalia duck hunting trip,

105; surveillance program, 143, 147, 149
LeCraft Henderson, Karen, 24
Legislative veto, viii
Leonard, William J., 22, 156
Levin, Carl, 12
Levy, Robert, 141
Lieberman, Joseph, 9, 15, 80, 95; Cheney-Scalia duck hunting trip, 105; Presidential Records Act, 157
Lincoln, Abraham, 49, 131, 132
Lundquist, Andrew, 63, 121

Madison. James, 38
McCarthy, Joseph, 132
McConnell, Michael, 146, 150, 159–60
Metcalf, Lee, 116–18
Miers, Harriet, 53
Monigan, John S., 117
Moss, John E., 2
Moyers, Bill, 2
Moynihan, Daniel Patrick, 4
Mueller, Richard S., III, 139, 149

National Archives, 22, 31, 44, 46, 50, 51
National Commission on Terrorist Attacks upon the United States, 94, 104
National energy task force, x, xi, 5, 6, 16, 59–62; FACA lawsuit against vice president, 82, 97–98, 100–102, 108–11, 114, 119, 120–21; FOIA lawsuit, 76–80, 99; GAO investigation and lawsuit against vice president, 63–74, 82–84, 89
National Newspaper Association, 28
National Nuclear Security Administration, 19
National Resources Defense Council, 67; FACA lawsuit against vice president and energy task force, 100; FOIA lawsuit against vice president

and energy task force, 74, 76–77, 99; release of energy task force records, 79, 82, 87, 94
national security, xii, 1–3, 4, 5, 9, 16, 23; civil liberties, 131
National Security Agency, xi, 19; Bush's surveillance program, xii, 124, 126, 129–30, 137–40, 160–61; domestic spying abuses, 123; new surveillance technologies, 134; operations of, 132–33; opposition to surveillance program, 135–39, 141–43, 149; revisions to surveillance law, 144–47, 150–51; telephone companies, 142, 147, 159; violation of FISA, 129–30, 134–36, 139, 141–43
National Security Archive, 8, 19, 26, 28
National Security Council, 9, 55, 71
Nixon, Richard M., xi, 5, 36, 57, 71; administration of, 4, 118; assertion of executive privilege, 44, 46, 102, 110, 118, 120; open government, 33; presidential tapes and records of, ix, 35, 37–40, 47–49, 73, 82, 111, 112; resignation of presidency, 39; surveillance of political enemies, 131
Nixon-Sampson agreement, 39, 56
Nixon v. Administrator of General Services, 36, 39, 42, 46–48, 53, 82, 110
North, Oliver, 130

Office of Professional Responsibility, 143
Olson, Theodore B., 73, 83, 102–3, 108
OpenTheGovernment.org, 28–29
Operation TIPS (Terrorism Information and Prevention System), 14
Ose, Doug, 50–51

105–7; civil liberties, invasion of, 129; FACA lawsuit against vice president and energy task force, 91, 97, 101–2, 108–14, 118–20; GAO lawsuit against vice president, 88–89; *Hamdi v. Rumsfeld*, 125–26, 128; Paula Jones case, 102–3; presidential election of 2000, 61; steel seizure case, 128; *United States v. Curtis-Wright Export Corporation*, 130

Surveillance, xi, xii; warrantless domestic spying, 123–29, 131, 133–34, 135–39, 141

Taft, William Howard, 48
Taliban, 133
Tatel, David S., 24
Tenet, George, 136, 137
Terrorist Surveillance Program, 124
Thomas, Clarence, 112
Total Awareness Program, 125
Tower, John, 54, 56
Trading with the Enemy Act, 132
Truman, Harry, 128

United States v. Curtis-Wright Export Corporation, 130
United States v. Nixon, 40, 102–3, 110, 120
U.S. archivist, 20, 36, 42, 44, 46–49, 51–52, 55
U.S. Congress: Authorization to Use Military Force, 125–26; constitutional powers, 130; elections, xii, 141; Executive Order 13233, 50–51, 53; FACA, x, 12, 97; failure to check executive power, viii, 133; FISA, revisions of, 127, 144, 149–52, 159–61; FISA, political debate over, 140–41; FOIA, amendments and revisions of, 2, 7,

32, 155; GAO investigation of and lawsuit against vice president and energy task force, 59, 65–66, 70–75, 84–86, 91–92; Homeland Security Act, 11–15; investigation of Attorney General Alberto Gonzales, 149, 157; oversight of executive branch, 33, 93–94; passage of open government laws, vii; Patriot Act, 10; power to regulate executive surveillance activities, 129–30; Presidential Records Act, ix, 6, 35, 37, 41–43, 51–53, 157–58; seizure of Nixon tapes and records, 39; subpoena to vice president, 148

Vietnam War, vii, 4

Walker, David M., 59, 64–67, 70; GAO lawsuit against vice president and energy task force, 85–86, 88–91, 94–95
Walker v. Cheney, 59–60, 71–77, 80, 82–94, 98, 109, 113, 119
War Powers Act, viii
Washington, George, ix, 37, 38
Watergate, 2, 4, 36, 38, 39, 58, 82, 102, 112
Waxman, Henry A., 22, 50, 53; energy task force, 63–65, 68–71, 83; GAO lawsuit against vice president and energy task force, 75, 86–87, 89–90, 94; investigation of missing White House e-mail, 158–59
White, Byron, 40
White House e-mail, 37, 54–56, 90, 155, 158–59
Will, George, 140
Wilson, Woodrow, 48, 132

Yoo, John, 135–38

About the Author

BRUCE P. MONTGOMERY is Associate Professor and Faculty Director of Archives at the University of Colorado at Boulder. He is the founding director of the UCB Human Rights Initiative and a founding member of the International Federation of Human Rights Centers and Archives. He has served as an analyst of classified documents for the U.S. government. He is the author of *Subverting Open Government: White House Materials and Executive Branch Politics*. Articles by Montgomery on this topic have appeared in many journals and newspapers, including *Presidential Studies Quarterly* and the *Washington Post*.